Web Data Management and Electronic Commerce

Web Data Management
and Electronic Commerce

Management

and Electronic
Commerce

Bhavani Thuraisingham, Ph.D.

CRC Press
Boca Raton   London   New York   Washington, D.C.

Library of Congress Cataloging-in-Publication Data

Thuraisingham, Bhavani M.
    Web data management and electronic commerce / Bhavani Thuraisingham.
       p. cm.
    Includes bibliographical references and index.
    ISBN 0-8493-2204-9 (alk. paper)
    1. Web databases. 2. Database management. 3. Electronic commerce.
    I. Title.
    QA76.9.W43T49 2000
    005.75'8—dc21   00-037827
                                                                     CIP

© 2000 by CRC Press LLC

No claim to original U.S. Government works
International Standard Book Number 0-8493-2204-9
Library of Congress Card Number 00-037827
Printed in the United States of America 1 2 3 4 5 6 7 8 9 0
Printed on acid-free paper

PREFACE

Recent developments in information systems technologies have resulted in computerizing many applications in various business areas. Data have become a critical resource in many organizations, and, therefore, efficient access to data, sharing the data, extracting information from the data, and making use of the information has become an urgent need. As a result, there have been many efforts on not only integrating the various data sources scattered across several sites, but extracting information from these databases in the form of patterns, and trends have also become important. These data sources may be databases managed by database management systems, or they could be data warehoused in a repository from multiple data sources. The advent of the World Wide Web (WWW) in the mid-1990s has resulted in even greater demand for managing data, information and knowledge effectively. There is now so much data on the web that managing it with conventional tools is becoming almost an impossibility. New tools and techniques are needed to effectively manage this data. Therefore, to provide the interoperability as well as warehousing between the multiple data sources and systems, and to extract information from the databases and warehouses on the web, various tools are being developed.

The focus of this book is on managing the large quantities of data on the web as well as on applying various data management techniques to a specific application: electronic commerce. That is, this book will be devoted to the emerging technology area called web data management with special emphasis on electronic commerce. In general, data management includes managing the databases, interoperability, migration, warehousing, and mining. For example, the data on the web have to be managed and mined to extract information and patterns and trends. Data could be in files, relational databases, or other types of databases such as multimedia databases. Data may be structured or unstructured.

There are hardly any texts on web data management, although there are several articles now in research journals and magazines. The purpose of this book is to discuss complex ideas in web data management in a way that can be understood by someone who wants a background in this area. Technical managers as well as those interested in technology will benefit from this book. We focus on a data-centric view in describing web technologies. The concepts are explained with electronic commerce as an application area. We repeatedly stress the importance of having good data on the web. Toward this end, we discuss various data management technologies critical to the web.

This book is divided into three parts. Part I describes supporting technologies for web data management. Without the underlying concepts such as querying and transactions, one cannot develop data and information management as a technology area for the web. We start with a discussion of database systems technologies followed by a discussion of data mining technologies. Then we describe various interoperability aspects including a discussion of distributed, heterogeneous, federated and client-server databases. Object technologies and security technologies are discussed next. Object technologies include object-programming languages, object databases, object-based design and analysis, distributed objects, and components and framework. Security technologies include access control mechanisms, secure operating systems, secure databases, and secure networks. While there are many other technologies for web data management, such as multimedia, visualization, and collaboration, for the purposes of this book we consider the five supporting technologies discussed in Part I to be critical. We do address some of the other technologies including multimedia and knowledge management in latter parts of this book. These other technologies are built from the basic supporting technologies. Finally we provide an overview of web technologies. Since this book is all about the web, we do not consider web technologies to be a supporting technology unlike some of the other technologies we have discussed. Nevertheless the web is central to this entire book and we need to give some introduction to the web. Therefore, we have chosen to do it in Part I under supporting technologies.

Part II describes the core data and information management related technologies for the web. We start with a discussion of database management for the web. In particular, we discuss the various functions including query processing, transaction management, metadata management, storage management, and security and integrity management. We also provide an overview of data modeling for web databases. Following this we discuss interoperability of heterogeneous database systems on the web. An overview of Java Database Connectivity which is a standard developed by Sun's Javasoft and is being adopted by most database system vendors will be given. Next we focus on architectures for the web including three-tier computing. We also include a discussion of digital libraries. Then we discuss issues of data mining on the web. Both mining web data to extract information as well as mining usage patterns to help users will be addressed. Next we discuss security and privacy problems on the web. The discussion of security here will focus mainly on data management aspects and privacy concerns through data mining. Note that security will also be given more consideration in Part III when we address electronic commerce, and in particular various web security concerns. Following the discussion on security and privacy, we describe metadata for the web. While the discussion on metadata can be applied to web data management as well as data management in general, metadata management is becoming increasingly important for the web. Then a discussion of XML (Extensible Markup Language) will be given. Note that XML is a standard being developed by the World Wide Web Consortium (W3C) for data modeling and document exchange on the web. XML is rapidly becoming one of the most important developments for web data management. We also give a note on ontologies in our discussion of metadata.

While early chapters of Part II focus on data management related technologies for the web, latter chapters of Part II focus on other emerging information management technologies for the web. We start with a discussion of collaboration, multimedia, training and some other important technologies for the web. For example, various broadcasting corporations and news sources are increasingly posting their data on the web. Therefore efficient multimedia data management techniques are important. Visualization on the web will also be addressed. This will be followed by a discussion of knowledge management for the enterprise. Knowledge management is becoming critical for many organizations and we will provide an overview of how intranets are promoting knowledge management in organizations. We also discuss decision support within this context. Next we provide a discussion of distributed agents for managing and locating resources on the web. We end Part II with a discussion of some of the emerging tools for web data and information management. Note that we had first planned to divide the current Part II into two parts. That is, to group the data management related technologies into one part and the information management related technologies into another. However, after thinking about it, it was difficult for us to draw a line between data management and information management. For example, consider data mining; some say that it is part of data management while some others say that it is part of information management. Therefore, we decided to group both data and information management technologies for the web into one part.

While Part I focuses on supporting technologies and Part II focuses on important data and information management technologies, Part III will focus on a specific application that is of interest to many and that is electronic commerce (also called e-commerce). This is all about carrying out business on the web such as buying and selling products as well as advertising products. We provide an overview of electronic commerce systems and discuss models, architectures and functions for e-commerce. We also discuss legal and ethical considerations for e-commerce and discuss the difference between e-commerce and e-business. While telecommunications is not really part of information management, due to its importance, we also provide a brief overview of the application of telecommunications in e-commerce and the web. In addition, the increasing popularity of the Java programming language for e-commerce will also be discussed. Part III also describes how the various data and information management technologies described in Part II can be applied for electronic commerce. Some suggestions on how to build an e-commerce organization are also given. Then we focus on two important topics for e-commerce; one is e-commerce security and the other is e-commerce transactions.

Note that there are also other emerging applications on the web such as entertainment and training. One could train individuals thousands of miles away through the web. Furthermore, entertainment on the web is becoming a huge business. In a way training and entertainment applications on the web can also be considered to be part of electronic commerce. That is electronic commerce in a broad sense encompasses almost all aspects of web interaction. Although there are different terms cropping up such as e-learning (electronic learning) and e-procurement (electronic procurement). While there are tremendous advantages with electronic commerce there are also dangerous problems. The most important aspect is security. With Internet banking and similar applications, it is especially important to provide appropriate security measures. Therefore, we give attention to security and privacy issues. Note that various security mechanisms such as digital signatures are being proposed for electronic commerce and we provide an overview of these techniques. We give considerable attention to security in all three parts of this book. Part I provides some background information on security, Part II discusses security and privacy aspects of data mining through the web, and Part III discusses e-commerce security and web security. There is also another great worry about displaying inappropriate material on the web via techniques employed for electronic commerce. There have been numerous discussions on this. It appears that in addition to technological solutions one also needs to implement appropriate policies and procedures to protect children and others from such inappropriate material. Legal aspects also play an important role here.

This book also includes three appendices. Appendix A provides an overview of data management and our framework for data management. This will show where web data management fits into this framework. Appendix B provides an overview of some networking concepts. The Internet is built on various networking standards and therefore networking is an essential part of web data management and electronic commerce. Note that telecommunications is also becoming critical for the web and e-commerce. As mentioned earlier, we discuss some aspects in Part III of this book. We have stressed in this book that e-commerce is only part technology; the other part is business oriented. E-commerce is now being used to carry out enterprise business process management. Therefore, an overview of enterprise business process management will be given in Appendix C. Although this topic has not received much attention in the past relating to e-commerce and e-business, we can expect to hear a lot about this in the future.

Although our first two books *Data Management Systems Evolution and Interoperation* and *Data Mining: Technologies, Techniques, Tools and Trends* would serve as excellent sources of reference to this book, this book is fairly self-contained. We have provided a reasonably comprehensive overview of the various background material necessary to understand the web in Part I. However, some of the details on this background information, especially on data management and mining, can be found in our previous texts.

We have tried to obtain information on products and standards that are current. However, as we have stressed over and over again in our books, vendors and researchers are continually updating their systems and, therefore, the information valid today may not be accurate tomorrow. We urge the reader to contact the vendors and get up-to-date information. Note that many of the products are trademarks of various corporations. If we know or have heard of such trademarks we have used all capital italic letters for the product when we first introduce it in this book. Again due to the rapidly changing nature of the computer industry, we encourage the reader to contact the vendors to obtain up-to-date information on trademarks and ownership of the various products.

We have tried our best to obtain references from books, journals, magazines, and conference and workshop proceedings, and given only a few URLs to web pages as references. Although we tried not to give URLs as references, we found that it was almost impossible to write a text about the web without giving URLs as references. URLs contain excellent reference material, but some of them may not be available even when this book goes into print. Therefore, we also encourage the reader to check the web from time to time for current information on web data management developments, prototypes, and products. There is now a conference series devoted to this topic and it is called the WWW conference and is held annually around the world. As mentioned earlier, there is also a consortium that has been formed called W3C. This consortium develops various standards for the web such as security and data models. There is so much of information out there and this information is changing so rapidly that we found it quite challenging to write this book.

We would like to stress to managers and executives that to be competitive one needs to maintain a web site for an organization. This is an excellent way to create information sharing. However, managers should not rush into developing web sites. They should think about the audience, what information to post, security issues, as well as ways that the organization would benefit the most before embarking on a web project. A web site has to be maintained continually and therefore resources, both man power and funds, are needed for this.

We repeatedly use the terms data, data management, and database systems and database management systems in this book. We elaborate on these terms in one of the appendices. We define data management systems to be systems that manage the data, extract meaningful information from the data, and make use of the information extracted. Therefore, data management systems include database systems, data warehouses, and data mining systems. Data could be structured data such as those found in relational databases, or it could be unstructured such as text, voice, imagery, and video. There have been numerous discussions in the past to distinguish between data, information, and knowledge. In our previous books on data management and mining, we did not attempt to clarify these terms. We simply stated that data could be just bits and bytes or it could convey some meaningful information to the user. However, with the web and also with increasing interest in data, information and knowledge management as separate areas, in this book we take a different approach to data, information and knowledge by differentiating between these terms as much as possible. For us data are usually some value, like numbers, integers, and strings. Information is obtained when some meaning or semantics is associated with the data such as John's salary is 20K. Knowledge is something that you acquire through reading and learning. That is, data and information can be transferred into knowledge when uncertainty about the data and information is removed from someone's mind. It should be noted that it is rather difficult to give strict definitions of data, information and knowledge. Sometimes we will use these terms interchangeably also. Our framework for data management helps clarify some of the differences. It should also be noted that although we have chosen to call this book web data management instead of web information management or web knowledge management, we do discuss information and knowledge management technologies for the web. To be consistent with the terminology in our previous books, we will also distinguish between database systems and database management systems. A database management system is that component which manages the database containing persistent data. A database system consists of both the database and the database management system.

This book provides a fairly comprehensive overview of web data management technologies and electronic commerce applications. It is written for technical managers and executives as well as for technologists interested in learning about the subject. Various people have approached me and asked questions as to what web data management is all about. Therefore, I decided to write this book so that the complicated ideas can be expressed in a simplified manner and yet provide much of the information needed. This was also the reason for writing my previous books on data management and then data mining. It should be noted that like many areas in data management, unless someone has practical experience in carrying out experiments and working with the various tools it is difficult to get an appreciation of what is out there and how to go about developing web sites. Therefore, we encourage the reader not only to read the information in this book and take advantage of the references mentioned here, but we also urge the reader, especially those who are interested in developing web sites, to work with the tools out there.

Web data management is still a relatively new technology and includes many other technologies. Therefore, as the various technologies and integration of these technologies mature, we can expect to see progress in web data management. That is, not only can we expect to access relational databases on the web, we can also manage multimedia databases, warehouses, and mining data on the web. We can expect rapid developments with respect to many of the ideas, concepts, and techniques discussed in this book. We urge the reader to keep up with all the developments in this emerging and useful technology area. It should be noted that this book is intended to provide the background information as well as some of the key points and trends in web data management and electronic commerce.

It should also be noted that electronic commerce is one of the fastest growing technologies. Not only is there much interest in text-based electronic commerce, we expect voice-based electronic commerce to explode over the next few years. Furthermore, the models for electronic commerce will also be changing due to the various laws and regulations that we can expect to be developed. This is also because electronic commerce will be occurring across states and countries and therefore state, federal and international rules and regulations will have to be enforced.

There is so much to write about web data management and e-commerce that we could be writing this book forever. That is, while we have tried to provide as much information as possible in this book, there is so much more to write about. Daily we hear about e-commerce on the news, various television programs, and in conversations. There will be no limits to this subject as we enter the new millennium. My advice to the readers is to keep up with the developments, determine what is important and what is not, and be knowledgeable about this subject. It will not only help us in our business lives and careers but also in our personal lives such as personal investments, travel, selecting schools and many other activities.

The views and conclusions expressed in this book are those of the author and do not reflect the views, policies, or procedures of the author's institution or sponsors. I thank my management for providing an environment where it is exciting and challenging to work, my professors and teachers for having given me the foundations upon which to build my skills, my sponsors and colleagues, all others who have supported my education and my work, and especially those who have reviewed various portions of this book. Last but not least I thank my husband Thevendra and my son Breman for being so patient with me while I wrote this book and for their continuing encouragement and support.

Bhavani Thuraisingham, Ph.D.
Bedford, Massachusetts

About the Author

Bhavani Thuraisingham, Ph.D., recipient of IEEE Computer Society's prestigious 1997 Technical Achievement Award for her outstanding and innovative work in secure data management, is a chief scientist in data management at MITRE Corporation's Information Technology Directorate in Bedford, Massachusetts. In this position she provides technology directions in data, information and knowledge management for the Information Technology Directorate of MITRE's Air Force Center. In addition, she is also an expert consultant in computer software to MITRE's work for the Internal Revenue Service. Her current work focuses on data mining as it relates to multimedia databases and database security, distributed object management with emphasis on real-time data management, and web data management applications in electronic commerce. She also serves as adjunct professor of computer science at Boston University and teaches a course in advanced data management and data mining.

Prior to her current position at MITRE in May 1999, she was the department head in data management and object technology in MITRE's Information Technology Division in the Intelligence Center for four years. In this position she was responsible for the management of about 30 technical staff in four key areas: distributed databases, multimedia data management, data mining and knowledge management, and distributed objects and quality of service. Prior to that, she had held various technical positions including lead, principal, and senior principal engineer, and was head of MITRE's research in Evolvable Interoperable Information Systems as well as Data Management, and co-director of MITRE's Database Specialty Group. She managed fifteen research projects under the Massive Digital Data Systems effort for the Intelligence Community and was also a team member of the AWACS modernization research project between 1993 and 1999. Before that she led team efforts on the designs and prototypes of various secure database systems for government sponsors between 1989 and 1993.

Prior to joining MITRE in January 1989, Dr. Thuraisingham worked in the computer industry between 1983 and 1989. She was first a Senior Programmer/Analyst with Control Data Corporation for over two years working on the design and development of the CDCNET product and later she was a Principal Research Scientist with Honeywell Inc. for over three years conducting research, development, and technology transfer activities. She was also an adjunct professor of computer science and a member of the graduate faculty at the University of Minnesota between 1984 and 1988. Prior to starting her industrial experience and after completing her Ph.D., she was a visiting faculty member first in the Department of Computer Science, at the New Mexico Institute of Technology, and then at the Department of Mathematics at the University of Minnesota between 1980 and 1983. Dr. Thuraisingham has a B.Sc, M.Sc, M.S., and also received her Ph.D. degree from the United

Kingdom at the age of 24. She is a senior member of the IEEE as well as a member of the ACM, the British Computer Society, and AFCEA. She has a certification in Java programming and has also completed a Management Development Program.

Dr. Thuraisingham has published over three hundred and fifty technical papers and reports, including over fifty journal articles, and is the inventor of three U.S. patents for MITRE on database inference control. She also serves on the editorial boards of various journals, including IEEE Transactions on Knowledge and Data Engineering, the Journal of Computer Security, and Computer Standards and Interfaces Journal. She gives tutorials in data management, including data mining and warehousing, object databases, and web databases, and currently teaches courses at both the MITRE Institute and the AFCEA Educational Foundation annually. She has chaired or co-chaired several conferences and workshops including IFIP's 1992 Database Security Conference, ACM's 1993 Object Security Workshop, ACM's 1994 Objects in Healthcare Information Systems Workshop, IEEE's 1995 Multimedia Database Systems Workshop, IEEE's 1996 Metadata Conference, AFCEA's 1997 Federal Data Mining Symposium, IEEE's 1998 COMPSAC Conference, IEEE's 1999 WORDS Workshop, and will be chairing IFIP's 2000 Database Security Conference and IEEE's 2001 ISADS Conference. She is a member of OMG's real-time special interest group, founded the C4I special interest group, and has served on panels in data management and mining. She has edited several books as well as special journal issues and was the consulting editor of the Data Management Handbook series by CRC's Auerbach Publications for 1996 and 1997. She is the author of the books *Data Management Systems Evolution and Interoperation* and *Data Mining: Technologies, Techniques, Tools and Trends* by CRC Press.

Dr. Thuraisingham has given invited presentations at several conferences including recent keynote addresses at the Second Pacific Asia Data Mining Conference '98, SAS Institute's Data Mining Technology Conference '99, IEEE Artificial Neural Networks Conference '99, and IEEE Tools in AI Conference '99. She has also delivered the featured addresses at AFCEA's Federal Database Colloquium from 1994 through 1999. Her presentations are worldwide including in the United States, Canada, United Kingdom, France, Germany, Italy, Spain, Switzerland, Austria, Belgium, Sweden, Finland, Norway, The Netherlands, Greece, Ireland, South Africa, India, Hong Kong, Taiwan, Japan, Singapore, New Zealand, and Australia. She also gives seminars and lectures at various universities around the world including at the University of Cambridge in England.

To My Advisors:

John Cleave, University of Bristol, U.K.

and

Roger Hindley, University of Wales, Swansea, U.K.

For your help and guidance during my graduate education and for the continued encouragement I get from you

TABLE OF CONTENTS

CHAPTER 1

INTRODUCTION

1.1 TRENDS

Recent developments in information systems technologies have resulted in computerizing many applications in various business areas. Data have become a critical resource in many organizations, and, therefore, efficient access to data, sharing the data, extracting information from the data, and making use of the information has become an urgent need. As a result, there have been many efforts on not only integrating the various data sources scattered across several sites, but extracting information from these databases in the form of patterns, and trends have also become important. These data sources may be databases managed by database management systems, or they could be data warehoused in a repository from multiple data sources. The advent of the World Wide Web (WWW) in the mid 1990s has resulted in even greater demand for managing data, information and knowledge effectively. There is now so much data on the web that managing it with conventional tools is becoming almost an impossibility. New tools and techniques are needed to effectively manage this data. Therefore, to provide the interoperability as well as warehousing between the multiple data sources and systems, and to extract information from the databases and warehouses on the web, various tools are being developed.

The focus of this book is on managing the large quantities of data on the web as well as on applying the data management techniques to a specific application: electronic commerce. That is, this book will be devoted to the emerging technology area called web data management with special emphasis on electronic commerce. In general, data management includes managing the databases, interoperability, migrating, warehousing, and mining. For example, the data on the web have to be managed and mined to extract information and patterns and trends. Data could be in files, relational databases, or other types of databases such as multimedia databases. Data may be structured or unstructured.

We repeatedly use the terms data, information, and knowledge in this book. Data could be structured data such as those found in relational databases, or it could be unstructured such as text, voice, imagery, and video. There have been numerous discussions in the past to distinguish between data, information, and knowledge. In our previous books on data management and mining, we did not attempt to clarify these terms. We simply stated that data could be just bits and bytes or it could

1

convey some meaningful information to the user. However, with the advent of the web, and also with increasing interest in data, information and knowledge management on the web as separate technology areas, in this book we take a different approach to data, information and knowledge by differentiating between these terms as much as possible. For us data are usually some values like numbers, integers, and strings. Information is obtained when some meaning or semantics is associated with the data such as John's salary is 20K. Knowledge is something that you acquire through reading and learning. That is, data and information can be transferred into knowledge when uncertainty about the data and information is removed from someone's mind. It should be noted that it is rather difficult to give strict definitions of data, information and knowledge. Sometimes we will use these terms interchangeably also.

The organization of this chapter is as follows. We discuss data, information, and knowledge in Section 1.2. A brief introduction to the World Wide Web is the subject of Section 1.3. Supporting technologies for the web is discussed in Section 1.4. Then we discuss data management related technologies in Section 1.5. Emerging information management technologies is the subject of Section 1.6. Introduction to electronic commerce is given in Section 1.7. Note that Sections 1.4, 1.5, 1.6 and 1.7 will be elaborated in Parts I, II, and III of this book.[1] The organization of this book is the subject of Section 1.8. To put this all together we describe a framework for web data management. This framework helps us to give some context to the various web data management technologies. Finally, the chapter is summarized in Section 1.9, which also includes a discussion of directions.

1.2 DATA, INFORMATION AND KNOWLEDGE

Data, information, and knowledge are becoming key resources in an enterprise. As mentioned earlier, by data we usually mean the raw bits and bytes such as the number 20 or the string ZZZ. Data can be converted to information, such as the number 20 is John's salary. Then there is knowledge and this is the information that one acquires and what one does with it. If I know that John's salary is 20K and can use it for some useful purpose, then I have acquired some knowledge. Knowledge will include data, information, as well as the usage of this information. With knowledge, one can make intelligent decisions. In general there is really no clear-cut distinction between data, information and knowledge. Some

---

[1] We could have separated 1.5 and 1.6 into two parts. After some thought we decided to combine both data and information management technologies into one, as the distinction we feel was rather subjective.

say that information is a superset of data, and knowledge is a superset of information. Some say that information encompasses everything (see for example the discussion in [THUR99a]).

The emergence of the World Wide Web has made us make distinctions between data, information and knowledge. Data management, information management and knowledge management are emerging as distinct technology areas. Some have said that information management encompasses data and knowledge management. Data, information and knowledge are now easily available to millions of people due to the web. There is data everywhere and one soon gets overloaded with information. Efficient access to the data and information has become critical. Furthermore, with people sharing the data and information on the web, knowledge and experiences also get shared. Therefore data management, information management and knowledge management have become critical technologies for the web. Furthermore, since there are now so many transactions, such as buying and selling goods being carried out on the web, various data, information and knowledge management technologies are now being applied to important application areas such as electronic commerce.

Figure 1-1 illustrates our rather subjective view of data, information, and knowledge management. We find it convenient to say that data are subsumed by information, which is subsumed by knowledge. This book addresses all three aspects. While Part II mainly focuses on data management, both knowledge management and information management aspects are discussed in Part III. As mentioned earlier, there have been numerous debates about this subject. For example, where does data mining fit in? Is it data management or is it information management? Since you extract information out of the data some say that it is information management. But data mining is all about making sense out of the data in the databases. In that case some argue that it is data management. For our convenience we have put data mining as part of data management, and so is data warehousing. Technologies such as visualization, collaboration, machine translation are what we call information management. As mentioned earlier, different groups have different views as to where these technologies belong. That is, classification of the various technologies as to whether they belong to data management, information management or knowledge management is rather subjective.

1.3 INTRODUCTION TO THE WORLD WIDE WEB

The inception of the web took place at CERN in Switzerland by a group of physicists. Timothy Bernes-Lee, who is considered to be the father of the web, now heads the World Wide Web Consortium (W3C). The consortium specifies standards for the web including data models, query languages, and security.

Around the time the WWW emerged in the early 1990s, a group of graduate students at the University of Illinois developed a browser, which was called MOSAIC. This was around 1993-4. A company called Netscape Communications then marketed MOSAIC and since then various browsers as well as search engines have emerged. These search engines, the browsers, and the servers all now constitute the WWW. The Internet became the transport medium for communication.

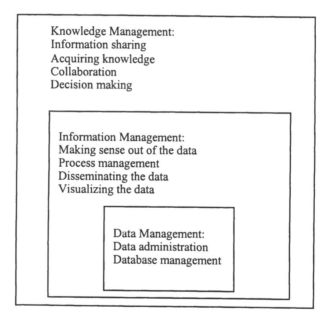

Figure 1-1. Data, Information, and Knowledge Management: One View

Various protocols for communication such as HTTP (Hypertext Transfer Protocol) and languages for creating web pages such as HTML (Hypertext markup language) also emerged. Perhaps one of the significant developments is the Java programming language by Sun Microsystems. The work is now being continued by Javasoft, a subsidiary of Sun. Java is a language that is very much like C++ but avoids all the disadvantages of C++ like pointers. It was developed as a programming language to be run platform independent. It was soon found that this was an ideal language for the web. So now there are various Java applications as well as what is known as Java applets. Applets are Java programs residing in a machine and can be called by a web page running on a separate machine. Therefore applets can be embedded into web pages to perform all kinds of features. Of course there are additional security restrictions as applets could come from untrusted machines. Another concept is a servlet. Servlets run on web servers and perform specific functions such as delivering web pages for a user request. Figure 1-2 illustrates the WWW environment.

Middleware for the web is continuing to evolve. If the entire environment is Java, that is connecting Java clients to Java servers, then one could use RMI (Remote Method Invocation) by Javasoft. If the platform consists of heterogeneous clients and servers then one could use Object Management Group's CORBA (Common Object Request Broker Architecture) for interoperability. Some of these technologies will be discussed in Part I.

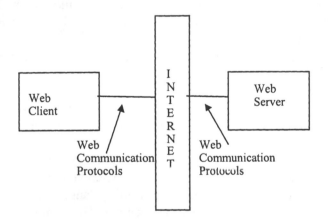

Figure 1-2. World Wide Web

Developments on the web are exploding. The advances are being made at such a rapid pace that it is becoming extremely difficult to maintain up-to-date knowledge. Much of the focus is on managing the large quantities of data, information, and knowledge on the web. Therefore, tools and techniques are being developed to manage this data, information, and knowledge. Various data management operations such as query processing and transaction management are being examined for the web. Security and privacy is getting increasing attention. Mining and extracting information is also becoming a major development. Various browsers and tools are being developed to scan and peruse the information. Multimedia on the web is also getting a lot of interest. Ultimately all this is leading to providing effective electronic commerce-based activities on the web.

1.4 SUPPORTING TECHNOLOGIES FOR WEB DATA MANAGEMENT

There are various supporting technologies for the web. We discuss some of them. One of the key supporting technologies is database systems. There are lots and lots of data on the web; some of them stored in files and some in databases. This data has to be managed effectively. Therefore, query processing, transaction management, storage management and metadata management all play a key role in web data management.

Another technology that is becoming critical for the web is data mining. Data mining is the process of forming conclusions from premises often previously unknown from large quantities of data. There are two aspects here. One is to mine the data on the web and extract useful information and the other is to mine the web usage patterns to give guidance to the user.

Interoperability is a third important technology. The different data sources on the web have to interoperate with each other. The data could also be warehoused. Interoperation may be based on client-server technology where web clients interact with web servers, or it could be based on some federated model where groups of servers form a federation and communicate with each other.

Object technology is another important area for the web. All types of object technologies, such as databases, design and analysis methods, distributed object management, programming languages, and components and frameworks are becoming critical. For example, the most popular programming language for the web is Java and this is an object-based language. Components are becoming a necessity for developing middleware for the web. Distributed object management systems provide the backbone for interoperability between web clients and servers.

The importance of security technologies for the web cannot be overemphasized. With more and more transactions and business being carried out on the web it is critical that the information be secured. Furthermore, privacy of the individuals has to be protected. Security techniques such as digital signatures and certificates are gaining wide acceptance.

Figure 1-3 illustrates these supporting web technologies. We have called them the basic technologies. One can build on them to develop other technologies for the web. These include information technologies such as visualization, multimedia processing, and collaboration. We will elaborate on these information management technologies in the next section. Note that Part I will discuss the supporting technologies in more detail. Data management technologies directly related to the web will be given more detailed considerations in Part II. Emerging information technologies for the web will also be the subject of Part II. Applications of all these technologies will be addressed in Part III.

1.5 DATA MANAGEMENT RELATED TECHNOLOGIES FOR THE WEB

The previous section discussed supporting technologies in general for the web. In particular database systems and data mining were given some consideration; this section elaborates on the various data management technologies directly relevant to the web.

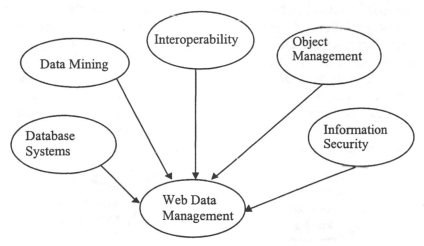

Figure 1-3. Supporting Technologies for the Web

Web database systems are springing up all over the place. Database system vendors are connecting their systems to the web. Furthermore, database systems technologies are being used to manage the data on the web. These include query management, transaction processing and metadata management.

Web data mining is becoming increasingly important. As mentioned in the previous section one can mine the data on the web and extract information. On the other hand one can use mining to obtain patterns and trends about a user and then give advice to the user. Closely related to mining is privacy and security. With web mining, one can now extract all kinds of information about individuals and violate privacy. Therefore, appropriate technologies have to be developed and laws enforced.

While metadata management is usually considered to be part of data management, with so much recent interest on using metadata for all kinds of applications such as legacy migration and interoperability, metadata management for the web is taking its own shape and form. Metadata can be mined to extract information. Various data management techniques may be used to manage the metadata also. With the web, the amounts of metadata could be large. Metadata could include various policies and procedures, information about the resources, information about the agents on the web as well as information about the data sources. Ontologies, a way of specifying various concepts, relationships, and entities, is an area that is exploding. Various standards organizations are proposing ontologies for web data management.

Finally different standards are emerging for web data management. Javasoft's Java Database Connectivity (JDBC) was the first step to connect relational database to the web. The most popular standard for web data management is XML (Extensible Markup Language). Some claim that XML is becoming the data model for web databases. Essentially XML is a standard way of expressing documents so that they can be exchanged on the web. But XML has evolved to such a great extent that various ontologies are now being expressed in XML. Figure 1-4 illustrates how all these data management technologies come together for web data management.

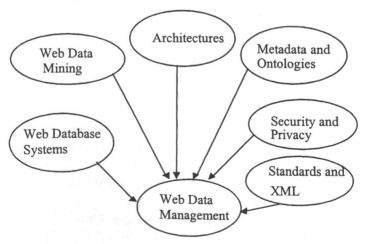

Figure 1-4. Data Management Technologies for the Web

1.6 EMERGING INFORMATION MANAGEMENT TECHNOLOGIES FOR THE WEB

Various information and knowledge management technologies are emerging for the web. In fact we feel that knowledge management became a technology area mainly due to the web. The idea behind knowledge management is to develop tools and techniques to capture the knowledge of an organization. Knowledge is power and capturing and using knowledge and expertise puts organizations at a tremendous advantage over their competitors. Knowledge management process includes creating knowledge, storing and representing knowledge, effectively using and sharing the knowledge and updating the knowledge. The Web in the form of Internet and Intranets is a vehicle for knowledge management.

Numerous other information technologies are being applied for web data management. These include visualizing the data on the web for better management, managing and mining multimedia data, collaborating and sharing information on the web, conducting training classes on the web and many other technologies such as digital libraries, machine language translation, intelligent agents and mediators, as well as information extraction. Publish and subscribe models are gaining popularity for managing the large quantities of data on the web. Figure 1-5 illustrates how all these various information and knowledge management techniques are being used for web data management.

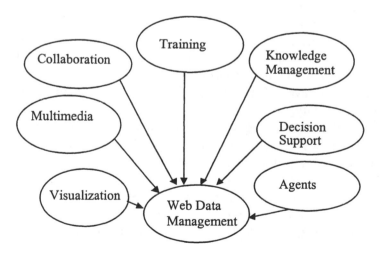

Figure 1-5. Information Technologies for the Web

The ultimate goal is to have various tools and techniques available for managers, educators, policy makers, and technologists to make effective decisions. That is, decision-making and decision support are technologies that are gaining a lot of interest with respect to web data management. All this will help toward effective enterprise data/information/knowledge management.

1.7 ELECTRONIC COMMERCE

Now that we have described the various technologies for the web, the main question is what are the applications that benefit from the web? We hear about training and collaboration on the web, entertainment on the web, and having a lookup service on the web. All this amounts to one thing and that is ELECTRONIC COMMERCE, which we will refer to from now on as E-COMMERCE. Perhaps the single most important activity that has resulted from the web is e-commerce. So, what is e-commerce? Generally it is an activity that is used to conduct business on the web. Once we had email and electronic communication facilities, one of the important developments was EDI (electronic data interchange). However, with the advent of the web, EDI is sort of being overtaken by e-commerce.[2] What sort of business can you carry out on the web? Almost anything, the web can be used to purchase products. The web can be used to market your products. The web can also be used to provide entertainment and training. In fact many elementary school children are benefiting from the web and there are programs now that use the web as a vehicle for teaching classes. Distance learning is really taking off. One can also conduct operations and surgeries via the web and this is now being known as telemedicine. While text-based communication is still dominant, it is expected that soon voice-based communication will prevail. One only needs a smart phone to carry out any business activity.

All of the technologies we have described in this book contribute extensively toward electronic commerce. One can apply data management technologies for managing the data, transaction management for carrying out web transactions, security for protecting e-commerce activities, and mining to learn about competitors' products. Figure 1-6 illustrates the various components of electronic commerce. Part III of this book will explore electronic commerce in more detail.

---

[2] In Part III we will introduce e-business (electronic business) and discuss its relationship to e-commerce.

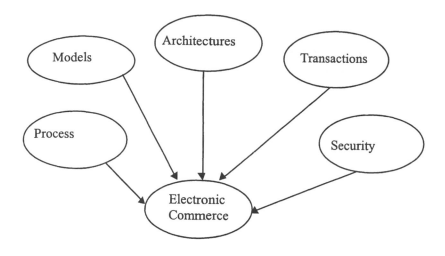

Figure 1-6. Components for Electronic Commerce

1.8 ORGANIZATION OF THIS BOOK

This book covers the essential web topics in web data management and electronic commerce in three parts: Supporting Technologies, Data and Information Management Technologies, and Electronic Commerce. To explain our ideas more clearly, we illustrate a web data management framework in Figure 1-7. This framework has three layers. Layer 1 is the Supporting Technologies Layer. It describes the various supporting technologies that contribute to web data management. These include database management, data mining, objects, interoperability and security. Layer 2 is the Data and Information Management Technologies Layer. This layer describes the various data management concepts and techniques for the web including web databases, web mining, security and privacy, metadata, and emerging standards. This layer also describes emerging information management technologies for the web such as knowledge management and decision support, multimedia and collaboration, and agents. Layer 3 is the Application Layer and is all about e-commerce.

Each layer is described in a part of this book. Part I, consisting of six chapters, describes the various supporting technologies. Chapter 2 describes database systems technology. This includes a discussion of data modeling, architectures, and functions. We believe it is the developments in database technologies that have mainly contributed to the existence of web data management as a technical area now. Chapter 3 describes what data mining is all about. Chapter 4 discusses technologies for interoperability such as client-server architectures and heterogeneous database integration. Chapter 5 discusses object technologies including object databases and distributed object systems. Chapter 6 focuses on security and provides a background on various security concepts and techniques. Finally, Chapter 7, while not directly related

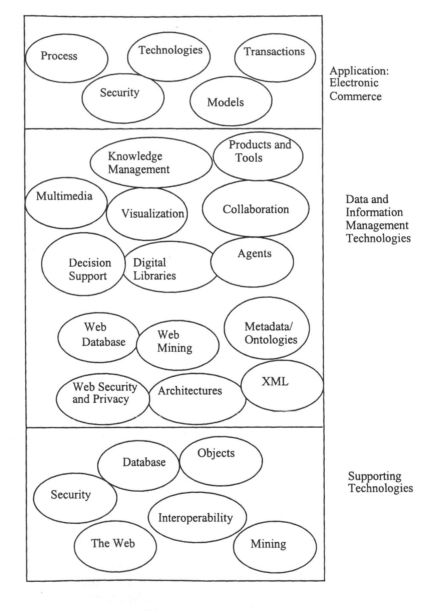

Figure 1.7. Framework for Web Data Management

to a supporting technology, gives an introduction to the World Wide Web. We included this discussion for completion and have it in Part I, as we did not find another suitable place for this important topic.

Part II, consisting of eight chapters, addresses data and information management technologies for the web. Chapter 8 is on web database management. In particular, functions for web data management, interoperability issues, architectures, as well as integrating structured and unstructured databases, are discussed. In addition, digital libraries are also addressed in this chapter. Chapter 9 describes web data mining. Both mining web data to extract useful information as well as mining web usage patterns to give guidance to the user are mentioned. Security and privacy aspects of the web are the subject of Chapter 10. More consideration is given to privacy issues in this chapter, as security will be addressed under e-commerce in Part III. Chapter 11 describes the essential points in managing metadata for the web as well as ontologies for web data management. Emerging standards for the web such as XML are also addressed. While Chapters 8, 9, 10, and 11 address data management technologies for the web, emerging information management technologies for the web are addressed in the next three chapters. Chapter 12 describes some other information technologies such as collaboration and multimedia services for the web. In addition, topics such as training, visualization, and real-time performance issues are also addressed. Chapter 13 describes knowledge management and decision support functions. As mentioned earlier, knowledge management has evolved as a technology area mainly due to the advent of the web. Agents for the web is the subject of Chapter 14. An overview of some of the tools for web data and information management will be given in Chapter 15.[3]

While Parts I and II address technologies, Part III addresses the important application area of e-commerce. Chapter 16 provides an overview of e-commerce and discusses the process, models, architectures and functions. Data and information management technologies for e-commerce are the subject of Chapter 17. Essentially this chapter examines the technologies discussed in Part II and shows the relationship to e-commerce. Security implications are the subject of Chapter 18. Managing transactions for e-commerce is the subject of Chapter 19. Figure 1-8 illustrates the chapters in which the components of the framework in Figure 1-7 are addressed in this book. We summarize the

---

[3] Note that we could have separated the contents of Part II into two parts, first of which would have addressed more data management technologies and the second would have addressed information management technologies. However we could not draw a clear distinction between the two. Therefore we merged all eight chapters into one part.

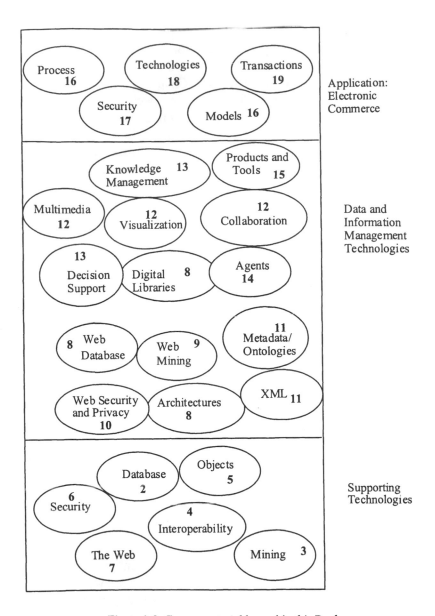

Figure 1-8. Components Addressed in this Book

book and provide a discussion of challenges and directions in Chapter 20. Each of the chapters in Parts I, II, and III, in other words Chapters 2 through 19, starts with an overview of the chapter and ends with a summary of the chapter. Each part also begins with an introduction and ends with a conclusion. Finally, we have three appendices that provide useful background information. As we will see, both data management and networking technologies play a major role in web data management. Appendix A provides an overview of trends in data management technology, and in Appendix B, we provide an overview of the developments and trends in networking technology. We stress in this book that e-commerce is only part technology. A major part of e-commerce is related to business. Various business functions are being carried out electronically. One such aspect of the business of an organization is enterprise business processing. Therefore, in Appendix C we provide an overview of various enterprise business processes. We can expect to hear a lot about this topic related to e-commerce in the future. We also provide a fairly comprehensive list of references in the section on references. We have obtained these references from various journals, conference and workshop proceedings, and magazines. In addition, each appendix also has its own set of references. We end this book with an Index.

1.9 HOW DO WE PROCEED?

This chapter has provided an introduction to web data management. We first discussed data, information and knowledge. Then we provided a brief introduction to the web. Supporting technologies for web data management were described next. These included database systems, data mining, interoperability, object management, and information security. Then we focussed on data management related technologies for the web. In particular, web database management, web mining, security and privacy issues, metadata and ontologies, and emerging standards were discussed. The next topic was about emerging information technologies for the web which included knowledge management, distributed agents, multimedia and collaboration. Finally we discussed a key application area and that is electronic commerce. Parts I, II, and III of this book elaborate on Sections 1.4, 1.5, 1.6 and 1.7. The organization of this book was detailed in Section 1.8 which also included a framework for organization purposes. Our framework is a three-layer framework and each layer is addressed in a part of this book.

This book provides the information for a reader to get familiar with web data management. Many important topics are covered so that the reader has some idea as to what web data management is all about. For an in-depth understanding of the various topics covered in this book, we recommend the reader to the references we have given. Various papers and articles have appeared on web data management and related areas. We reference many of these throughout this book. Some of the interesting discussions have been published in the proceedings of the World Wide Web conference series. The World Wide Web consortium (W3C) has also been responsible for tremendous advances on the web. The URL for this consortium at the time this book goes to press is www.w3c.org.

There is so much to write about web data management and e-commerce that we could be writing this book forever. That is, while we have tried to provide as much information as possible in this book, there is so much more to write about. Daily we hear about e-commerce on the news, various television programs, and in conversations. There is going to be no limit to this subject as we enter the new millennium. My advice to the reader is to keep up with the developments, discern what is important and what is not, and be knowledgeable about this subject. It will not only help people in their business lives but also in their personal lives such as personal investments and other activities.

Part I

Supporting Technologies for Web Data Management

Introduction to Part I

Part I, consisting of six chapters, describes supporting technologies for web data management. Chapter 2 provides an overview of database system technology and discusses the impact of the web on this technology. In particular, data modeling and architectures, database system functions such as query processing, transaction management and metadata management are discussed. In Part II we will see that web impacts data modeling and architectures, as well as database functions.

Chapter 3 provides an overview of data mining. In particular, technologies for data mining, data mining techniques, and emerging directions are discussed. Web data mining is an important aspect of data mining and has many applications in electronic commerce. Web data mining will be addressed in Part II while its applications to e-commerce will be addressed in Part III.

Chapter 4 discusses interoperability aspects. In particular, distributed databases, heterogeneous database integration, and client-server databases are discussed. Architectures for such systems are being applied for interoperability on the web and will be addressed in Part II.

Chapter 5 provides an overview of object technology. Object technology includes object databases, object-oriented programming languages, object-oriented design and analysis techniques, distributed object systems, and components and frameworks. All of these object technologies have applications in web data management.

Chapter 6 describes security issues. It starts with a discussion of access control and then describes secure systems. The focus is mainly on secure databases as the emphasis of this book is on web data management. Emerging trends in security are also discussed. It should be noted that security is one of the critical technologies for the web and e-commerce.

While Chapters 1 through 6 focus on supporting technologies for the web, Chapter 7 provides an introduction to the web. In particular, the evolution of the web as well as aspects of corporate information infrastructures are discussed.

CHAPTER 2

DATABASE SYSTEMS TECHNOLOGY

2.1 OVERVIEW

Database systems play a key role in web data management. Having good data is key to effective web data management, and, therefore, we give considerable attention to database systems in this book. It should be noted that we are taking quite a data-oriented perspective to the web.

Database systems technology has advanced a great deal during the past four decades from the legacy systems based on network and hierarchical models to relational and object-oriented database systems based on client-server architectures. This chapter provides an overview of the important developments in database systems relevant to the contents of this book. Much of the discussion in the remainder of this book builds on the information presented in this chapter.

As stated in Appendix A, we consider a database system to include both the database management system (DBMS) and the database (see also the discussion in [DATE90]). The DBMS component of the database system manages the database. The database contains persistent data. That is, the data are permanent even if the application programs go away.

The organization of this chapter is as follows. In Section 2.2, relational data models, as well as entity relationship models are discussed. In Section 2.3 various types of architectures for database systems are described. These include an architecture for a centralized database system, schema architecture, as well as functional architecture. Database design issues are discussed in Section 2.4. Database administration issues are discussed in Section 2.5. Database system functions are discussed in Section 2.6. These functions include query processing, transaction management, metadata management, storage management, maintaining integrity and security, and fault tolerance. The impact of the web is the subject of Section 2.7. The chapter is summarized in Section 2.8.[4]

---

[4] There are other data management technologies. For example data warehousing is discussed in the chapter on data mining. Distributed, heterogeneous, and client-server data management are discussed in the chapter on interoperability.

2.2 RELATIONAL AND ENTITY-RELATIONSHIP DATA MODELS

2.2.1 Overview

It is widely accepted among the data modeling community that the purpose of a data model is to capture the universe that it is representing as accurately, completely, and naturally as possible [TSIC82]. Various data models have been proposed and we have provided an overview in our previous book [THUR97]. In this section we discuss the essential points of the relational data model as it is the most widely used today. In addition we also discuss entity-relationship data model, as some of the ideas have been used in object models and, furthermore, entity relationship models are being used extensively in database design. There do exist many other models such as logic-based models, hypersemantic models and functional models. Discussion of all of these models is beyond the scope of this book. We do provide an overview of an object model in Chapter 5, as object technology is essential for the web.

2.2.2 Relational Data Model

With the relational model [CODD70], the database is viewed as a collection of relations. Each relation has attributes and rows. For example, Figure 2-1 illustrates a database with two relations EMP and DEPT. EMP has four attributes: SS#, Ename, Salary, and D#. DEPT has three attributes: D#, Dname, and Mgr. EMP has three rows, also called tuples, and DEPT has two rows. Each row is uniquely identified by its primary key. For example, SS# could be the primary key for EMP and D# for DEPT. Another key feature of the relational model is that each element in the relation is an atomic value such as an integer or a string. That is, complex values such as lists are not supported.

EMP

SS#	Ename	Salary	D#
1	John	20K	10
2	Paul	30K	20
3	Mary	40K	20

DEPT

D#	Dname	Mgr
10	Math	Smith
20	Physics	Jones

Figure 2-1. Relational Database

Various operations are performed on relations. The SELECT operation selects a subset of rows satisfying certain conditions. For example, in the relation EMP, one may select tuples where the salary is more than 20K. The PROJECT operation projects the relation onto some attributes. For example, in the relation EMP one may project onto the attributes Ename and Salary. The JOIN operation joins two relations over some common attributes. A detailed discussion of these operations is given in [DATE90] and [ULLM88].

Various languages to manipulate the relations have been proposed. Notable among these languages is the ANSI Standard SQL (Structured Query Language). This language is used to access and manipulate data in relational databases [SQL3]. There is wide acceptance of this standard among database management system vendors and users. It supports schema definition, retrieval, data manipulation, schema manipulation, transaction management, integrity, and security. Other languages include the relational calculus first proposed in the Ingres project at the University of California at Berkeley [DATE90]. Another important concept in relational databases is the notion of a view. A view is essentially a virtual relation and is formed from the relations in the database. For further details we refer to [DATE90].

2.2.3 Entity-Relationship Data Model

One of the major drawbacks of the relational data model is its lack of support for capturing the semantics of an application. This resulted in the development of semantic data models. The entity-relationship (ER) data model developed by Chen [CHEN76] can be regarded to be the earliest semantic data model. In this model, the world is viewed as a collection of entities and relationships between entities. Figure 2-2 illustrates two entities, EMP and DEPT. The relationship between them is WORKS.

Relationships can be either one-one, many-one, or many-many. If it is assumed that each employee works in one department and each department has one employee, then WORKS is a one-one relationship. If it is assumed that an employee works in one department and each department can have many employees, then WORKS is a many-one relationship. If it is assumed that an employee works in many departments, and each department has many employees, then WORKS is a many-many relationship.

Figure 2-2. Entity-Relationship Representation

Several extensions to the entity-relationship model have been proposed. One is the entity-relationship-attribute model where attributes are associated with entities as well as relationships, and another has introduced the notion of categories into the model (see for example the discussions in [ELMA85], YANG88]). It should be noted that ER models are used mainly to design databases. That is, most database CASE tools are based on the ER model, where the application is represented using such a model and subsequently the database (possibly relational) is generated.[5] Current database management systems are not based on the ER model. That is, unlike the relational model, ER models did not take off in the development of database management systems.

2.3 ARCHITECTURAL ISSUES

This section describes various types of architectures for a database system. First we illustrate a very high-level centralized architecture for a database system. Then we describe a functional architecture for a database system. In particular, the functions of the DBMS component of the database system are illustrated in this architecture. Then we discuss the ANSI/SPARC's three-schema architecture, which has been more or less accepted by the database community [DATE90]. Finally, we describe extensible architectures.[6]

Figure 2-3 is an example of a centralized architecture. Here, the DBMS is a monolithic entity and manages a database, which is centralized. Functional architecture illustrates the functional modules of a DBMS. The major modules of a DBMS include the query processor, transaction manager, metadata manager, storage manager, integrity manager, and security manager. The functional architecture of the DBMS component of the centralized database system architecture (of Figure 2-3) is illustrated in Figure 2-4.

---

[5] CASE stands for Computer Aided Software Engineering.

[6] Note that distributed architectures for data management are discussed in Chapter 4 where we address distributed, heterogeneous, and legacy databases.

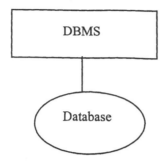

Figure 2-3. Centralized Architecture

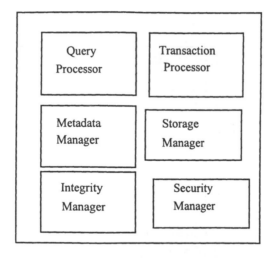

Figure 2-4. Functional Architecture for a DBMS

Schema describes the data in the database. It has also been referred to as the data dictionary or contents of the metadatabase. Three-schema architecture was proposed for a centralized database system in the 1960s. This is illustrated in Figure 2-5. The levels are the external schema, which provides an external view, the conceptual schema, which provides a conceptual view, and the internal schema, which provides an internal view. Mappings between the different schemas must be provided to transform one representation into another. For example, at the external level, one could use ER representation. At the logical or conceptual level, one could use relational representation. At the physical level, one could use a representation based on B-Trees.[7]

There is also another aspect to architectures, and that is extensible database architectures. For example, for many applications, a DBMS may have to be extended with a layer to support objects or to process rules or to handle multimedia data types or even to do mining. Such an extensible architecture is illustrated in Figure 2-6.

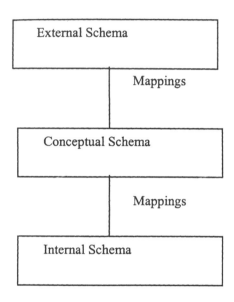

Figure 2-5. Three-Schema Architecture

2.4 DATABASE DESIGN

Designing a database is a complex process. Much of the work has been on designing relational databases. There are three steps, which are illustrated in Figure 2-7. The first step is to capture the entities of the application and the relationships between the entities. One could use a model such as the entity-relationship model for this purpose. More recently, object-oriented data models, which are part of object-oriented design and analysis methodologies, are becoming popular to represent the application.

The second step is to generate the relations from the representations. For example, from the entity-relationship diagram of Figure 2-2, one

---

[7]   Note that a B-Tree is a representation scheme used to physically represent the data. However, it is at a higher level than the bits and bytes level. For a discussion on physical structures and models, we refer to [DATE90].

could generate the relations EMP, DEPT, and WORKS. The relation WORKS will capture the relationship between employees and departments.

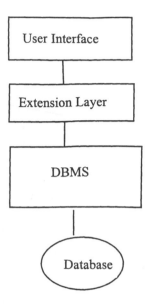

Figure 2-6. Extensible DBMS

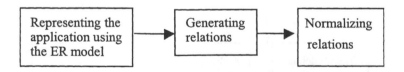

Figure 2-7. Database Design Process

The third step is to design good relations. This is the normalization process. Various normal forms have been defined in the literature (see, for example, [MAIE83] and [DATE90]). For many applications, relations in third normal form would suffice. With this normal form, redundancies, complex values, and other situations that could cause potential anomalies are eliminated.

2.5 DATABASE ADMINISTRATION

A database has a database administrator (DBA). It is the responsibility of the DBA to define the various schemas and mappings. In addition, the functions of the administrator include auditing the database as well as implementing appropriate backup and recovery procedures.

The DBA could also be responsible for maintaining the security of the system. In some cases, the system security officer (SSO) maintains security. The administrator should determine the granularity of the data for auditing. For example, in some cases there is tuple (or row) level auditing while in other cases there is table (or relation) level auditing. It is also the administrator's responsibility to analyze the audit data.

Note that there is a difference between database administration and data administration. Database administration assumes there is an installed database system. The DBA manages this system. Data administration functions include conducting data analysis, determining how a corporation handles its data, and enforcing appropriate policies and procedures for managing the data of a corporation. Data administration functions are carried out by the data administrator. For a discussion of data administration, we refer to [DMH94, DMH95, DMH96, DMH98, DOD94, DOD95]. Figure 2-8 illustrates various database administration issues.

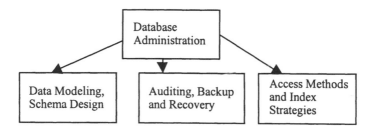

Figure 2-8. Some Database Administration Issues

2.6 DATABASE MANAGEMENT SYSTEM FUNCTIONS

2.6.1 Overview

The functional architecture of a DBMS was illustrated in Figure 2-4. The functions of a DBMS carry out its operations. A DBMS essentially manages a database, and it provides support to the user by enabling him to query and update the database. Therefore, the basic functions of a DBMS are query processing and update processing. In some applications such as banking, queries and updates are issued as part of transactions. Therefore transaction management is also another function of a DBMS. To carry out these functions, information about the database has to be maintained. This information is called metadata. The function that is associated with managing the metadata is metadata management. Special techniques are needed to manage the data stores that actually store the data. The function that is associated with managing these techniques is storage management. To ensure that the above functions are carried out properly and that the user gets accurate data, there are some additional functions. These include security management, integrity management, and fault management (i.e., fault tolerance).

The above are some of the essential functions of a DBMS. However, more recently there is emphasis on extracting information from the data. Therefore, other functions of a DBMS may include providing support for data mining, data warehousing, and collaboration.

This section focuses only on the essential functions of a DBMS. These are query processing, transaction management, metadata management, storage management, maintaining integrity, security control, and fault tolerance. Note that we do not have a special section for update processing, as we can handle it as part of transaction management. We discuss each of the essential functions in Sections 2.6.2 to 2.6.7.

2.6.2 Query Processing

Query operation is the most commonly used function in a DBMS. It should be possible for users to query the database and obtain answers to their queries. There are several aspects to query processing. First of all, a good query language is needed. Languages such as SQL are popular for relational databases. Such languages are being extended for other types of databases. The second aspect is techniques for query processing. Numerous algorithms have been proposed for query processing in general and for the JOIN operation in particular (see also [KIM85]). Also, different strategies are possible to execute a particular query. The costs for the various strategies are computed, and the one with the least cost is usually selected for processing. This process is called query optimization. Cost is generally determined by the disk access. The goal is to minimize disk access in processing a query.

As stated earlier, users pose a query using a language. The constructs of the language have to be transformed into the constructs understood by the database system. This process is called query transformation. Query transformation is carried out in stages based on the various schemas. For example, a query based on the external schema is transformed into a query on the conceptual schema. This is then transformed into a query on the physical schema. In general, rules used in the transformation process include the factoring of common subexpressions and pushing selections and projections down in the query tree as much as possible. If selections and projections are performed before the joins, then the cost of the joins can be reduced by a considerable amount.

Figure 2-9 illustrates the modules in query processing. The user interface manager accepts queries, parses the queries, and then gives them to the query transformer. The query transformer and query optimizer communicate with each other to produce an execution strategy. The database is accessed through the storage manager. The response manager gives responses to the user.

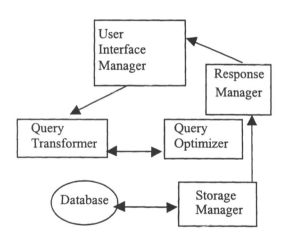

Figure 2-9. Query Processor

2.6.3 Transaction Management

A transaction is a program unit that must be executed in its entirety or not executed at all. If transactions are executed serially, then there is a performance bottleneck. Therefore, transactions are executed concurrently. Appropriate techniques must ensure that the database is consistent when multiple transactions update the database. That is, transactions must satisfy the ACID (Atomicity, Consistency, Isolation, and Durability) properties. Major aspects of transaction management are serializability, concurrency control, and recovery. We discuss them briefly in this section. For a detailed discussion of transaction management we refer to [DATE90] and [ULLM88]. A good theoretical treatment of this topic is given in [BERN87].

Serializability: A schedule is a sequence of operations performed by multiple transactions. Two schedules are equivalent if their outcomes are the same. A serial schedule is a schedule where no two transactions execute concurrently. An objective in transaction management is to ensure that any schedule is equivalent to a serial schedule. Such a schedule is called a serializable schedule. Various conditions for testing the serializability of a schedule have been formulated for a DBMS.

Concurrency Control: Concurrency control techniques ensure that the database is in a consistent state when multiple transactions update the database. Three popular concurrency control techniques which ensure the serializability of schedules are locking, time-stamping, and validation.

Recovery: If a transaction aborts due to some failure, then the database must be brought to a consistent state. This is transaction recovery. One solution to handling transaction failure is to maintain log files. The transaction's actions are recorded in the log file. So, if a transaction aborts, then the database is brought back to a consistent state by undoing the actions of the transaction. The information for the undo operation is found in the log file. Another solution is to record the actions of a transaction but not make any changes to the database. Only if a transaction commits should the database be updated. There are some issues, however. For example, the log files have to be kept in stable storage. Various modifications to the above techniques have been proposed to handle the different situations.

When transactions are executed at multiple data sources, then a protocol called two-phase commit is used to ensure that the multiple data sources are consistent. Figure 2-10 illustrates the various aspects of transaction management.

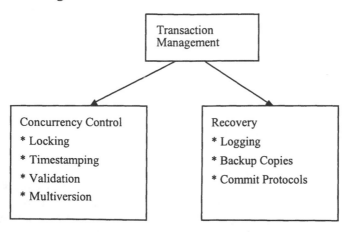

Figure 2-10. Some Aspects of Transaction Management

2.6.4 Storage Management

The storage manager is responsible for accessing the database. To improve the efficiency of query and update algorithms, appropriate access methods and index strategies have to be enforced. That is, in generating strategies for executing query and update requests, the access methods and index strategies that are used need to be taken into consideration. The access methods used to access the database would depend on the indexing methods. Therefore, creating and maintaining appropriate index file is a major issue in database management systems. By using an appropriate indexing mechanism, the query processing algorithms may not have to search the entire database. Instead, the data to be retrieved could be accessed directly. Consequently, the retrieval algorithms are more efficient. Figure 2-11 illustrates an example of an indexing strategy where the database is indexed by projects.

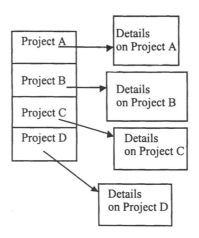

Figure 2-11. An Example Index on Projects

Much research has been carried out on developing appropriate access methods and index strategies for relational database systems. Some examples of index strategies are B-Trees and Hashing [DATE90]. Current research is focusing on developing such mechanisms for object-oriented database systems with support for multimedia data.

2.6.5 Metadata Management

Metadata describes the data in the database. For example, in the case of the relational database illustrated in Figure 2-1, metadata would include the following information: the database has two relations, EMP and DEPT; EMP has four attributes and DEPT has three attributes, etc.

One of the main issues is developing a data model for metadata. In our example, one could use a relational model to model the metadata also. The metadata relation REL shown in Figure 2-12 consists of information about relations and attributes.

In addition to information about the data in the database, metadata also includes information on access methods, index strategies, security constraints, and integrity constraints. One could also include policies and procedures as part of the metadata. In other words, there is no standard definition for metadata. There are, however, efforts to standardize metadata [META96]. Metadata becomes a major issue with some of the recent developments in data management such as digital libraries. Some of the issues are discussed in Part II of this book.

Relation REL

Relation	Attribute
EMP	SS#
EMP	Ename
EMP	Salary
EMP	D#
DEPT	D#
DEPT	Dname
DEPT	Mgr

Figure 2-12. Metadata Relation

Once the metadata is defined, the issues include managing the metadata. What are the techniques for querying and updating the metadata? Since all of the other DBMS components need to access the metadata for processing, what are the interfaces between the metadata manager and the other components? Metadata management is fairly well understood for relational database systems. The current challenge is in managing the metadata for more complex systems such as digital libraries and Internet database systems.

2.6.6 Database Integrity

Concurrency control and recovery techniques maintain the integrity of the database. In addition, there is another type of database integrity and that is enforcing integrity constraints. There are two types of integrity constraints enforced in database systems. These are application independent integrity constraints and application specific integrity constraints. Integrity mechanisms also include techniques for determining the quality of the data. For example, what is the accuracy of the data and that of the source? What are the mechanisms for maintaining the quality of the data? How accurate is the data on output? In [AFSB83] we only discussed the enforcement of application independent and application specific integrity constraints. Our focus was on the relational data model. For a discussion of integrity based on data quality, we refer to [MIT]. Note that data quality is very important for mining and warehousing. If the data that is mined is not good, then one cannot rely on the results. We revisit this in Chapter 6.

Application independent integrity constraints include the primary key constraint, the entity integrity rule, referential integrity constraint, and the various functional dependencies involved in the normalization process (see the discussion in [DATE90]).

Application specific integrity constraints are those constraints that are specific to an application. Examples include "an employee's salary cannot decrease" and "no manager can manage more than two departments." Various techniques have been proposed to enforce application specific integrity constraints. For example, when the database is updated, these constraints are checked and the data are validated. Aspects of database integrity are illustrated in Figure 2-13.

2.6.7 Database Security

In this section we focus on discretionary security since this is the area that we are interested in with respect to warehousing and mining.[8] The major issues in security are authentication, identification, and enforcing appropriate access controls. For example, what are the mechanisms for identifying and authenticating the user? Will simple password mechanisms suffice? With respect to access control rules, languages such as SQL have incorporated GRANT and REVOKE statements to grant and revoke access to users. For many applications simple GRANT and REVOKE statements are not sufficient. There may be more complex authorizations based on database content. Negative authorizations may also be needed. Access to data based on the roles of the user is also being investigated.

Numerous papers have been published on discretionary security in databases. These can be found in various security-related journals and

---

[8] Note that multilevel security issues for database systems were addressed in [AFSB83].

conference proceedings (see, for example, [IFIP]). Some aspects of database security are illustrated in Figure 2-14.

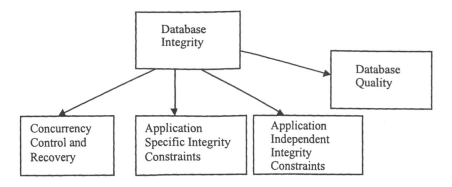

Figure 2-13. Some Aspects of Database Integrity

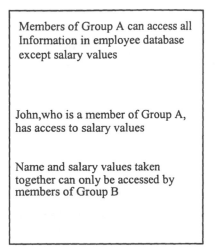

Figure 2-14. Access Control Rules

2.6.8 Fault Tolerance

The previous two sections discussed database integrity and security. A closely related feature is fault tolerance. It is almost impossible to guarantee that the database will function as planned. In reality, various faults could occur. These could be hardware faults or software faults. As mentioned earlier, one of the major issues in transaction management is to ensure that the database is brought back to a consistent state in the presence of faults. The solutions proposed include maintaining appropriate log files to record the actions of a transaction in case its actions have to be retraced.

Another approach to handling faults is checkpointing. Various checkpoints are placed during the course of database processing. At each checkpoint it is ensured that the database is in a consistent state. Therefore, if a fault occurs during processing, then the database must be brought back to the last checkpoint. This way it can be guaranteed that the database is consistent. Closely associated with checkpointing are acceptance tests. After various processing steps, the acceptance tests are checked. If the techniques pass the tests, then they can proceed further. Some aspects of fault tolerance are illustrated in Figure 2-15.

```
Checkpoint A
Start Processing
*

*

Acceptance Test
If OK, then go to Checkpoint  B
Else Roll Back to Checkpoint A


Checkpoint B
Start Processing
*

*
```

Figure 2-15. Some Aspects of Fault Tolerance

2.7 IMPACT OF THE WEB

The explosion of the users on the Internet and the increasing number of world wide web servers with large quantities of data are rapidly advancing database management on the web. For example, the heterogeneous information sources have to be integrated so that users access the servers in a transparent and timely manner. Security and privacy is becoming a major concern. So are other issues such as copyright protection and ownership of the data. Policies and procedures have to be set up to address these issues.

Database management functions for the web include those such as query processing, metadata management, storage management, transaction management, security, and integrity. In [THUR96a] we have examined various database management system functions and discussed the impact of Internet database access on these functions. Some of the issues are discussed in more detail in Chapter 8. Figure 2-16 illustrates applications accessing various database systems on the web.

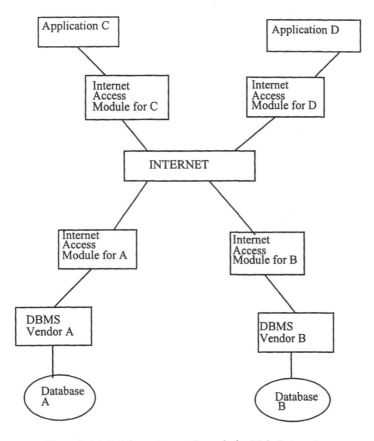

Figure 2-16. Database Access through the Web (Internet)

2.8 SUMMARY

This chapter has discussed various aspects of database systems and provided a lot of background information to understand the other chapters in this book. We began with a discussion of various data models. We chose relational and entity-relationship models as they are more relevant to what we have addressed in this book. Then we provided an overview of various types of architectures for database systems. These include functional and schema architectures. Note that we have focused on centralized systems. Distributed database system issues will be discussed in Chapter 4. Next we discussed database design aspects and database administration issues. This chapter also provided an overview of the various functions of database systems. These include query processing, transaction management, storage management, metadata management, security, integrity, and fault tolerance.[9] Finally we discussed briefly the impact of the web on database management.

Many of the chapters in this book discuss various data management system aspects related to the web. These include data mining and warehousing, interoperability, metadata management and ontologies, multimedia databases, and security and privacy implications.

---

[9]   Various texts have been published on database systems. Examples include [KORT86], [ULLM88], [DATE90], and [THUR97].

CHAPTER 3

DATA MINING

3.1 OVERVIEW

Data mining is another important technology for the web. The increasing number of databases on the web has to be mined to extract useful information. Data mining is the process of posing various queries and extracting useful information, patterns, and trends often previously unknown from large quantities of data possibly stored in databases. Essentially, for many organizations, the goals of data mining include improving marketing capabilities, detecting abnormal patterns, and predicting the future based on past experiences and current trends. There is clearly a need for this technology. There are large amounts of current and historical data being stored. Therefore, as databases become larger, it becomes increasingly difficult to support decision making. In addition, the data could be from multiple sources and multiple domains. There is a clear need to analyze the data to support planning and other functions of an enterprise.

Various terms have been used to refer to data mining as shown in Figure 3-1. These include knowledge/data/information discovery and knowledge/data/information extraction. Note that some define data mining to be the process of extracting previously unknown information while knowledge discovery is defined as the process of making sense out of the extracted information. In this book we do not differentiate between data mining and knowledge discovery. It is difficult to determine whether a particular technique is a data mining technique. For example, some argue that statistical analysis techniques are data mining techniques. Others argue they are not and that data mining techniques should uncover relationships that are not straightforward. For example, with data mining, a medical supplies company could increase sales by targeting certain physicians in its advertising who are likely to buy the products, or a credit bureau may limit its losses by selecting candidates who are not likely to default on their payments. Such real-world experiences have been reported in various papers (see, for example, [GRUP98]). In addition, data mining could also be used to detect abnormal behavior. For example, an intelligence agency could determine abnormal behavior of its employees using this technology.

Some of the data mining techniques include those based on rough sets, inductive logic programming, machine learning, and neural networks, among others. The data mining problems include classification (finding rules to partition data into groups), association (finding rules to make associations between data), and sequencing (finding rules to order data). Essentially one arrives at some hypothesis, which is the information extracted, from examples and patterns observed. These patterns are observed from posing a series of queries; each query may depend on the responses obtained to the previous queries posed. There have been several developments in data mining. These include tools by corporations such as Lockheed Martin, Inc. (see, for example, [SIMO95]).

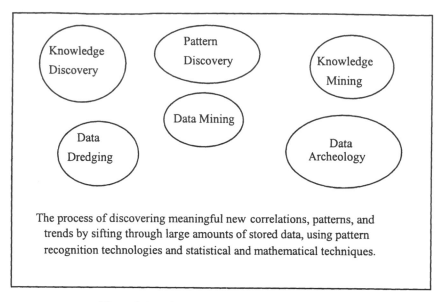

Figure 3-1. Different Definitions of Data Mining

This chapter is organized as follows. Technologies that contribute to data mining are discussed in Section 3.2. Essential concepts in data mining including techniques are discussed in Section 3.3. Trends in data mining are the subject of Section 3.4. Note that the contents of our previous book, *Data Mining: Technologies, Techniques, Tools and Trends*, is an elaboration of each of the three Sections: 3.2, 3.3, and 3.4. In Section 3.5 we describe data warehousing and its relationship to data mining. Impact of the web is the subject of Section 3.6. The chapter is summarized in Section 3.7.

3.2 DATA MINING TECHNOLOGIES

Data mining is an integration of multiple technologies as illustrated in Figure 3-2. These include data management such as database management, data warehousing, statistics, machine learning, decision support, and others such as visualization and parallel computing.[10] We briefly discuss the role of each of these technologies. It should however be noted that while many of these technologies such as statistical packages and machine learning algorithms have existed for many decades, the ability to manage the data and organize the data has played a major role in making data mining a reality.

Data mining research is being carried out in various disciplines. Database management researchers are taking advantage of the work on deductive and intelligent query processing for data mining. One of the areas of interest is to extend query processing techniques to facilitate data mining. Data warehousing is also another key data management technology for integrating the various data sources and organizing the data so that it can be effectively mined.

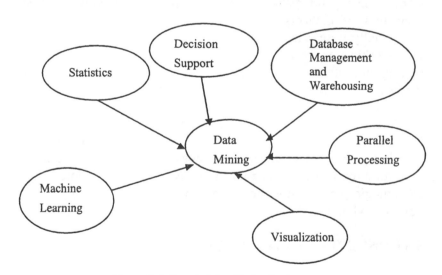

Figure 3-2. Data Mining Technologies

Researchers in statistical analysis are integrating their techniques with machine learning techniques to develop more sophisticated statistical techniques for data mining. Various statistical analysis

---

[10]   We have distinguished between data management and database management and also between data, information, and knowledge. Our definitions are given in Appendix A as well as in [THUR97].

packages are now being marketed as data mining tools. There is some dispute over this. Nevertheless, statistics is a major area contributing to data mining.

Machine learning has been around for a while. The idea here is for the machine to learn various rules from the patterns observed and then apply these rules to solve the problems. While the principles used in machine learning and data mining are similar, with data mining one usually considers large quantities of data to mine. Therefore, integration of database management and machine learning techniques are needed for data mining.

Researchers from the computer visualization field are approaching data mining from another perspective. One of their areas of focus is to use visualization techniques to aid the data mining process. In other words, interactive data mining is a goal of the visualization community.

Decision support systems are a collection of tools and processes to help managers make decisions and guide them in management. For example, tools for scheduling meetings, organizing events, spreadsheets, view graph tools, and performance evaluation tools are examples of decision support systems. Decision support has theoretical underpinnings in decision theory.

Finally, researchers in the high performance computing area are also working on developing appropriate techniques so that the data mining algorithms are scalable. There is also interaction with the hardware researchers so that appropriate hardware can be developed for high performance data mining.

It should be noted that several other technologies are beginning to have an impact on data mining including collaboration, agents, and distributed object management. A discussion of all of these technologies is beyond the scope of this book. We have focused on some of the key technologies here. Furthermore, we emphasize that having good data is key to good mining.

3.3 CONCEPTS AND TECHNIQUES IN DATA MINING

There are a series of steps involved in data mining. These include getting the data organized for mining, determining the desired outcomes to mining, selecting tools for mining, carrying out the mining, pruning the results so that only the useful ones are considered further, taking actions from the mining, and evaluating the actions to determine benefits. These steps will be discussed in detail in this book. We briefly review some of the outcomes and techniques.

There are various types of data mining. By this we do not mean the actual techniques used to mine the data, but what the outcomes will be. Some of these outcomes are discussed in [AGRA93], and we will elaborate them in this book. They have also been referred to as data mining tasks. We describe a few here.

In one outcome of data mining, called "classification," records are grouped into some meaningful subclasses. For example, suppose an automobile sales company has some information that all the people in its list who live in City X own cars worth more than 20K. They can then assume that even those who are not on their list, but live in City X, can afford to own cars costing more than 20K. This way the company classifies the people living in City X.

A second outcome of data mining is "sequence detection." That is, by observing patterns in the data, sequences are determined. Here is an example of sequence detection: after John goes to the bank, he generally goes to the grocery store.

A third outcome of data mining is "data dependency analysis." Here, potentially interesting dependencies, relationships, or associations between the data items are detected. For example, if John, James, and William have a meeting, then Robert will also be at that meeting. It appears it is this type of mining that is of much interest to many.

A fourth outcome of mining is "deviation analysis." For example, John went to the bank on Saturday, but he did not go to the grocery store after that. Instead he went to a football game. With this type, anomalous instances and discrepancies are found.

As mentioned earlier, various techniques are used to obtain the outcomes of data mining. These techniques could be based on rough sets, fuzzy logic, inductive logic programming, or neural networks, among others, or they could simply be some statistical technique. We discuss these techniques later in this book. Furthermore, different approaches have also been proposed to carry out data mining including top-down mining as well as bottom-up mining. Data mining outcomes, techniques and approaches are illustrated in Figure 3-3 and will be elaborated later in this book.

Numerous developments have been made in data mining over the past few years. Many of these focus on relational databases. That is, the data is stored in relational databases and mined to extract useful information and patterns. We have several research prototypes and commercial products. The research prototypes include those developed at IBM's (International Business Machines) Almaden Research Center and at Simon Fraser University. The prototypes and products employ various data mining techniques including neural networks, rule based reasoning, and statistical analysis. The various data mining tools in the form of prototypes and products will also be discussed in this book.

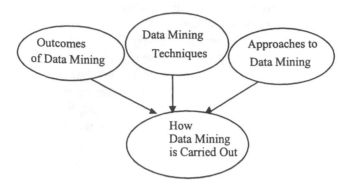

Figure 3-3. Aspects of Data Mining

3.4 DIRECTIONS AND TRENDS IN DATA MINING

While several developments have been made, there are also many challenges. For example, due to the large volumes of data, how can the algorithms determine which technique to select and what type of data mining to do? Furthermore, the data may be incomplete and/or inaccurate. At times there may be redundant information, and at times there may not be sufficient information. It is also desirable to have data mining tools that can switch to multiple techniques and support multiple outcomes. Some of the current trends in data mining include the following and are illustrated in Figure 3-4:

- Mining distributed, heterogeneous, and legacy databases
- Mining multimedia data
- Mining data on the World Wide Web
- Security and privacy issues in data mining
- Metadata aspects of mining

In many cases the databases are distributed and heterogeneous in nature. Furthermore, much of the data is in legacy databases. Mining techniques are needed to handle these distributed, heterogeneous, and legacy databases. Next, current data mining tools operate on structured data. However, there are still large quantities of data that are unstructured. Data in the multimedia databases are often semistructured or unstructured. Data mining tools have to be developed for multimedia databases. Next, the explosion of data and information on the World Wide Web necessitates the development of tools to manage and mine the data so that only useful information is extracted. Therefore, developing mining tools for the World Wide Web will be an important area. Privacy issues are becoming critical for data mining [THUR96b]. Users now have sophisticated tools to make inferences and deduce information to which they are not authorized. Therefore, while data mining tools help solve many problems in the real world, they could also invade the privacy of individuals. Throughout our previous book [THUR97] we repeatedly stressed the importance of metadata for data management. Metadata also plays a key role in data mining [THUR98a].

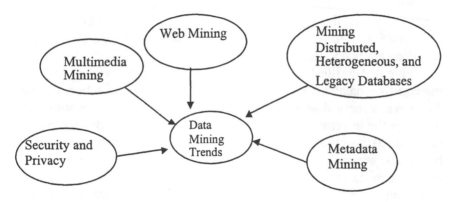

Figure 3-4. Data Mining Trends

In addition to the trends in the above areas, there are also several challenges. These include handling dynamic data, sparse data, incomplete and uncertain data, as well as determining which data mining algorithm to use and on what data to operate. In addition, mining multiple languages is also a challenge. Researchers are addressing these challenges.

3.5 DATA WAREHOUSING AND ITS RELATIONSHIP TO DATA MINING

Data warehousing is one of the key data management technologies to support data mining. Several organizations are building their own warehouses. Commercial database system vendors are marketing warehousing products. In addition, some companies are specializing only in developing data warehouses. What then is a data warehouse? The idea behind this is that it is often cumbersome to access data from the heterogeneous databases. Several processing modules need to cooperate with each other to process a query in a heterogeneous environment. Therefore, a data warehouse will bring together the essential data from the heterogeneous databases. This way the users need to query only the warehouse.

As stated by Inmon [INMO93], data warehouses are subject-oriented. Their design depends to a great extent on the application utilizing them. They integrate diverse and possibly heterogeneous data sources. They are persistent. That is, the warehouse is very much like a database. They vary with time. This is because as the data sources from which the warehouse is built get updated, the changes have to be reflected in the warehouse. Essentially data warehouses provide support to decision support functions of an enterprise or an organization. For example, while the data sources may have the raw data, the data warehouse may have correlated data, summary reports, and aggregate functions applied to the raw data.

Figure 3-5 illustrates a data warehouse. The data sources are managed by database systems A, B, and C. The information in these databases is merged and put into a warehouse. There are various ways to merge the information. One is to simply replicate the databases. This does not have any advantages over accessing the heterogeneous databases. The second case is to replicate the information, but to remove any inconsistencies and redundancies. This has some advantages, as it is important to provide a consistent picture of the databases. The third approach is to select a subset of the information from the databases and place it in the warehouse. There are several issues here. How are the subsets selected? Are they selected at random or is some method used to select the data? For example, one could take every other row in a relation (assuming it is a relational database) and store these rows in the warehouse. The fourth approach, which is a slight variation of the third approach, is to determine the types of queries that users would pose, then analyze the data and store only the data that is required by the user. This is called on-line analytical processing (OLAP) as opposed to on-line transaction processing (OLTP).

With a data warehouse, data may often be viewed differently by different applications. That is, the data is multidimensional. For example, the payroll department may want data to be in a certain format while the project department may want data to be in a different format. The warehouse must provide support for such multidimensional data.

In integrating the data sources to form the warehouse, a challenge is to analyze the application and select appropriate data to be placed in the warehouse. At times, some computations may have to be performed so that only summaries and averages are stored in the data warehouse.

Note that it is not always the case that the warehouse has all the information for a query. In this case, the warehouse may have to get the data from the heterogeneous data sources to complete the execution of the query. Another challenge is what happens to the warehouse when the individual databases are updated? How are the updates propagated to the warehouse? How can security be maintained? These are some of the issues that are being investigated.

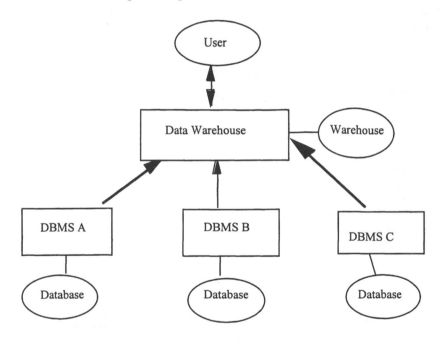

Figure 3-5. Data Warehouse Example

In our tutorials on data warehousing and mining, we are often asked the question do we really want to build a warehouse or do we want to integrate the data sources? For example, what is the difference between warehousing and interoperability? It should be noted that a warehouse is built for decision support. Therefore, the data in the warehouse may not reflect the changes made in the data sources in a timely fashion. If the data sources are changing rapidly and if the user wants to see the changes, then a warehouse may not make much sense, and one may want to simply integrate the heterogeneous data sources. However, in many cases one could have both; that is, a warehouse as well as database systems that interoperate with each other.

We are also often asked the question as to the difference and/or relationship between warehousing and mining. Note that while data

warehousing formats the data and organizes the data to support management functions, data mining attempts to extract useful information as
well as predicts trends from the data. Figure 3-6 illustrates the relationship between data warehousing and data mining. Note that having a
warehouse is not necessary to do mining, as data mining can be applied
to databases also. However, warehouse structures the data in such a way
as to facilitate mining; so, in many cases it is highly desirable to have a
data warehouse to carry out mining. The relationship between warehousing, mining and database systems is illustrated in Figure 3-7.

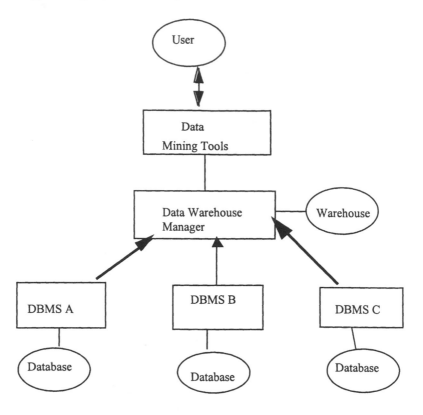

Figure 3-6. Data Mining vs. Data Warehousing

The answer to the question where does warehousing end and mining begin is rather subjective. There are certain questions that warehouses can answer. Furthermore, warehouses have built in decision
support capabilities. Some warehouses carry out predictions and trends.
In this case warehouses carry out some of the data mining functions. In
general, we believe that in the case of a warehouse the answer is in the
database. The warehouse has to come up with query optimization and

access techniques to get the answer. For example, consider questions like "how many red cars did physicians buy in 1990 in New York?" The answer is in the database. However, for a question like "how many red cars do you think physicians will buy in 2005 in New York?" the answer may not be in the database. Based on the buying patterns of physicians in New York and their salary projections, one could predict the answer to this question.

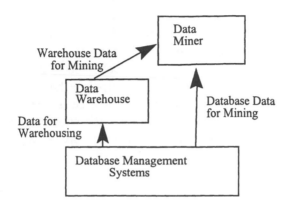

Figure 3-7. Database Systems, Data Warehousing and Mining

Essentially, a warehouse organizes the data effectively so the data can be mined. The question then is do you absolutely have to have a warehouse to mine the data? The answer we give is that it is very good to have a warehouse, but it does not mean we must have a warehouse to mine. A good DBMS that manages a database effectively could also be used. Also, with a warehouse one often does not have transactional data. Furthermore, the data may not be current; therefore the results obtained from mining may not be current. If one needs up-to-date information, then one could mine the database managed by a DBMS, which also has transaction processing features. Mining data that keeps changing often is a challenge. Typically mining has been used for decision support data. Therefore, there are several issues that need further investigation before we can carry out what we call real-time data mining. For now at least, we believe that having a good data warehouse is critical to do good mining for decision support functions. Note that one could also have an integrated tool that carries out both data warehousing and data mining functions. We call such a tool a data warehouse miner and this is illustrated in Figure 3-8.

3.6 IMPACT OF THE WEB

Mining the data on the web is one of the major challenges faced by the data management and mining community as well as those working on web information management and machine learning. There is so much data and information on the web that extracting the useful and relevant information for the user is the real challenge here. When one scans through the web it becomes quite daunting, and soon we get overloaded with data. The question is, how do you convert this data into information and subsequently knowledge so that the user only gets what he wants? Furthermore, what are the ways of extracting information previously unknown from the data on the web? More importantly how can mining the usage patterns on the web improve the capability of an organization? In other words, electronic commerce is one of the major beneficiaries of web mining. Web mining is the subject of Chapter 9. Figure 3-9 illustrates how the data mining tools may be applied to web databases.

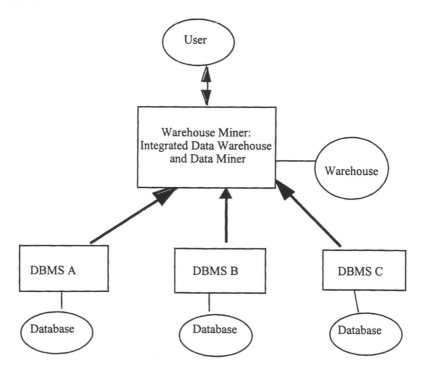

Figure 3-8. Integrated Data Warehousing and Data Mining

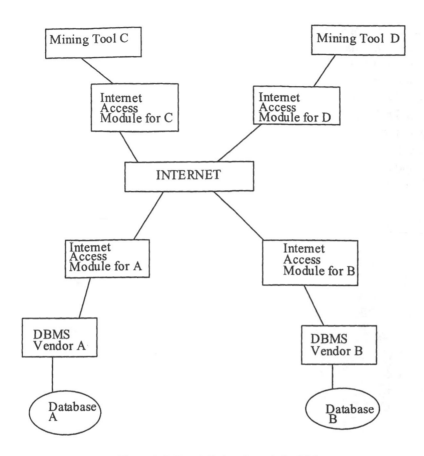

Figure 3-9. Data Mining through the Web

3.7 SUMMARY

This chapter has provided an introduction to data mining. We first discussed various technologies for data mining, and then we provided an overview of the concepts in data mining. These concepts include the outcomes of mining, the techniques employed, and the approaches used. The directions and trends, such as mining heterogeneous data sources, mining multimedia data, mining web data, metadata aspects, and privacy issues, were addressed next. Finally, we provided an overview of data warehousing and its relationship to data mining.

Note that in this book we have given just enough information for the reader to understand some data mining topics related to the web such as web mining and web privacy. For more details we refer to [THUR98a] and [THUR00]. Many important topics were covered in [THUR98a] so that the reader has some ideas as to what data mining is all about. For an in-depth understanding of the various topics in data mining we also recommend the reader to the numerous papers and articles that have appeared in data mining and related areas. We reference many of these throughout this book. Some of the interesting discussions on data mining have appeared in [TKDE93], [TKDE96], [ACM96a], [SIGM96], [KDD95], [KDD96], [KDD97], [KDD98], [PAKD97], and [PAKD98]. In addition, data mining papers have also appeared at various data management conferences (see, for example, [DE98], [SIGM98], and [VLDB98]). Recently, a federal data mining symposium series has been established [AFCE97]. In addition to [THUR98a], books in data mining include [ADRI96] and [BERR97].

CHAPTER 4

INTEROPERABILITY

4.1 OVERVIEW

While chapter 2 described concepts in database systems essential to web data management and chapter 3 discussed data mining and its impact on the web, this chapter describes interoperability technologies that are also essential to understanding web data management. The different database systems have to interoperate with each other on the web. Therefore, in this chapter we discuss various types of multi-database systems. First we provide an overview of distributed databases. Then we discuss interoperability of heterogeneous database systems. Multi-database systems also include federated database systems and client-server databases. All these database systems have to operate in the web environment. Finally we provide an overview of the issues involved in migrating legacy database systems. This is because the legacy databases and applications on the web also have to be migrated to take advantage of new hardware and software.

During the mid-1970s focus shifted toward distributed database systems from centralized database systems. This was partly due to the developments in computer networking technology. A distributed database system is essentially a collection of homogeneous database systems connected through a network. While homogeneous distributed database systems provided many challenges in the late 1970s and early 1980s, in the 1980s much of the focus was on integrating heterogeneous database systems. Autonomy is also a major consideration in accessing remote databases. The owner or an administrator of a database system would want to have as much autonomy as possible to carry out his operations. At the same time he would want to gain maximum access to remote databases. That is, the administrators of the different database systems would have to cooperate with one another to share each other's data. Autonomy and cooperation are conflicting goals and therefore a balance between the two has to be achieved. Research into handling heterogeneity and autonomy has led to the development of federated database systems (FDS). Such a system has been defined to be a collection of cooperating database systems, which are possibly autonomous and heterogeneous. The idea of client-server databases where clients of any vendor access servers of any vendor became very popular in the late 1980s and throughout the 1990s. A lot of focus in the 1990s was also on migrating legacy databases.

This chapter provides an overview of the different types of multi-database systems and discusses the impact of the web on these systems. Section 4.2 discusses distributed database systems. Section 4.3 describes heterogeneous database integration. Section 4.4 addresses challenges in federated database management. Section 4.5 discusses client-server databases. Migrating legacy databases and applications is the subject of Section 4.6. Other types of middleware such as message oriented (MOM) and transaction processors/monitors (TP) are discussed in Section 4.7. Finally, the impact of the web on these databases and systems is the subject of Section 4.8. The chapter is summarized in Section 4.9.

4.2 DISTRIBUTED DATABASES

Although many definitions of a distributed database system have been given, there is no standard definition. Our discussion of distributed database system concepts and issues has been influenced by the discussion in [CERI84]. A distributed database system includes a distributed database management system (DDBMS), a distributed database, and a network for interconnection. The DDBMS manages the distributed database. A distributed database is data that is distributed across multiple databases. Our choice architecture for a distributed database system is a multi-database architecture, which is tightly coupled. This architecture is illustrated in Figure 4-1. We have chosen such an architecture, as we can explain the concepts for both homogeneous and heterogeneous systems based on this approach. In this architecture, the nodes are connected via a communication subsystem and local applications are handled by the local DBMS. In addition, each node is also involved in at least one global application, so there is no centralized control in this architecture. The DBMSs are connected through a component called the Distributed Processor (DP). In a homogeneous environment, the local DBMSs are homogeneous while in a heterogeneous environment, the local DBMSs may be heterogeneous.

Distributed database system functions include distributed query processing, distributed transaction management, distributed metadata management, and enforcing security and integrity across the multiple nodes [BELL92]. The DP is a critical component of the DDBMS. It is this module that connects the different local DBMSs. That is, each local DBMS is augmented by a DP. The modules of the DP are illustrated in Figure 4-2. The components are the Distributed Metadata Manager (DMM), the Distributed Query Processor (DQP), the Distributed Transaction Manager (DTM), the Distributed Security Manager (DSP), and the Distributed Integrity Manager (DIM). DMM manages the global metadata. The global metadata includes information on the schemas which describe the relations in the distributed database, the way the relations are fragmented, the locations of the fragments, and the constraints enforced. DQP is responsible for distributed query processing; DTM is responsible for distributed transaction management; DSM is responsible for enforcing global security constraints; and DIM is responsible for maintaining integrity at the global level. Note that the modules of DP communicate with their peers at the remote nodes. For example, the DQP at node 1 communicates with the DQP at node 2 for handling distributed queries.

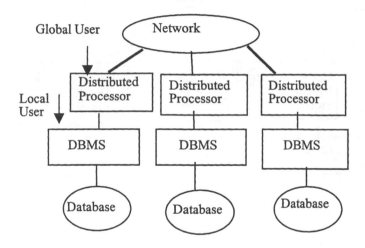

Figure 4-1. An Architecture for a DDBMS

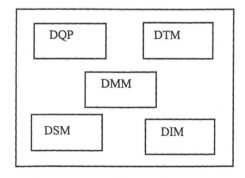

Figure 4-2. Modules of DP

4.3 HETEROGENEOUS DATABASE INTEGRATION

Figure 4-3 illustrates an example of interoperability between heterogeneous database systems. The goal is to provide transparent access, both for users and application programs, for querying and executing transactions (see, for example, [IEEE91], [ACM90], and [WIED92]). Note that in a heterogeneous environment, the local DBMSs may be heterogeneous. Furthermore, the modules of the DP have both local DBMS specific processing as well as local DBMS independent processing. We call such a DP a heterogeneous distributed processor (HDP). Some of these issues are discussed in more detail in [THUR97].

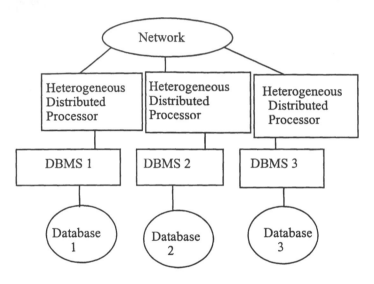

Figure 4-3. Interoperability of Heterogeneous Database Systems

There are several technical issues that need to be resolved for the successful interoperation between these diverse database systems. Note that heterogeneity could exist with respect to different data models, schemas, query processing techniques, query languages, transaction management techniques, semantics, integrity, and security. There are two approaches to interoperability. One is the federated database management approach where a collection of cooperating, autonomous, and possibly heterogeneous component database systems, each belonging to one or more federations, communicates with each other. The other is the client-server approach where the goal is for multiple clients to communicate with multiple servers in a transparent manner.

Our previous book on *Data Management Systems Evolution and Interoperation* addresses both aspects to interoperability [THUR97]. Various aspects of heterogeneity are also addressed in that book. We are often asked the question as to when one should interconnect heterogeneous database systems through an HDP and when one should integrate them through a data warehouse. For on-line transaction processing applications the interoperability approach is the answer whereas for decision support applications the warehousing approach is the answer. For some other applications one would need both as illustrated in Figure 4-4.

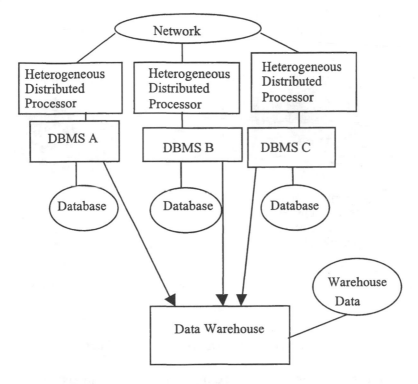

Figure 4-4. Interoperability and Warehousing

4.4 FEDERATED DATABASES

As stated by Sheth and Larson [SHET90], a federated database system is a collection of cooperating but autonomous database systems belonging to a federation. That is, the goal is for the database management systems which belong to a federation to cooperate with one another and yet maintain some degree of autonomy. Note that to be consistent with the terminology, we distinguish between a federated database management system and a federated database system. A federated database system includes both a federated database management system, the local DBMSs, and the databases. The federated database management system is that component which manages the different databases in a federated environment.

Figure 4-5 illustrates a federated database system. Database systems A and B belong to federation F1 while database systems B and C belong to federation F2. We can use the architecture illustrated in Figure 4-3 for a federated database system. In addition to handling heterogeneity, the HDP also has to handle the federated environment. That is, techniques have to be adapted to handle cooperation and autonomy. We have called such an HDP an FDP (Federated Distributed Processor). An architecture for an FDS is illustrated in Figure 4-6.

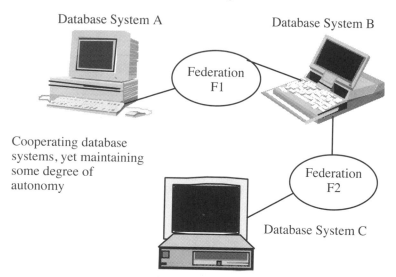

Figure 4-5. Federated Database Management

Figure 4-7 illustrates an example of an autonomous environment. There is communication between components A and B and between B and C. Due to autonomy, it is assumed that components A and C do not wish to communicate with each other. Now, component A may get requests from its own user or from component B. In this case, it has to decide which request to honor first. Also, there is a possibility for component C to get information from component A through component B. In such a situation, component A may have to negotiate with component B before it gives a reply to component B. The developments to deal with autonomy are still in the research stages. The challenge is to handle transactions in an autonomous environment. Transitioning the research into commercial products is also a challenge.

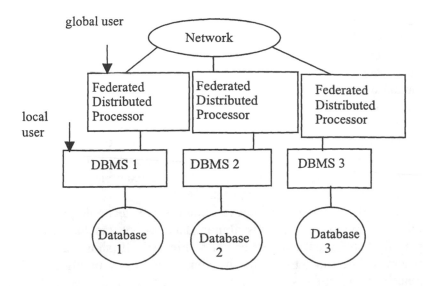

Figure 4-6. Architecture for a Federated Database System

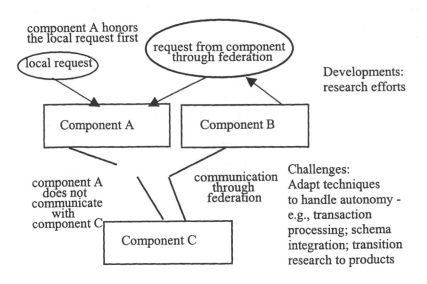

Figure 4-7. Autonomy

4.5 CLIENT-SERVER DATABASES

Earlier sections described interoperability between heterogeneous database systems and focused on the federated database systems approach. In this approach, different database systems cooperatively interoperate with each other. This section describes another aspect of interoperability which is based on the client-server paradigm. Major database system vendors have migrated to an architecture called the client-server architecture. With this approach, multiple clients access the various database servers through some network. A high level view of client-server communication is illustrated in Figure 4-8. The ultimate goal is for multi-vendor clients to communicate with multi-vendor servers in a transparent manner. A specific example of client-server communication is illustrated in Figure 4-9.

One of the major challenges in client-server technology is to deter-mine the modules of the distributed database system that need to be placed at the client and server sides. Figure 4-10 shows an approach where all the modules of the distributed processor of Figure 4-2 are placed at the client side, while the modules of the local DBMS are placed at the server side. Note that with this approach the client does a lot of processing and this is called the "fat client" approach. There are other options also. For example, some of the modules of the distributed processor could be part of the server in which case the client would be "thinner".

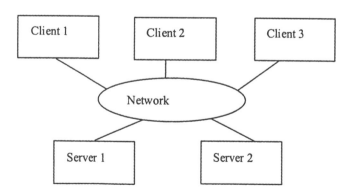

Figure 4-8. Client-Server Architecture-based Interoperability

In order to facilitate the communication between multiple clients and servers, various standards are being proposed. One example is the International Standards Organization's (ISO) Remote Database Access

(RDA) standard. This standard provides a generic interface for communication between a client and a server. Microsoft Corporation's Open
Database Connectivity (ODBC) is also becoming increasingly popular
for clients to communicate with the servers. OMG's CORBA provides

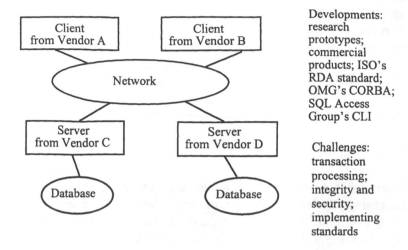

Developments:
research
prototypes;
commercial
products; ISO's
RDA standard;
OMG's CORBA;
SQL Access
Group's CLI

Challenges:
transaction
processing;
integrity and
security;
implementing
standards

Figure 4-9. Example Client-Server Architecture

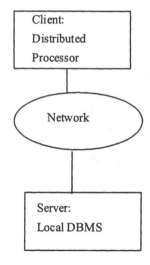

Figure 4-10. An Approach to Place the Modules

specifications for client-server communication based on object technology. Here, one possibility is to encapsulate the database servers as
objects and the clients to issue appropriate requests and access the

servers through an Object Request Broker. Other standards include IBM's DRDA (Distributed Relational Database Access) and the SQL Access Group's Call Level Interface (CLI).[11] While much of the developments have been in query processing, the challenges are in transaction processing, semantic heterogeneity, integrity, and security.

In our previous book [THUR97] we described various aspects of client-server interoperability, in particular, technical issues for client-server interoperability, architectural approaches, three of the standards proposed for communication between clients and servers such as RDA, ODBC, and CORBA, as well as metadata aspects. A good reference is [ORFA94]. We will revisit distributed object management systems such as CORBA in the chapter on object management.

4.6 MIGRATING LEGACY DATABASES AND APPLICATIONS

Many database systems developed some twenty to thirty years ago are becoming obsolete. These systems use older hardware and software. Between now and the next few decades, many of today's information systems and applications will also become obsolete. Due to resource and, in certain cases, budgetary constraints, new developments of next generation systems may not be possible in many areas (see, for example, [BENS95]). Therefore, current systems need to become easier, faster, and less costly to upgrade and less difficult to support. Legacy database system and application migration is a complex problem, and many of the efforts underway are still not mature. While a good book has been published recently on this subject [BROD95], there is no uniform approach for migration. Since migrating legacy databases and applications is becoming a necessity for most organizations, both government and commercial, one could expect a considerable amount of resources to be expended in this area in the near future. The research issues are also not well understood.

Migrating legacy applications and databases also has an impact on heterogeneous database integration. Typically a heterogeneous database environment may include legacy databases as well as some of the next generation databases. In many cases, an organization may want to migrate the legacy database system to an architecture like the client-server architecture and still want the migrated system to be part of the heterogeneous environment. This means that the functions of the

---

[11] It is now part of the Open Group. Note that the products and standards have evolved over the years and are continually changing. We encourage the reader to keep up with the developments. Much of the information can be obtained on the web.

heterogeneous database system may be impacted due to this migration process.

Two candidate approaches have been proposed for migrating legacy systems. One is to do all of the migration at once. The other is incremental migration. That is, as the legacy system gets migrated, the new parts have to interoperate with the old parts. Various issues and challenges to migration are discussed in [THUR97]. In the next section we will address how legacy databases could be mined. Figure 4-11 illustrates an incremental approach to migrating legacy databases through the use of object request brokers.

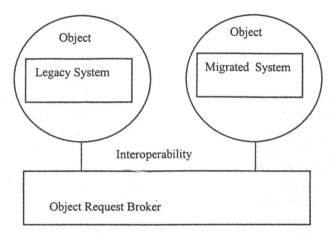

Figure 4-11. Migrating Legacy Databases

4.7 OTHER TYPES OF MIDDLEWARE

The previous sections have addressed the use of distributed object management technology for integrating different databases and systems. Other types of middleware include message oriented middleware (MOM) and transaction processors/monitors (TP).

MOM is essentially middleware for client-server communication. The components reside in both the client and the server. It supports interoperability between heterogeneous systems. It also supports asynchronous communication between clients and servers. It reduces master-slave communication by queuing messages when clients or servers are busy. The messages are delivered when the clients and servers become available. This way the client will not have to wait until the server completes execution.

TPs are dedicated systems performing mainly transaction processing. Tandem was among the first to develop TPs. Since then various

TPs have been developed. These TPs can now perform thousands of transactions per second. BEA's Tuxedo is a middleware system that was developed with the goal of scaling to numerous nodes and working well with the web. Later in Part II we will discuss BEA's Web Logic product that works with Tuxedo to provide a rich set of services to the e-commerce customer.

We expect the web to be the integration platform of the various types of middleware as shown in Figure 4-12. That is, the DOMs, MOMs, and TPs all have to work together on the web. We are not there yet, but we feel that this is the direction the industry is moving toward. One can also expect to see one system with plug and play components for DOM, MOM, and TP.

4.8 IMPACT OF THE WEB

The web has impacted all of the multi-database technologies. There are distributed databases on the web and these databases have to be integrated. For example, the two Oracle database systems may need to communicate with one another with the Internet as the transport mechanism and process queries in a distributed manner. The databases on the web may be heterogeneous. Therefore, the various functions of heterogeneous database integration will play a major role in web database integration. Some of the database systems on the web may form federations. We hear of corporations sharing information through Intranets and Extranets. At present, web technology is still based on a client-server computing paradigm. That is, the web clients communicate with web servers to get web pages and other data. However, in the future one could envisage client-server technology to get more limited as users could simply use a dumb terminal and get all of the resources

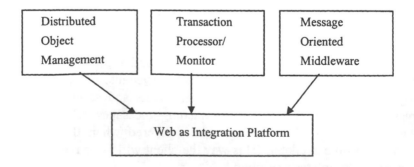

Figure 4-12. Other Types of Middleware

from the web. Finally, web databases may be legacy in nature and therefore these databases have to be migrated to take advantage of new hardware and software.

One key technology that will be central to managing multi-databases on the web is objects. We briefly talked about distributed object-based client-server interoperability. More and more web infra-structures are taking advantage of distributed object computing. In the next chapter we will examine objects in more detail and discuss how they help web data management. Figure 4-13 illustrates a scenario where multi-database systems interoperate on the web.

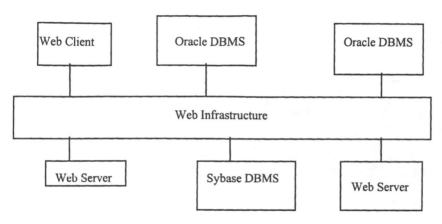

Figure 4-13. Web Database Interoperability

4.9 SUMMARY

This chapter has addressed various multi-database issues. We started with a discussion of distributed databases and then addressed heterogeneity. Federated database management was the next topic. This was followed by a discussion of client-server-based interoperability. Finally we addressed legacy database issues as well as some other types of middleware. For each type of multi-database system we discussed the impact of the web. As stated in this chapter as well as in the previous chapters, the numerous databases on the web have to be integrated and eventually mined to get useful information. Object technology plays a major role with this integration. The various types of object technolo-gies will be the subject of Chapter 5.

CHAPTER 5

OBJECT TECHNOLOGY

5.1 OVERVIEW

Object Technology, also referred to as OT or OOT (Object-Oriented Technology), encompasses different technologies. These include object-oriented programming languages, object database management systems, object-oriented design and analysis, distributed object management, and components and frameworks. The underlying theme for all these types of object technologies is the object model. That is, the object model is the very essence of object technology. Any object system is based on some object model, whether it is a programming language or a database system. The interesting aspect of an object model is that everything in the real world can be modeled as an object.

The organization of this chapter is as follows. In Section 5.2 we describe the essential properties of object models (OODM). Object-oriented programming languages (OOPL) is the subject of Section 5.3. Object database systems will be discussed in Section 5.4 (OODB). Object-oriented design and analysis (OODA) will be discussed in Section 5.5. Distributed object management (DOM) is the subject of Section 5.6. Section 5.7. describes components and frameworks (C&F). Finally, in Section 5.8 we discuss the impact of the web. More specifically, the impact of object technology on web data management will be discussed. The chapter is summarized in Section 5.9. Figure 5-1 illustrates the various types of object technologies (OOT). OODM is common to all these technologies.

5.2 OBJECT DATA MODEL

Since the birth of object technology sometime during the 1970s, numerous object models have been proposed. In fact some recent object models trace back to the language Simula in the 1960s. Initially these models were to support programming languages such as Smalltalk. Later these models were enhanced to support database systems as well as other complex systems. This section provides an overview of the essential feature of object models. Note that many of the features presented here are common for object models developed for different types of systems such as programming languages, database systems, modeling and analysis, and distributed object management systems.

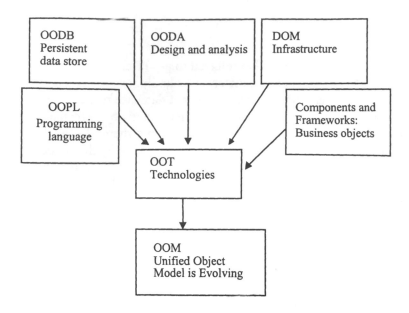

Figure 5-1. Object Technologies

While there are no standard object models, the Unified Modeling Language (UML) proposed by the prominent object technologies (Rumbaugh, Booch and Jacobson) has gained increasing popularity and has almost become the standard object model in recent years. Our discussion of the object model has been influenced by much of our work in object database systems as well as the one proposed by Won Kim et al. [BANE87]. We call it an object-oriented data model.[12]

The key points in an object-oriented model are encapsulation, inheritance, and polymorphism. With an object-oriented data model, the database is viewed as a collection of objects [BANE87]. Each object has a unique identifier called the object-ID. Objects with similar properties are grouped into a class. For example, employee objects are grouped into EMP class while department objects are grouped into DEPT class as shown in Figure 5-2. A class has instance variables describing the properties. Instance variables of EMP are SS#, Ename, Salary, and D#, while the instance variables of DEPT are D#, Dname, and Mgr. The

---

[12] Two types of object models have been proposed for databases. One is the object-oriented data model proposed for object-oriented databases and the other is the object-relational data model proposed for object-relational databases. We discuss the object-oriented data model in this section. Object-relational models are discussed in the section on object database management.

objects in a class are its instances. As illustrated in the figure, EMP has three instances and DEPT has two instances.

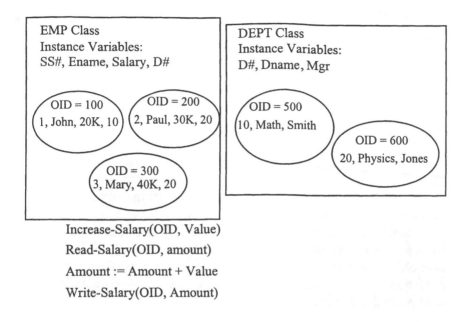

Figure 5-2. Objects and Classes

A key concept in object-oriented data modeling is encapsulation. That is, an object has well-defined interfaces. The state of an object can only be accessed through interface procedures called methods. For example, EMP may have a method called Increase-Salary. The code for Increase-Salary is illustrated in Figure 5-2. A message, say Increase-Salary(1, 10K), may be sent to the object with object ID of 1. The object's current salary is read and updated by 10K.

A second key concept in an object model is inheritance where a subclass inherits properties from its parent class. This feature is illustrated in Figure 5-3, where the EMP class has MGR (manager) and ENG (engineer) as its subclasses. Other key concepts in an object model include polymorphism and aggregation.[13] These features are discussed in [BANE87]. Further information can also be obtained in [THUR97]. Note that a second type of inheritance is when the instances of a class inherit the properties of the class.

---

[13]   Inheritance is also known as the IS-A hierarchy. Aggregation is also known as the IS-PART-OF hierarchy.

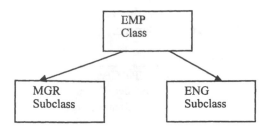

Figure 5-3. Class-Subclass Hierarchy

A third concept is polymorphism. This is the situation where one can pass different types of arguments for the same function. For example, to calculate the area, one can pass a sphere or a cylinder object. Operators can be overloaded also. That is, the add operation can be used to add two integers or real numbers.

Another concept is the aggregate hierarchy also called the composite object or the is-part-of hierarchy. In this case an object has component objects. For example, a book object has component section objects. A section object has component paragraph objects. Aggregate hierarchy is illustrated in Figure 5-4.

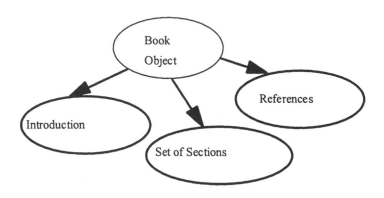

Figure 5-4. Aggregate Object

Objects also have relationships between them. For example, an employee object has an association with the department object, which is the department he is working in. Also, the instance variables of an object could take integers, lists, arrays, or even other objects as values. All of these concepts are discussed in the book by Cattell [CATT91]. Object Data Management Group is also proposing standards for object data models [ODMG93].

5.3 OBJECT-ORIENTED PROGRAMMING LANGUAGES

Object-oriented programming languages (OOPL) essentially go back to Simula in the 1960s. However, it really became popular with the advent of Smalltalk by Xerox Palo Alto Research Center in the late 1970s. Smalltalk is a pure object-oriented programming language where everything is considered to be an object. Implementations of Smalltalk were being developed throughout the 1980s. Around the mid 1980s, languages such as LISP and C were being made object-oriented by extending them to support objects. One such popular extension is the language C++. In the early to mid 1990s a lot of the programming was carried out in C++.

Around the 1990s Sun Microsystems wanted to develop a language for its embedded computing and appliance business that would not have all of the problems associated with C++ such as pointers. The resulting language first named Oak was eventually called Java. Java became immensely popular because of the Internet. The language developers at Sun realized that Java, because of its write-once run-anywhere property, could be an appropriate language for Internet programming. We find today that there is a huge demand for Java programmers and the numbers are increasing rapidly.

Figure 5-5 illustrates the evolution of object-oriented programming languages. Because of all of the features that object technology offers, like reuse because of inheritance, we believe that many of the future systems will be based on objects. For example with inheritance one can reuse code and modules for various systems. This is because software modules could inherit properties from other modules implemented as part of the class-subclass hierarchy.

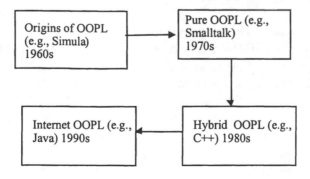

Figure 5-5. Evolution of OOPL

5.4 OBJECT DATABASE MANAGEMENT

5.4.1 Overview

We discuss three types of object database systems. One is object-oriented database system and these systems make object-oriented programming languages persistent. The second is extended-relational systems and these systems extend relational database systems with object layers. The third system is object-relational system where objects are nested within relations. We discuss each of these systems in the following sections.

5.4.2 Object-Oriented Database Systems

Object-oriented database management systems (OODBMS) were developed to make programming languages persistent. The early systems such as Gemstone and Objectstore made languages such as Smalltalk and C++ persistent. For example, Gemstone was originally designed to make Smalltalk persistent while Objectstore was designed to make C++ persistent. The idea was that with tight integration with programming languages it would be better for programming intensive applications rather then having a loose coupling between application programs and SQL–based relational databases. The tight integration between OODBMSs and application programs is illustrated in Figure 5-6. OODBMSs were also designed to support large and variable sized data blocks, multimedia data types, long-term lock and checkout of objects, high performance, and schema evolution (see [LOOM93]). These OODBMSs are currently in their second generation and can support relationships. The major focus at present is to make these OODBMSs the persistent store for web data management as well as distributed object management systems.

5.4.3 Extended-Relational Systems

While OODBMSs make programming languages persistent, relational systems are being extended to support objects. It is well understood that object management capability is needed to support complex data structures. At the same time languages such as SQL are standards languages. Therefore, one needs both the capability to manipulate relations as well as objects. One approach is to extend relational database systems with object layers as shown in Figure 5-7. In this approach, applications can access either objects or relations. Transformations between objects and relations are performed by the object manager. That is, the object database is in a way a virtual database. Objects eventually have to be transformed to relations and eventually these relations in the relational database are accessed through the relational DBMS.

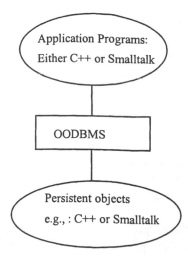

Figure 5-6. OODBMS

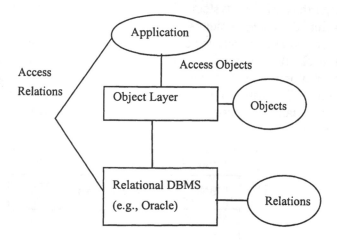

Figure 5-7. Extended-Relational Database System

Various relational database vendors such as Oracle, Sybase, and Informix are extending their database systems to support objects. These systems have been around for quite a few years. Such systems can support complex data structures and multimedia data types. While relational database vendors are migrating toward objects, OODBMS vendors are supporting relationships and SQL-like query languages.

Eventually we believe that there will be a middle ground between relations and objects

5.4.4 Object-Relational Systems

Object-relational database systems were developed to overcome some of the problems with relational and object-oriented database systems. The relational data model is based on well-defined principles. Furthermore, a notable feature of relational database systems is the query language. The SQL language, developed initially for relational databases, is an ANSI standard. However, relational data models cannot support complex objects which are needed for new generation applications such as CAD/CAM and multimedia. On the other hand, object-oriented data models can support complex structures. However, in general, object-oriented database systems do not have good support for querying.

To overcome these problems, relational database vendors are building some sort of support for objects as discussed in the earlier section. Object-oriented database vendors are developing better query interfaces as well as better support to represent relationships. In addition, a third kind of system, object-relational database system, has been developed. These systems provide support both for relations and objects. Note that there is no standard object-relational model. With one approach, the relations are extended so that the data elements are no longer atomic. That is, the data elements could be complex objects. Figure 5-8 illustrates this concept where the book relation has an attribute called components. This attribute describes the components of the book.

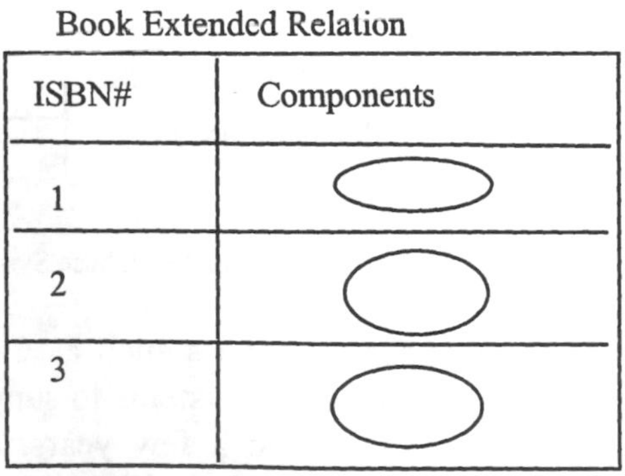

Book Extended Relation

ISBN#	Components
1	$\bigcirc$
2	$\bigcirc$
3	$\bigcirc$

Figure 5-8. Object-Relational Model

Object-relational database systems are essentially database systems that manage object relations. These database systems support SQL languages extended to support complex constructs as well as object languages that have SQL-like capabilities. Object-relational systems are still young and we can expect them to mature over the next few years. Several object-oriented database system products, as well as a few object-relational database system prototypes, are discussed in [ACM91].

5.5 OBJECT-ORIENTED DESIGN AND ANALYSIS

The previous two sections addressed object-oriented programming languages and object-oriented database management. Around the same time (i.e., in the 1980s) there was a lot of interest in using object technology to design and analyze applications. Prior to that various analysis techniques such as structured analysis and Jackson diagrams were used to analyze the application. At the same time entity relationship models were very popular to represent the entities of the application and the relationships between them.

With the advent of OOT, interest increased on using objects to model and analyze applications. Various design and analysis methodologies were being proposed. Notable among them were the method of Booch, Usecases by Jacobson and OMT (Object Modeling Technique) by Rumbaugh et al. There was so much debate about this subject that at the 1993 OOPSLA (Object-Oriented Programming Systems, Languages and Applications) Conference there was an extremely contentious debate on this subject.

Surprisingly, within the next two years it was announced that the three groups were merging and were producing a unified methodology. This unified methodology is called UML (Unified Modeling Language) [FOWL97]. UML has essential features from the three approaches and is now more or less a standard for object modeling and analysis. Figure 5-9 illustrates the convergence of the three approaches. Essentially in object-oriented design and analysis methodologies like, say, OMT, an object model, similar to the one we have proposed in this chapter, is used to represent the static parts of the application. A dynamic model is used to capture the interactions between the entities and the timing and synchronization of events, and a functional model generates the methods. In addition there is a system design phase where the various modules of the system are identified and during the object design phase the algorithms are designed. In the usecase method, the idea is to capture the user requirements with objects and do rapid prototyping. By combining all of the good features of the three prominent methods, UML has become the choice modeling methodology.

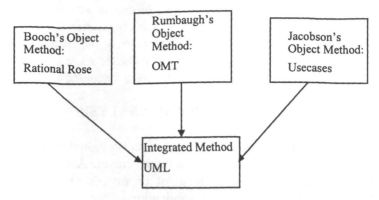

Figure 5-9. OODA Approaches

A closely related development in the mid-1990s is the design patterns methodology. Design patterns is all about extracting patterns in the modeling methodology that are often reused for various applications. For example, consider a general ledger application. This application would use objects and communication between objects in a standard way. Once you capture this pattern, then this pattern can be reused for various general ledger applications by, say, different users and corporations. Design patterns has simply exploded as an area and various people have published their patterns for different systems and applications. There are also web-based user and discussion groups on patterns.

5.6 DISTRIBUTED OBJECT MANAGEMENT

5.6.1 Overview
Various types of distributed object management systems have been proposed in the literature for interoperability. We discussed them briefly in our previous book [THUR97]. In Section 5.6.1 we provide an overview of distributed objects and in Section 5.6.2 we discuss a special distributed object management approach, which is the Object Management Group's CORBA (Common Object Broker Architecture).

5.6.2 Distributed Object Management Approach
Distributed object management (DOM) technology is becoming increasingly used to interconnect heterogeneous databases, systems, and applications. With this approach, the various systems and applications

are encapsulated as objects and the objects communicate with each other through exchanging messages. Figure 5-10 provides a high level view of interoperability based on DOM technology. Here, three components A, B, and C are encapsulated as objects and communicate with each other through the DOM system.[14]

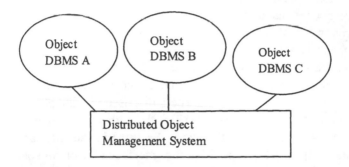

Figure 5-10. Interoperability-based on Distributed Object Management

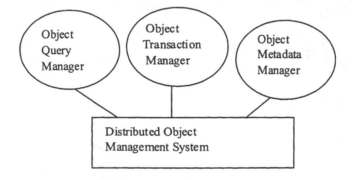

Figure 5-11. Distributed Object Management for Component Integration

DOM technology can also be used for finer grained encapsulation. For example, mediators, repositories, and DBMSs can be encapsulated so that different DBMSs interoperate. This is illustrated in Figure 5-11. What is key here is that each system must have well defined interfaces using a common interface definition language. What is inside each encapsulated object is transparent to the remote object. This technology is also being used for migrating legacy databases and applications. For a detailed discussion of DOM technology, we refer to [ORFA96]. Examples of DOM technology include OMG's CORBA and Microsoft's DCOM, and more recently Sun Microsystems JINI can also be

---

[14]   Internet-based component integration is discussed in Part II.

regarded to be a DOM technology. Since this text is not about DOM, in the next section we discuss only CORBA. Again we have selected this, as we are most familiar with this approach.

5.6.3 CORBA

An example of a distributed object management (DOM) system that is being used as a middleware to connect heterogeneous database systems is a system based on OMG's CORBA.[15] CORBA is a specification that enables heterogeneous applications, systems, and databases to interoperate with each other. As stated in [OMG95], there are three major components to CORBA. One is the object model which essentially includes most of the constructs discussed in Chapter 2, the second is the Object Request Broker (ORB) through which clients and servers communicate with each other, and the third is the Interface Definition Language (IDL) which specifies the interfaces for client server communication. Figure 5-12 illustrates client server communication through an ORB. Here, the clients and servers are encapsulated as objects. The two objects then communicate with each other. Communication is through the ORB.

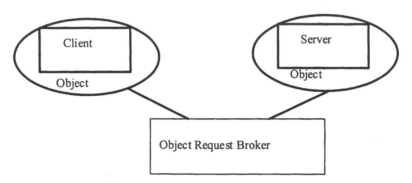

Figure 5-12. Interoperability through ORB

Furthermore, the interfaces must conform to IDL. Since heterogeneous database management is of interest to us, our goal is for heterogeneous database systems to interoperate with each other through the ORB. Figure 5-13 illustrates this integration. Essentially nodes A, B, and C are encapsulated as objects. They communicate through the ORB. Note that in this example we have assumed a coarse-grained encapsula-

---

15   Note that middleware is referred to as the intermediate layer which lies between the operating systems and the applications. This layer connects different systems and applications.

tion where entire nodes are encapsulated as objects. One could encapsulate portions of the modules. For example, Figure 5-14 illustrates a

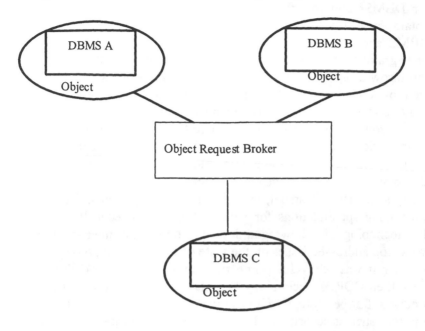

Figure 5-13. Heterogeneous Database Integration through ORB

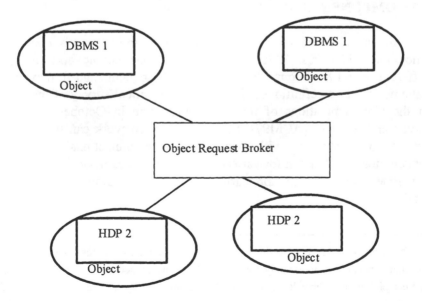

Figure 5-14. Finer-grained Encapsulation

case where the DBMSs and the HDPs (i.e. the heterogeneous distributed processor) are encapsulated separately. Here we have four objects, two for DBMSs and two for the HDPs. One can continue this way and obtain even finer-grained encapsulation where the modules of the DBMS and modules of the HDP are encapsulated. The advantage of finer-grained encapsulation is that it facilitates migration. That is, one can throw away an HDP and replace it with newer modules. However, the more objects there are, the more messages are sent through the ORB and this will have an impact on the performance.

Various special interest groups and task forces are coming up with specifications based on CORBA. These include specifications for security, real-time processing, and Internet access. In addition, there is also work carried out on developing specifications for vertical domains such as medical, financial, and transportation domains. OMG is also developing specifications for various business objects. It appears that this technology is showing a lot of promise for interoperability. A workshop addressed issues on the state of CORBA technology and as to whether it was ready for prime time in 1994 [OOPS94].[16] However, since then CORBA technology has matured and there are now several products. Furthermore, OMG is actively involved in specifying services for areas such as security, real-time, and fault tolerance.

5.7 COMPONENTS AND FRAMEWORKS

This is one of the latest object technologies and has really taken off since the mid-1990s. When talking to various people and reading different texts I have found that the terms components and frameworks have no standard definitions. There was an excellent survey of the field in the Communications of the ACM magazine in October 1997 by Fayad and Schmidt [ACM97]. In a sense a framework can be considered to be a skeleton with classes and interconnections. One then instantiates this skeleton for various applications. Frameworks are being developed for different application domains including financial and medical.

---

[16] Note that OMG is a consortium of over 800 corporations. Another DOM technology that is becoming increasingly popular is Microsoft Corporation's Distributed OLE (Object Linking and Embedding) and COM (Component Object Model). The future of these technologies will be clearer in the next few years (see, for example, [ORFA96]). In [THUR97] we provided a brief overview of Microsoft's database access product OLE/DB. Note that the names of the various distributed object management system products are also evolving.

Components on the other hand are classes, objects and relationships between them that can be reused. Components can be built for different applications. There are components for financial applications, medical applications and telecommunication applications. These components are also called business objects. One can also develop general-purpose components. For example, a database system can be developed as a collection of components for query processing, transaction management and metadata management. Figure 5-15 illustrates components for data management. In this figure it is assumed that various vendors produce different components for data management. These components have to be integrated to produce a DBMS. Figure 5-16 illustrates components for three-tier client-server processing and we will revisit this illustration in Part II.

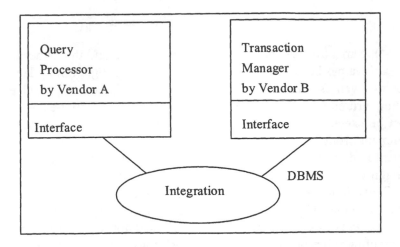

Figure 5-15. Component Integration for Database Management

5.8 IMPACT OF THE WEB

Now that we have explained all the key points in object technology, let us examine the impact of the web. More specifically let us examine how the web is impacted by object technology. First of all object databases (OODB) can be used like any other database to interface to the web. Object databases can also be a persistent store for various resources on the web. Note that one can also use relational database systems. However, object database systems, with their representational power, are capable of storing, say, richer data structures.

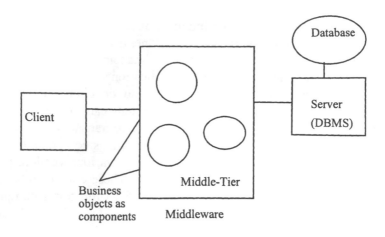

Figure 5-16. Three-Tier Components

One area that has made a big impact is OOPL and this is because of Java. Java has become more or less the standard programming language for the web. Various applications programs, applets, and servlets are being written in Java.[17] Java applets can be embedded in web pages and can be executed when the web page is brought into the browser environment from the server. This is a significant development. Object-oriented design and analysis (OODA) methodologies are being used to design web-based applications. Distributed object systems (DOM) such as CORBA are being used as infrastructures for web-based integration. For example, Netscape browser uses ORBs for its infrastructure. Components and frameworks are being used for web-based three-tier computing. One popular component technology is Sun Microsystem's Enterprise Java Beans (EJB). We now hear of various types of beans being developed for different web-based applications and these beans are based on EJB. Figure 5-17 illustrates how objects are being impacted by the web and vice versa.

5.9 SUMMARY

This chapter has summarized some of the important object technology developments that have taken place over the past three decades. We started with object models, the very essence of object technology. Then we discussed the evolution of OOPLs. This was followed by a discussion of various types of object database systems. Object-oriented design and analysis was given some consideration. Next we provided an

---

[17] We will explain applets and servlets in a later chapter.

overview of distributed object management. Finally the emerging area of frameworks and components was discussed. The impact of this technology on the web is tremendous. We will see throughout this book how OT is being applied.

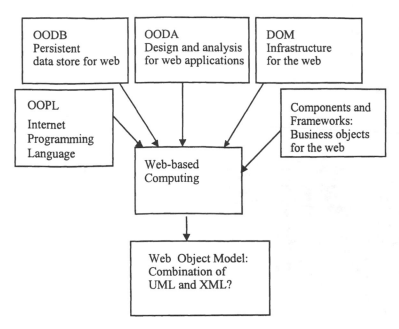

Figure 5-17. Web-based Computing and OT

CHAPTER 6

DATA AND INFORMATION SECURITY

6.1 OVERVIEW

The number of computerized databases has been increasing rapidly over the past three decades. The advent of the Internet as well as networking capabilities has made the access to data and information much easier. For example, users can now access large quantities of information in a short space of time. As more and more tools and technologies are being developed to access and use the data, there is also now an urgent need to protect the data. Many government and industrial organizations have sensitive and classified data that has to be protected. Various other organizations such as academic institutions also have sensitive data about their students and employees. As a result, techniques for protecting the data stored in Database Management Systems (DBMSs) have become an urgent need.

Over the past three decades various developments have been made on securing the databases. Much of the early work was on statistical database security. Then, in the 1970s, as research in relational databases began, attention was directed toward access control issues. In particular, work on discretionary access control models began. While some work on mandatory security started in the late 1970s, it was not until the Air Force summer study in 1982 that many of the efforts in multilevel secure database management systems were initiated [AFSB83]. This resulted in the development of various secure database system prototypes and products. In the 1990s, with the advent of new technologies such as digital libraries, the World Wide Web, and collaborative computing systems, there was much interest in security not only with the government organizations, but also with the commercial industry.

This chapter provides an overview of the various developments in information security with special emphasis on database security. In Section 6.2 we discuss basic concepts such as access control for information systems. Section 6.3 provides an overview of secure systems. Secure database systems will be discussed in Section 6.4. Since much of this book is on web data management, we give some consideration to secure database systems. Emerging trends is the subject of section 6.5. Impact of the web is given in Section 6.6. The chapter is summarized in Section 6.7. For a detailed discussion of the information in this chapter we refer to [FERA00].

6.2 ACCESS CONTROL AND OTHER SECURITY CONCEPTS

Access control models include those for discretionary security and mandatory security. In this section we discuss both aspects of access control and also consider other issues.

In discretionary access control models, users or groups of users are granted access to data objects. These data objects could be files, relations, objects or even data items. Access control policies include rules such as User U has read access to Relation R1 and write access to Relation R2. Access control could also include negative control where user U does not have read access to Relation R.

In mandatory access control subjects that act on behalf of users are granted access to objects based on some policy. A well-known policy is the Bell and La Padula policy [BELL75] where subjects are granted clearance levels and objects have sensitivity levels. The set of security levels form a partially ordered lattice where Unclassified < Confidential < Secret < TopSecret. The policy has two properties and are the following. A subject has read access to an object if its clearance level dominates that of the object. A subject has write access to an object if its level is dominated by that of the object.

Other types of access control include role-based access control. Here access is granted to users depending on their roles and the functions they perform. For example, personnel managers have access to salary data while project mangers have access to project data. The idea here is generally to give access on a need-to-know basis.

While the early access control policies were formulated for operating systems, these policies have been extended to include other systems such as database systems, networks and distributed systems. For example, a policy for networks includes policies for not only reading and writing but also for sending and receiving messages.

Other security policies include administration policies. These policies include those for ownership of data as well as how to manage and distribute the data. Database administrators as well as system security officers are involved in formulating the administration policies.

Security policies also include policies for identification and authentication. Each user or subject acting on behalf of a user has to be identified and authenticated possibly using some password mechanisms. Identification and authentication becomes more complex for distributed systems. For example, how can a user be authenticated at a global level?

The steps to developing secure systems include developing a security policy, developing a model of the system, designing the system, and verifying and validating the system. The methods used for verification depend on the level of assurance that is expected. Testing and risk analysis is also part of the process. These activities will eliminate or assess the risks involved. Figure 6-1 illustrates various types of security policies.

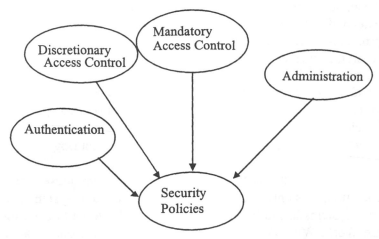

Figure 6-1. Secure Policies

6.3 SECURE SYSTEMS

In the previous section we discussed various policies for building secure systems. In this section we elaborate on various types of secure systems.

Much of the early research in the 1960s and 1970s were on securing operating systems. Early security policies such as the Bell and LaPadula policy were formulated for operating systems. Subsequently secure operating systems such as Honeywell's SCOMP and MULTICS were developed (see IEEE83]). Other policies such as those based on noninterference also emerged in the early 1980s.

While early research on secure database systems was reported in the 1970s it was not until the early 1980s that active research began in this area. Much of the focus was on multilevel secure database systems. The security policy for operating systems was modified slightly. For example, the write policy for secure database systems was modified to state that a subject has write access to an object if the subject's level is that of the object. Since database systems enforced relationships between data and had semantics, there were additional security concerns. For example, data could be classified based on content, context and time. The problem of posing multiple queries and inferring sensitive information from the legitimate responses became a concern. This problem is now known as the inference problem. Also, research was carried out not only on securing relational systems but also object systems.

Research on computer networks began in the late 1970s and throughout the 1980s and beyond. The networking protocols were extended to incorporate security features. The result was secure network protocols. The policies include those for reading, writing, sending and receiving messages. Research on encryption and cryptography has received much prominence due to networks and the Internet. Security for stand-alone systems was extended to include distributed sytems. These systems included distributed databases and distributed operating systems. Much of the research on distributed systems now focuses on securing the Internet, known as web security, as well as securing systems such as distributed object management systems.

As new systems emerge, such as data warehouses, collaborative computing systems, multimedia systems and agent systems, security for such systems has to be investigated. With the advent of the Internet and the World Wide Web, security is being given serious consideration by not only the government organizations but also commercial organiza-tions. With e-commerce it is important to protect the company's intellectual property. Figure 6-2 illustrates various types of secure systems.

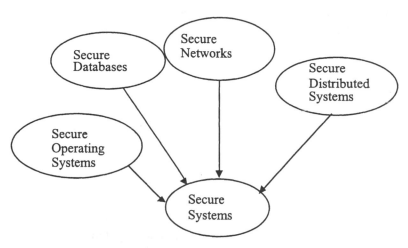

Figure 6-2. Secure Systems

6.4 SECURE DATABASE SYSTEMS

Work on discretionary security for databases began in the 1970s when security aspects were investigated for System R at IBM Almaden

Research Center. Essentially the security properties specified the read and write access that a user may have to relations, attributes, and data elements. In the 1980s and 1990s security issues were investigated for object systems. Here the security properties specified the access that users had to objects, instance variables, and classes. In addition to read and write, method execution access was also specified.

Since the early 1980s much of the focus was on multilevel secure database management systems. These systems essentially enforce the mandatory policy discussed in Section 6.2 with the modification described in Section 6.3. Since the 1980s various designs, prototypes and commercial products of multilevel database systems have been developed. Ferrari and Thuraisingham give a detailed survey of some of the developments [FERA00]. Example efforts include the SeaView effort by SRI International and Lock Data Views effort by Honeywell. These efforts extended relational models with security properties. One challenge was to design a model where a user sees different values at different security levels. For example, at the Unclassified level an employee's salary may be 20K and at the secret level it may be 50K. In the standard relational model such ambiguous values cannot be represented due to integrity properties.

Note that several other significant developments have been made on multilevel security for other types of database systems. These include security for object database systems [THUR89]. In this effort, security properties specify read, write and method execution policies. Much work was also carried out on secure concurrency control and recovery. The idea here is to enforce security properties and still meet consistency without having covert channels. Research was also carried out on multilevel security for distributed, heterogeneous and federated database systems. Another area that received a lot of attention was the inference problem. For details on the inference problem we refer the reader to [THUR93]. For secure concurrency control we refer to the numerous algorithms by Bertino, Jajodia et al. (see, for example, [BERT97]). For information on secure distributed and heterogeneous databases as well as secure federated databases we refer to [THUR91] and [THUR94].

As database systems become more sophisticated, securing these system will become more and more difficult. Some of the current work focuses on securing data warehouses, multimedia databases, and web databases (see for example [IFIP97] and [IFIP98]). Figure 6-3 illustrates various types of secure database systems.

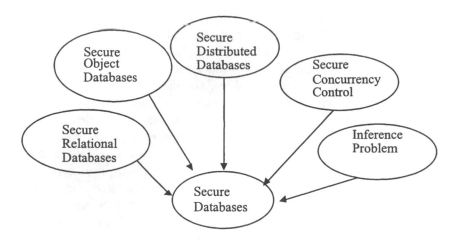

Figure 6-3. Secure Database Systems

6.5 EMERGING TRENDS

In the mid 1990s research in secure systems expanded to include emerging systems. These included securing collaborative computing systems, multimedia computing and data warehouses. Data mining resulted in new security concerns. Since users now have access to various data-mining tools, it could exacerbate the inference problem. This is because the data-mining tool may make correlations and associations which may be sensitive. On the other hand data mining could also help with security problems such as intrusion detection and auditing.

The advent of the web resulted in extensive investigations of security for digital libraries and electronic commerce. In addition to developing sophisticated encryption techniques, security research also focused on securing the web clients as well as servers. Programming languages such as Java were designed with security in mind. Much research was also carried out on securing agents.

Secure distributed system research focused on security for distributed object management systems. Organizations such as OMG started working groups to investigate security properties. As a result we now have secure distributed object management systems commercially available. Figure 6-4 illustrates the various emerging secure systems and concepts. More details are given in [FERA00].

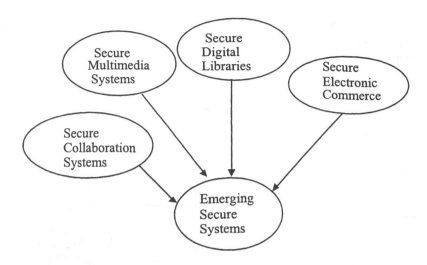

Figure 6-4. Emerging Secure Systems

6.6 IMPACT OF THE WEB

The advent of the web has greatly impacted security. Security is now part of mainstream computing. Government organizations as well as commercial organizations are concerned about security. For example, in a financial transaction, millions of dollars could be lost if security is not maintained. With the web, all sorts of information are available about individuals and therefore privacy may be compromised.

Various security solutions are being proposed to secure the web. In addition to encryption, focus is on securing clients as well as servers. That is, end-to-end security has to be maintained. Web security also has an impact on electronic commerce. That is, when one carries out transactions on the web it is critical that security is maintained. Information such as credit card numbers and social security numbers have to be protected.

All of the security issues discussed in the previous sections have to be considered for the web. For example, appropriate security policies have to be formulated. This is a challenge, as no one person owns the web. The various secure systems including secure operating systems, secure database systems, secure networks and secure distributed systems may be integrated in a web environment. Therefore, this integrated system has to be secure. Problems such as the inference problem may be exacerbated due to the various data mining tools. The various agents on the web have to be secure. In certain cases trade-offs need to be made between security and other features. That is, quality of service is an important consideration. In addition to technological solutions, legal aspects also have to be examined. That is, lawyers and engineers have to work together. Research on securing the web is just beginning. Figure 6-5 illustrates aspects of web security

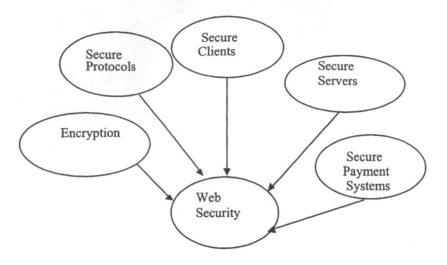

Figure 6-5. Aspects of Web Security

6.7 SUMMARY

This chapter has provided a brief overview of the developments in secure systems. We first discussed basic concepts in access control as well as discretionary and mandatory policies. Then, we provided an overview of secure systems. In particular secure operating systems, secure databases, secure networks, and secure distributed systems were discussed. Next we provided some details on secure databases. Finally we discussed some research trends and the impact of the web.

Directions in secure database systems will be driven by the developments on the World Wide Web. Database systems are no longer standalone systems. They are being integrated into various applications such as multimedia, electronic commerce, mobile computing systems, digital libraries, and collaboration systems. Therefore, security issues for all these new generation systems will be very important. Furthermore, there are many developments on various object technologies such as distributed object systems and components and frameworks. Security for such systems is being investigated. Eventually the security policies of the various subsystems and components have to be integrated to form policies for the entire systems. There will be many challenges in formulating policies for such systems. New technologies such as data mining will help security problems such as intrusion detection and auditing. However, these technologies can also violate the privacy of individuals. This is because adversaries can now use the mining tools and extract unauthorized information about various individuals. Finally, migrating legacy databases and applications will continually be a challenge. Security issues for such operations cannot be overlooked.

Essentially this chapter is a summary of a more detailed paper on secure database systems by Ferrari and Thuraisingham. This paper can be found in [FERA00].

CHAPTER 7

THE WORLD WIDE WEB

7.1 OVERVIEW

The developments about the Internet have been key to the development of the World Wide Web. Internet started out as a research project funded by the United States Department of Defense. Much of the work was carried out in the 1970s. It was at this time that there were numerous developments with networking. We began to see various networking protocols and products emerge. In addition standards groups such as International Standards Organzation proposed a layered stack of protocols for networking. The Internet research resulted in TCP/IP (Transmission Control Protocol/ Internet Protocol) for transport communication.

While networking concepts were advancing rapidly, data management technology emerged in the 1970s. Then in the 1980s the early ideas of Bush to organize and structure information in the 1940s started getting computerized. These ideas led to the development of hypermedia technologies. In the 1980s researchers thought that these hypermedia technologies would result in efficient access to large quantities of information, say, in library information systems. It was not until the early 1990s that researchers at CERN in Switzerland combined Internet and Hyperemia technologies, which resulted in the World Wide Web. The idea is for the various web servers scattered within and across corporations to be connected through Intranets and the Internet so that people from all over the world could have access to the right information at the right time. The advancement of various data and information management technologies contributed to the rapid growth of the World Wide Web. This book is all about various data and information management technologies for the web and applying these technologies for applications such as electronic commerce.

While the previous chapters of this part have focused on the key supporting technologies for the web, this chapter describes the web itself. In Section 7.2 we provide an overview of the evolution of the web. In Section 7.3 we discuss the role of Java. Hypermedia technologies are elaborated in Section 7.4. A note on the World Wide Web consortium is the subject of Section 7.5. Corporate Information Infrastructures will be discussed in Section 7.6. The chapter is summarized in Section 7.7.

7.2 EVOLUTION OF THE WEB

As mentioned in Chapter 1, the inception of the web took place at CERN in Switzerland. Although different people have been credited to be the father of the web, one of the early conceivers of the web was Timothy Bernes-Lee who was at CERN at that time. He now heads the World Wide Web Consortium (W3C). The consortium specifies standards for the web including data models, query languages, and security.

As soon as the WWW emerged in the early 1990s, a group of graduate students at the University of Illinois developed a browser, which was called MOSAIC. This was around 1993-4. A Company called Netscape Communications then marketed MOSAIC and since then various browsers as well as search engines have emerged. These search engines, and the browsers, the servers all now constitute the WWW. The Internet became the transport medium for communication.

Various protocols for communication such as HTTP (Hypertext Transfer Protocol) and languages for creating web pages such as HTML (Hypertext markup language) also emerged. Perhaps one of the significant developments is the Java programming language by Sun Microsystems. The work is now being continued by Javasoft, a subsidiary of Sun. Java is a language that is very much like C++ but avoids all the disadvantages of C++ like pointers. It was developed as a programming language to be run platform independent. It was soon found that this was an ideal language for the web. So now there are various Java applications as well as what is known as Java applets. Applets are Java programs residing in a machine that can be called by a web page running on a separate machine. Therefore applets can be embedded into web pages to perform all kinds of features. Of course there are additional security restrictions as applets could come from untrusted machines. Another concept is a servlet. Servlets run on web servers and perform specific functions such as delivering web pages for a user request. Applets and servlets will be elaborated later in this chapter.

Middleware for the web is continuing to evolve. If the entire environment is Java, that is connecting Java clients to Java servers, then one could use RMI (Remote Method Invocation) by Javasoft. If the platform consists of heterogeneous clients and servers then one could use Object Management Group's CORBA (Common Object Request Broker Architecture) for interoperability. Some argue whether client-server technology will be dead because of the web. That is, one may need different computing paradigms such as the federated computing model for the web. These aspects as well as various architectural aspects will be addressed in Part II.

Another development for the web is components and frameworks. We discussed some of them in the chapter on objects (i.e., Chapter 5). Component technology such as Enterprise Java Beans (EJB) is becoming very popular for componentizing various web applications. These applications are managed by what is now known as application servers. These application servers (such as BEA's Web Logic) communicate with database management systems through data servers (these data servers may be developed by the database vendors such as Object Design Inc.). Finally one of the latest technologies for integrating various applications and systems, possibly heterogeneous, through the web is Sun's JINI (see [ACM99]). It essentially encompasses Java and RMI as its basic elements. We address some of these technologies in Part II.

The web is continuing to expand and explode. Now there is so much data, information, and knowledge on the web that managing all this is becoming critical. Web information management is all about developing technologies for managing this information. One particular type of information system is a database system. In Part II of this book we provide some details on web database management. Then we discuss technologies for web information management. Finally in Part III we provide an overview of electronic commerce, the new way of doing business on the web and discuss the applications of web information management to electronic commerce. Figure 7-1 illustrates some of the web concepts we have discussed here.

One of the major problems with the Internet is information overload. Because humans can now access large amounts of information very rapidly, they can quickly become overloaded with information and in some cases the information may not be useful to them. Furthermore, in certain other cases, the information may even be harmful to the humans. The current search engines, although improving steadily, still give the users too much information. When a user types in an index word, many irrelevant web pages are also retrieved. What we need is intelligent search engines. The technologies that we have discussed in this book, if implemented successfully, would prevent this information overload problem. For example, agents may filter out information so that users get only the relevant information. Data mining technology could extract meaningful information from the data sources. Security technology could prevent users from getting information that they are not authorized to know. In addition to computer scientists, researchers in psychology, sociology, and other disciplines are also involved in examining various aspects of Internet database management. We need people in multiple disciplines to collaboratively work together to make the Internet a useful tool to human beings. One of the emerging goals of web technology is to provide appropriate support for data dissemination. This deals with getting the right data/information at the right time to the analyst/user (directly to the desktop if possible) to assist in carrying out various functions. Many of these technologies such as agents and data mining for the web will be addressed in Part II.

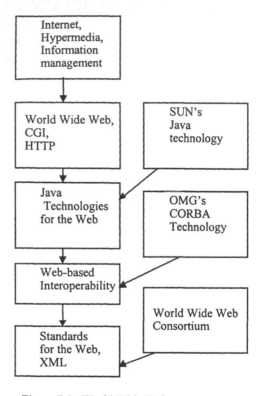

Figure 7-1. World Wide Web

7.3 THE ROLE OF JAVA

Various aspects of Java technology were discussed in the previous section. We elaborate on them here since Java and the web go hand in hand. Javasoft, a subsidiary of SUN Microsystems Inc., has developed a breakthrough product called Java.[18] Essentially Java is a programming language that was designed to overcome some of the limitations and problems with C++ such as dealing with pointers. Java was originally intended for embedded computing. Soon this language became one of the breakthrough products in computer science. While systems can be

---

18   Information on Java can be found in various web pages and text. An excellent reference is [JAVA].

coded in Java, it was soon found that Internet-based programming is facilitated a great deal with Java. Essentially, various programs can be written in Java and are called Java Applets. These Java applets are incorporated into HTML (Hypertext Markup Language) programs.[19] When the HTML programs are executed in an Internet browser environment, the embedded applets are executed. One could then download various Java applets and embed them into HTML programs. These applets when executed may solve specific problems. Several such applets are now available on the Internet. Executing applets on the Internet is illustrated in Figure 7-2.

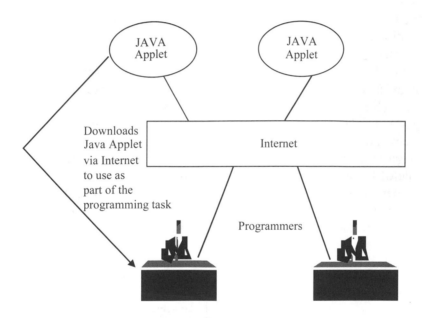

Figure 7-2. Java Programming over the Internet

As we have discussed in the previous section, other developments with Java technology include the notion of servlets. Servlets are similar to applets except that they execute in the server environment and the results are brought to the client. This way the client does not have to be concerned with applets coming from untrusted sources. Enterprise Java Beans that are components based on Java, Remote Method Invocation for communication between Java clients and servers, and finally JINI

---

19 Note that HTML is the language that is used for Internet programming. That is, web pages are written in HTML. These programs are executed through various browsers. Not all browsers can handle Java applets. However, we expect the number of browsers to handle Java applets to increase.

technology for integrating various heterogeneous embedded systems and applications are also emerging Java technologies. Many articles and books have appeared on various aspects of Java technology (see, for example, [ACM99]).

7.4 HYPERMEDIA TECHNOLOGY AND THE WEB

As we mentioned earlier, the growth of the web is due to technologies such as the Internet as well as those such as hypermedia and hypertext.[20] Early concepts of hypermedia systems were formulated in the 1940s. Many of these ideas were computerized only in the 1980s. However, the developments with Internet technology have really given a new direction and momentum to hypermedia technology. As a result hypermedia technology is key to the World Wide Web.

As illustrated in Figure 7-3, a hypermedia database management system essentially includes both a multimedia database management system (MM-DBMS) and a linker. The linker is the component of a hypermedia database system that facilitates browsing of various data sources. For example, by following links, it is possible for users to go through large amounts of information in a short space of time. An example of linking various data sources is illustrated in Figure 7-4. With the emergence of the Internet, many are now familiar with the various browsers that are now available. The relationships between the user, the browser, and the Internet is illustrated in Figure 7-5.

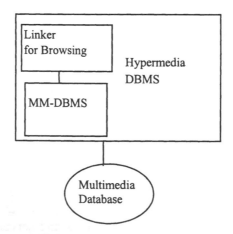

Figure 7-3. Hypermedia Database Management System

---

[20] Hypertext systems are based only on text while hypermedia systems may contain mixed media such as text, video and audio.

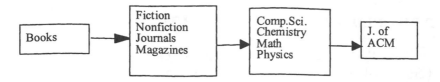

Figure 7-4. Linking Various Topics

While significant developments have been made, it is still very difficult for the users to manage these large quantities of data. With current browsers one can go from one topic to another by following links. One can also get quite lost in what has been called Cyberspace. Very quickly the whole task of browsing could become quite overwhelming. What is needed are "Intelligent Browsers" that will help the users to determine where they are, and how they can backtrack in a meaningful way. Agents will play a major role in intelligent browsing. In addition, appropriate metadata management techniques will also be critical. Metadata may include information about the various data sources as well as dynamic information such as the current status of various users browsing the data sources.

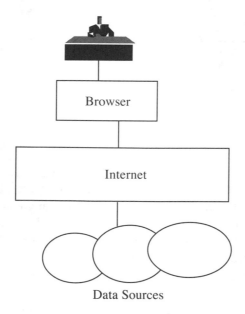

Figure 7-5. Browsing on the Internet

7.5 WORLD WIDE WEB CONSORTIUM

The World Wide Web Consortium (W3C) consists of several members including corporations such as Microsoft and Oracle. W3C was formed in 1996 to establish standards for the web. It has rapidly evolved into one of the most prominent consortiums. Because of the tremendous interest about the World Wide Web, this consortium is excepted to live for many more years.

W3C consists of many working groups promoting standards for different aspects of information management. The activities of the consortium can be found in www.w3c.org. The standards developed include those for security, data modeling, metadata, query language and interoperability. There are links from this consortium to other organizations such as the OMG. Figure 7-6 illustrates the various technical activities of W3C.

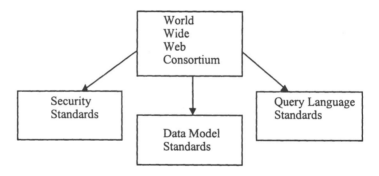

Figure 7-6. W3C Activities

One of the notable developments of W3C is XML (extensible markup language). XML is rapidly becoming the standard document exchange language. It is essentially a meta language for describing a document, which can then be interchanged on the web without any ambiguity. It promotes interoperability. Since the inception of XML, various groups are developing XML standards for different applications such as chemical, financial, and medical as well as for technologies such as multimedia and electronic commerce. For example, financial groups are specifying XML domain type definitions (DTDs) for financial documents, which include information about securities. Those working in the financial fields across states, countries and continents can then understand such documents. Many are convinced that XML will soon become the global language for the web. It will be used not only to exchange documents on the web but also to integrate heterogeneous databases and information sources on the web. More details of XML will be given in Part II.

7.6 CORPORATE INFORMATION INFRASTRUCTURES

The previous sections have described the evolution of the web and some of the main ideas behind the web. It should be noted that the remaining parts of this book will describe the various data and information technologies for the web and show how they may be applied for electronic commerce. These technologies are built on the supporting technologies of Part I. This section briefly describes why the web is so useful and how corporations are taking advantage of the web.

After the advent of the web, there was a national initiative called the NII (National Information Infrastructure) to develop technologies for the web. Subsequently, organizations such as the United States Department of Defense started initiatives like the DII (Defense Information Infrastructure). Corporations soon began developing their own information infrastructures.

The various corporate information infrastructures usually have two main components. One is for the internal use and built on Intranets and the other is for external use and built usually on the Internet. There are major security differences between the internal infrastructures and external infrastructures for a corporation. The external infrastructures have to go beyond the corporation's firewall (i.e., the security perimeter). Figure 7-7 illustrates both types of infrastructures for a corporation. The internal infrastructure may usually contain information about the employees, the projects and other pertinent information such as corporate news. The external infrastructure has information that the corporation wants to make public. This will include product announcement, links to other organizations as well as any information that would facilitate electronic commerce.

These corporate information infrastructures are key to the development and prominence of an organization. Over the past three to four years almost every major corporation in the world has created its information infrastructure especially in the developed countries. We can expect more and more corporations to go online in the future.

7.7 SUMMARY

This chapter has provided an overview of the World Wide Web. We started with a discussion of the evolution of the web and then discussed the importance of Java technology for the web. This was followed by a discussion of hypermedia technologies for the web. Then we provided an overview of the World Wide Web Consortium and then discussed the notion of Corporation Information Infrastructures.

This finishes the discussion of supporting technologies for the web as well as an introduction to the web itself. It also prepares us for the next part (i.e., Part II) of the book and that is on various data and information technologies for the web. These technologies are critical for the most important application for the web and that is electronic commerce. Electronic commerce will be the subject of Part III.

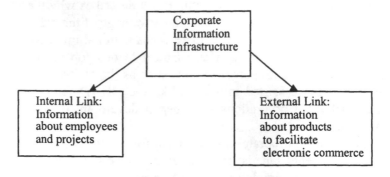

Figure 7-7. Corporate Information Infrastructure

Conclusion to Part I

Part I has described various supporting technologies. These include database systems, data mining, interoperability, objects, and security. In addition, an overview of the web was also provided.

In Part II we will see how these technologies will be applied to the web. Databases have to be accessed through the web. Furthermore, heterogeneous databases have to be integrated on the web. The data sources on the web have to be mined to extract information. The usage patterns on the web can also be mined to give web sites additional information. Object technology has contributed to the web a great deal. The most popular programming language for the web is Java and it is object-oriented. Security is critical for the web, as electronic commerce applications have to be secure.

With this background we are now in a position to explore the various data and information management technologies for the web in Part II.

Part II

Data and Information Management
Technologies for the Web

Introduction to Part II

Part II, consisting of seven chapters, describes data and information management for the web. Chapter 8 provides an overview of database systems technology for the web. In particular models, functions and architectures for web database management are discussed. A note on digital libraries is also provided.

Chapter 9 provides an overview of web data mining. In particular, a taxonomy for data mining is given first. Then both parts of the taxonomy are described. One is to mine the data on the web and the other is to mine usage patterns. Application to e-commerce will also be given.

Chapter 10 discusses security and privacy issues for the web. The main focus is privacy that can be compromised through data mining. An overview of the inference problem as well as potential solutions is discussed. Some security measures are also given.

Chapter 11 provides an overview of metadata. Definition of metdata, metadata on the web, metadata mining as well as some of the emerging areas such as XML and ontologies are discussed.

Chapter 12 describes collaboration and multimedia technologies for the web. In addition, some other technologies such as real-time processing, visualization and training are discussed.

Chapter 13 describes the emerging area of knowledge management. Sharing the knowledge of a corporation as well as technologies for knowledge management are given. In addition, an overview of decision support technologies is also provided.

Finally Chapter 14 describes agents for the web. Different types of agents as well as functions of agents are described.

CHAPTER 8

WEB DATABASE MANAGEMENT AND DIGITAL LIBRARIES: MODELS, FUNCTIONS AND ARCHITECTURES

8.1 OVERVIEW

The previous part described various key supporting technologies for web data management. This chapter describes what web data management is all about. Closely related to web data management is digital libraries and Internet database management.[21] Digital libraries are essentially digitized information distributed across several sites. The goal is for users to access this information in a transparent manner. The information could contain multimedia data such as voice, text, video, and images. The information could also be stored in structured databases such as relational and object-oriented databases.

The explosion of the users on the Internet and the increasing number of worldwide web servers are rapidly advancing digital libraries. This is because digital libraries are usually hosted on networks including the Internet. That is, users can access the various digital libraries across the Internet. There is no single technology for digital libraries. It is a combination of many technologies including heterogeneous database management, mass storage management, collaborative/workflow computing, multimedia database management, intelligent agents and mediators, and data mining. For example, the heterogeneous information sources have to be integrated so that users access the servers in a transparent and timely manner. Security and privacy is becoming a major concern for digital libraries. So are other issues such as copyright protection and ownership of the data. Policies and procedures have to be set up to address these issues.

Major national initiatives are under way to develop digital library technologies. The agencies funding digital library work include the National Science Foundation, the Defense Advanced Research Projects Agency, and the National Aeronautical and Space Administration [NSF95]. In addition, there are numerous projects funded by organizations such as the Library of Congress to develop digital library technologies (see, for example, [ACM95]). Various conferences and

---

[21] Note that we have used the term digital libraries and Internet/web database management interchangeably. Many of the issues for digital libraries are present for Internet database management. The Internet began as a research effort funded by the U.S. Government. It is now the most widely used network in the world.

workshops have also been established recently devoted entirely to digital libraries (see, for example, [DIGI95]).

Figure 8-1 illustrates the recent developments in data management technology to support digital libraries. Database management system vendors are now building interfaces to the Internet. Query languages like SQL are embedded into Internet access languages. In the example of Figure 8-1, DBMS vendors A and B make their data available to applications C and D. DBMS vendors are also developing interfaces to the Java programming environment (to be discussed in Section 8.2). Essentially what this all means is that heterogeneous databases are integrated through the Internet.

This chapter provides an overview of web data management functions with a special emphasis on digital libraries as an application area. In particular, models, functions and architectural aspects relating to web data management are discussed. The role of Java in web data management is the subject of Section 8.2. This will motivate the reader for accessing databases on the Internet. We introduce digital libraries in Section 8.3 as many of the models, functions and architectures apply for digital libraries. In particular, technology integration issues for digital libraries, potential uses with digital libraries including examples of digital libraries, locating resources, as well as Internet access and collaboration issues, are discussed. Database representation, such as data modeling, is discussed in Section 8.4. Database system functions for web data management are discussed in Section 8.5. These functions include query processing, metadata management, transaction management, integrity, and security. A note on semi-structured databases will be given in Section 8.6. Much of the remainder of the chapter will be devoted to various dimensions of architectures. Section 8.7 focuses on architectures for data management on the web. In particular, database access as well as three-tier computing is discussed. Interoperability will be elaborated in Section 8.8. Migration issues are discussed in section 8.9. Models of communications on the web, such as the publish and subscribe models, are discussed in Section 8.10. The impact of client-server computing on the web is the subject of Section 8.11. A note on federated computing is the subject of Section 8.12. The chapter is summarized in Section 8.13.

8.2 THE ROLE OF JAVA FOR WEB DATA MANAGEMENT

In Chapter 7 we discussed the role of Java for the web. Now, what is of interest to the data management community is accessing various database management systems from Java applications. Since more and more applications are now being written in Java, embedding SQL calls into Java is needed for Java programs to access relational database management systems. In the same way, to access object-oriented database management systems, embedding, say, OQL (object query language) calls into Java is needed. A standard called JDBC (Java Database Connectivity) has been developed for database access for Java programs. Clients as well as database servers build interfaces compliant with JDBC. An example approach to communication through JDBC is illustrated in Figure 8-2. Note that in many cases JDBC code may be implemented on top of ODBC (Open Database Connectivity - see for example [ODBC]). That is, ODBC server drivers may lie between the JDBC server code and the actual servers. A high level view of such a scenario is illustrated in Figure 8-3.

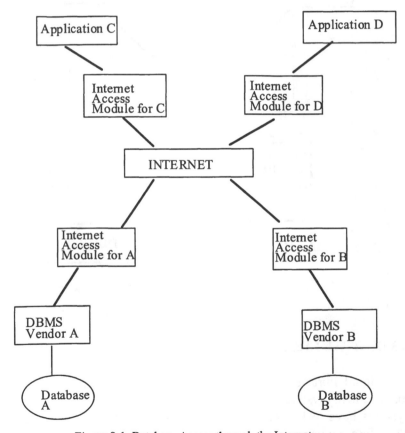

Figure 8-1. Database Access through the Internet

We have only briefly discussed the role of Java in Internet database management. Furthermore, it is only recently that standards like JDBC have been proposed, We can expect to scc major advances in this area in the near future. Furthermore, while we can expect the number of Java-based application programs to increase by a significant amount, we can also expect more and more database management systems (i.e., the servers) to be programmed in Java. For a discussion of JDBC, we refer to [JDBC].

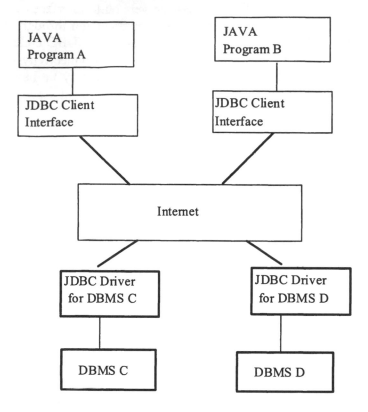

Figure 8-2. DBMS Access through JDBC

8.3 DIGITAL LIBRARIES

Digital libraries are essentially data management and information management systems that have to interoperate on the web. These systems have to be accessed by various users in an efficient manner. Therefore, sometimes digital libraries have been used interchangeably with web data and information management. All of the information we have provided in Part II is applicable to digital libraries.

Various technologies have to be integrated to develop digital libraries. Some of the important data management technologies for digital libraries are data mining, multimedia database management, and heterogeneous database integration. In addition, some of the other information management technologies such as agents, hypermedia, distributed object management, knowledge management, and mass storage are also important. Figure 8-4 illustrates the various digital library technologies.

Integration of these technologies is a major challenge. First of all, appropriate Internet access protocols have to be developed. In addition, interface definition languages play a major role in the interoperability of

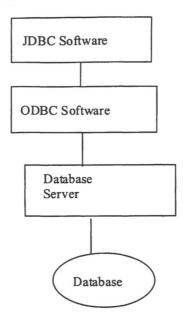

Figure 8-3. ODBC/JDBC Connection

different systems. Due to the large amount of data, integration of mass storage with data management will be critical. Data mining is needed to extract information from the databases. Multimedia technology combined with hypermedia technology is necessary for browsing multimedia data. Distributed object management will play a major role especially since the number of data sources to be integrated may be large.

An example of a digital library is illustrated in Figure 8-5. The idea here is that there are a certain number of sites participating in this library. Note that in theory the library could also have an unlimited number of users. However, many organizations want to share the data between a certain number of groups.

The information in the form of servers, databases, and tools belongs to the library. The participating sites could place this information or it could be placed by someone who is designated to maintain the library. Users then query and access the information in the library.

Figure 8-6 illustrates the use of agents to maintain the library. These agents locate resources for users, maintain the resources, and even filter out information so those users only get the information they want. Agents are essentially intelligent processes. They may communicate with each other in carrying out a specific task. The role of agents in query processing for digital libraries is illustrated in Figure 8-7.

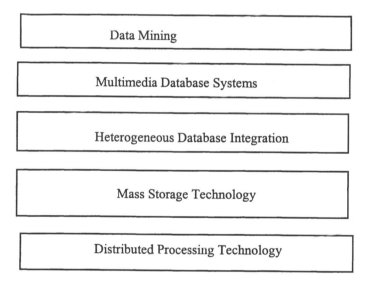

Figure 8-4. Some Technologies for Digital Libraries

One can also take advantage of the digital library technology for collaborative work environments. As illustrated in Figure 8-8, suppose an organization wants to develop some technology such as integrating heterogeneous databases. They access the WWW and find out the names of other organizations that already have developed such systems. They may like what is said about the system developed by organization B. They contact organization B and get a demonstration of the system through the Internet.

8.4 DATA REPRESENTATION AND MODELING

A major challenge for web data management researchers and practitioners is coming up with an appropriate data representation scheme.
The question is, is there a need for a standard data model for digital

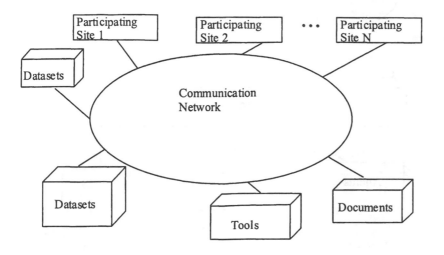

Figure 8-5. Digital Library: Example

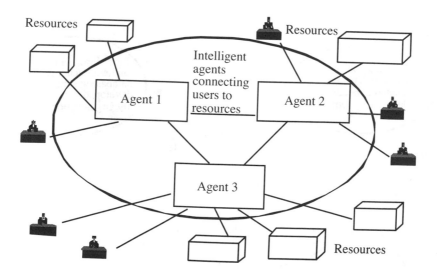

Figure 8-6. Agents for Locating Resources

libraries and Internet database access? Is it at all possible to develop such a standard? If so, what are the relationships between the standard model and the individual models used by the databases on the web?

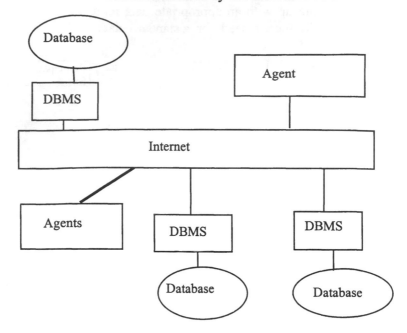

Figure 8-7. Agents for Query Processing

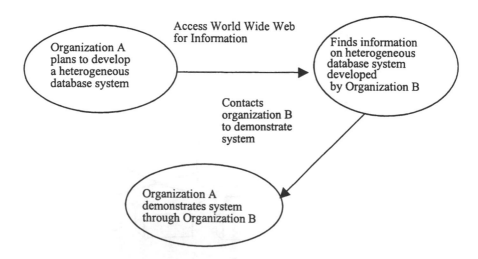

Figure 8-8. Collaboration through the Internet

Back in 1996 when we gave presentations at various conferences on data representation for web databases many felt that it would be impossible to come up with a standard notation. Some even felt that since relational representation was popular, one might need some form of relational notation and SQL-like language to access the various data sources on the web. There were also discussions on variations of an object model for the web. Representation schemes such as UML (see for example [FOWL97]) were emerging and it was thought that perhaps such schemes would be popular for web data modeling. At that time various data representation schemes such as SGML (Generalized Markup Language), HTML (Hypertext Markup Language), and ODA (Office Document Architecture) were being examined (see, for example, [ACM96b]). The question was are they sufficient or is another representation scheme needed?

The significant development for web data modeling came in the latter part of 1996 when the W3C was formed. This group felt that web data modeling was an important area and began addressing the data modeling aspects. Then sometime around 1997 interest in XML (Extensible Markup Language) began. This was an effort of the W3C. XML is not a data model. It is a metalanguage for representing documents. The idea is that if documents are represented using XML then these documents can be uniformly represented and therefore exchanged on the web. Since 1998 one of the significant developments for the web is XML. There are now numerous groups working on XML and proposing extensions to XML for different applications. We will revisit XML in Chapter 11. Figure 8-9 illustrates the evolution of data model discussion for web databases.

8.5 WEB DATABASE MANAGEMENT FUNCTIONS

Database management functions for the web include those such as query processing, metadata management, security, and integrity. In [THUR96c] we have examined various database management system functions and discussed the impact of Internet database access on these functions. Some of the issues are discussed here. Figure 8-10 illustrates the functions.

Querying and browsing are two of the key functions. First of all, an appropriate query language is needed. Since SQL is a popular language, appropriate extensions to SQL may be desired. XML-QL, to be discussed later, is moving in this direction. Query processing involves developing a cost model. Are there special cost models for Internet database management? With respect to browsing operation, the query processing techniques have to be integrated with techniques for follow-ing links. That is, hypermedia technology has to be integrated with database management technology.

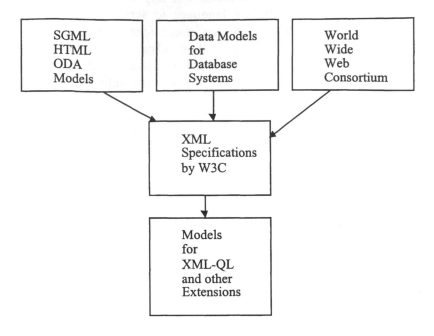

Figure 8-9. Data Modeling for the Web

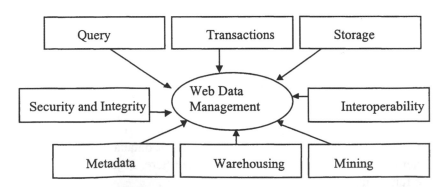

Figure 8-10. Web Database Functions

Updating digital libraries could mean different things. One could create a new web site, place servers at that site, and update the data managed by the servers. The question is, can a user of the library send information to update the data at a web site? The issue here is security privileges. If the user has write privileges, then he could update the databases that he is authorized to modify. Agents and mediators could be used to locate the databases as well as to process the update.

Transaction management is essential for many applications. There may be new kinds of transactions on the Internet. For example, various items may be sold through the Internet. In this case, the item should not be locked immediately when a potential buyer makes a bid. It has to be left open until several bids are received and the item is sold. That is, special transaction models are needed. Appropriate concurrency control and recovery techniques have to be developed for the transaction models.

Metadata management is a major concern for digital libraries. The question is, what is metadata? Metadata describes all of the information pertaining to the library. This could include the various web sites, the types of users, access control issues, and policies enforced. Where should the metadata be located? Should each participating site maintain its own metadata? Should the metadata be replicated or should there be a centralized metadata repository? Metadata in such an environment could be very dynamic especially since the users and the web sites may be changing continuously. The role of metadata will be described in Chapter 11.

Storage management for Internet database access is a complex function. Appropriate index strategies and access methods for handling multimedia data are needed. In addition, due to the large volumes of data, techniques for integrating database management technology with mass storage technology are also needed.

Security and privacy is a major challenge. Once you put the data at a site, who owns the data? If a user copies the data from a site, can he distribute the data? Can he use the information in papers that he is writing? Who owns the copyright to the original data? What role do digital signatures play? Mechanisms for copyright protection and plagiarism detection are needed. In addition, some of the issues discussed in [THUR97] on handling heterogeneous security policies will be of concern.[22]

Maintaining the integrity of the data is critical. Since the data may originate from multiple sources around the world, it will be difficult to keep tabs on the accuracy of the data. Data quality maintenance techniques need to be developed for digital libraries and Internet database

---

[22] Also, there has been a lot of discussions on the notion of a "firewall" to protect the internal information from external users. We do not address firewall issues in this chapter. For more details we refer the reader to [FIRE] and [CHES94].

access. For example, special tagging mechanisms may be needed to determine the quality of the data.

Other data management functions include integrating heterogeneous databases, managing multimedia data, and mining. Integrating various data sources will be the subject of Section 8.8. when we address interoperability. Managing multimedia data will be addressed in Chapter 12. Web mining will be discussed in Chapter 9. Some of the other functions we have addressed here such as data representation and metadata will be revisited in Chapter 11. We will also revisit these functions in Part III of this book.

8.6 SEMI-STRUCTURED DATABASES

Since Codd published his paper on the relational data model [CODD70], there has been a lot of work on developing various data models. These models mainly represent structured data. By structured data we mean data that has a well-defined structure such as data represented by tables. Here, each element belongs to a data type such as integer, string, real or boolean.

However, with multimedia data, there is very little structure. Text data could be lots of characters with no structure. Images could be a collection of pixels. Video and audio data also have no structure. That is, there is no organized way to represent such multimedia data. This type of data has come to be known as unstructured data.

It is nearly impossible to represent unstructured data. Therefore, to better represent such data, one introduces some structure to it. For example, text data could be represented as title, author, affiliation, and paragraphs. Such data are called semi-structured data. That is, semi-structured data are data that are not fully structured like relational structures, but they have partial structure.

During the past five years or so researchers have focussed on developing models to represent semi-structured data. Some of the early models were object-based. Object-relational models were also being proposed for semi-structured data. However, with the advent of the web and W3C, there is much interest to develop models for text data. One of the most popular representation schemes is XML. Note that XML is not a data model, but it is a metamodel to represent various documents. That is, documents such as memos, letters, books, and journal articles are represented with XML. In other words, XML defines the structure to represent such textual documents. We will revisit XML later on in the chapter on metadata.

The approach taken to represent text data with XML is being adopted to represent various types of data such as video, chemical structures, financial securities information, and medical imagery. XML extensions are also being proposed for e-commerce. In a way, all of these representations can be regarded to be representations for semi-structured data. Essentially semi-structured data models can be used to be the global data models in the integration of structured data with, say, text data as shown in Figure 8-11 or they can be used to directly represent semi-structured databases as shown in Figure 8-12. Some extensive research on semi-structured databases has been carried out at Stanford University in the Lore project [WIDO98]. Various other research efforts on semi-structured databases have also been reported [IEEE98]). With the advent of XML, we can expect research and practice of semi-structured databases to grow tremendously.

8.7 ARCHITECTURAL ASPECTS

8.7.1 Overview

There are various dimensions to web data management architectures and these dimensions will be discussed in the remainder of this chapter. Architectures include those for data access, interoperability, publish and subscribe, client-server, federation, and migration, among others.

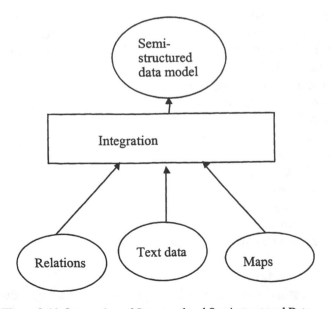

Figure 8-11. Integration of Structured and Semi-structured Data

Data access architectures will be the subject of this section. In particular, in this section we discuss architectures for data access and three-tier computing. Architectures for accessing databases on the web as well as an approach to three-tier computing on the web are discussed.

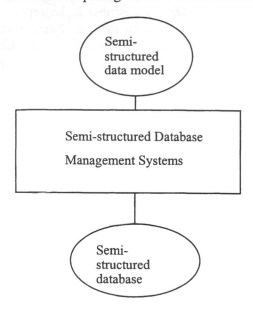

Figure 8-12. Representing Semi-structured Database

Section 8.8 will discuss interoperability of heterogeneous data sources on the web. Migration issues will be briefly addressed in Section 8.9. Models of communication such as publish and subscribe architectures will be the subject of Section 8.10. The impact of the web on client-server computing is the subject of Section 8.11. An alternative to client-server computing, which is federated computing, is the subject of Section 8.12.

At one time we had planned on having a separate chapter on architectures. However, after examining our discussions on database management in Chapter 2, which focussed on models, functions and architectures, we decided to include all of them in this chapter. As we learn more about the web, the information in this chapter can be elaborated into an entire book on web data management. That is, the core issues of web data management are summarized in this chapter.

8.7.2 Database Access
In the earlier sections of this chapter we gave a high level illustration of database access. One approach is to embed SQL calls into Java

programs and access relational databases via JDBC. The approaches have been extended to include object databases as well as object-relational databases.

While JDBC-based approaches are the way of the future, unfortunately many of the web clients cannot understand the concepts in relational databases. That is, web clients only understand the results of web servers and database management systems are not web servers in general. Therefore, as discussed in the various papers in the June 1998 issue of the IEEE Data Engineering Bulletin, one of the approaches currently being adopted for web database access is to use gateways between the database system and the web servers. These gateways will take the output of the database systems and then format it in a way that the web servers can manage. Then web clients and web servers can communicate with each other through the various protocols discussed in Part I. That is, as illustrated in Figure 8-13, when a client issues a request to the server, the data from the databases are retrieved via the gateway. The results are then delivered to the user.

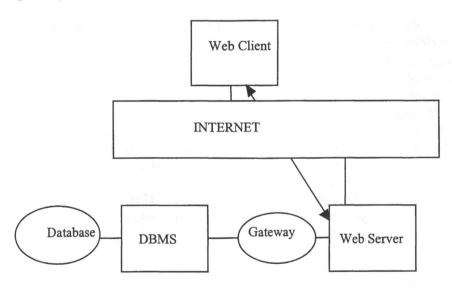

Figure 8-13. Database Access Via Gateways

One of the advantages of standards such as XML is to eliminate the need for such gateways. That is, if all of the documents are expressed in XML, then the database outputs will be represented using XML which can then be interpreted by web servers as well as clients. This way the need for gateways can be eliminated. This is illustrated in Figure 8-14.

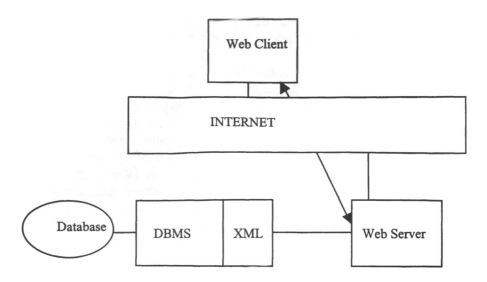

Figure 8-14. Database Access Without Gateways

When numerous applications have to access databases on the web performance becomes a major consideration. One of the trends these days is to use various application servers which are based on EJB technology discussed in Part I. Application servers can coordinate between the various applications. These application servers communicate either directly with the database systems or go through a data server. That is, a data server has two parts. One is access to the back-end database systems and the other is access to the application servers. The data server can schedule various transactions and access the back-end database system.

We illustrate such a system in Figure 8-15. This technology is becoming very popular and we are now seeing various application and data servers on the market.

8.7.3 Three-Tier Computing

Another concept that is extremely popular for the web is three-tier computing. We discussed some of these aspects in Part I. The front-end has the client and the logic for presentation. The middle-tier is the web-server. The third-tier is the database server.

We have used three-tier computing in a number of applications for data management as well as knowledge management. Figure 8-16 illustrates such an example. The client displays maps to the user. The web server is based on EJB technology and is a collection of business

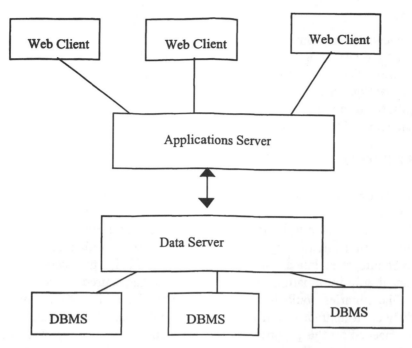

Figure 8-15. Application Server and Data Server

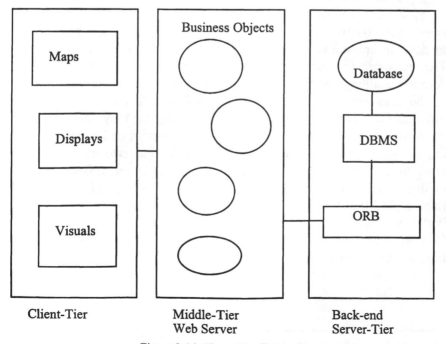

Figure 8-16. Three-Tier Computing

objects to carry out the functions of the application. One could use a database system to manage the web server objects. The back-end may be a relational database system.[23] Other aspects of middleware include transaction processing monitors (TP) and message-oriented middleware (MOM) discussed in Chapter 4. As mentioned earlier, in the future we can expect ORBs, TPs, and MOMs to be integrated.

8.8 INTEROPERABILITY

Heterogeneous database access, data warehousing, and data mining are important functions of digital libraries. The various heterogeneous data sources have to be integrated to provide transparent access to the user as illustrated in Figure 8-17. In some cases, the data sources have to be integrated into a warehouse. Data mining helps the users to extract meaningful information from the numerous data sources. Since the data in the libraries could have different semantics and syntax, it will be difficult to extract useful information. Sophisticated data mining tools are needed for this purpose. A discussion on interactive data mining and its impact on the World Wide Web is given in [THUR96c]. Figure 8-18 illustrates data warehousing and data mining on the Internet. Web mining is the subject of Chapter 9.

One way to interoperate heterogeneous databases is to use ORBs (see Figure 8-19). A major challenge in ORB-based interoperability is to develop appropriate interfaces between the ORB and the Internet. That is, extensions to IDL are needed for Internet database access. Another challenge with the Internet is to connect different components of the database management system. Different vendors may provide different components. For example, a query module may be developed by vendor A and a transaction module possibly with real-time processing capability may be developed by vendor B. The two modules may need to be accessed through the Internet. ORB technology would facilitate such integration also. This is illustrated in Figure 8-20. OMG's Internet SIG is focusing on ORB Interfaces to the Internet. As stated in Part I, alternatives to OMG's CORBA technology, such as Microsoft Corporation's Distributed OLE/COM, are also viable technologies for Internet database access.

---

[23] I thank Eric Hughes and Tim Frangioso for discussions and information on three-tier computing for the web.

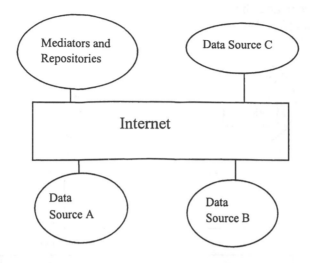

Figure 8-17. Integrating Data Sources on the Internet

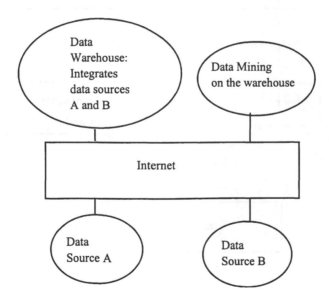

Figure 8-18. Data Warehousing and Mining on the Internet

8.9 A NOTE ON MIGRATION

In Part I we discussed various aspects of migrating legacy data-bases. We described both migrating databases as well as applications. For database migration one needs to develop schemas for the new environment and then migrate the data. This is the easier part of the migration effort. Migrating applications is more difficult.

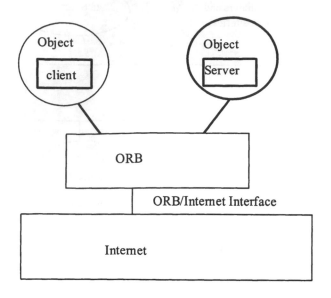

Figure 8-19. Internet-ORB-based Interoperability

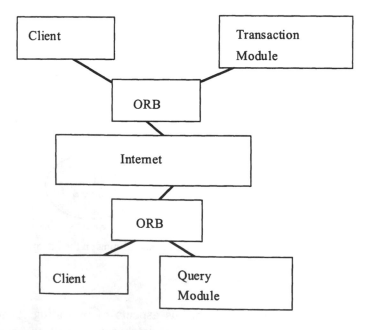

Figure 8-20. ORB-based Component Integration

The applications could be based on complex code and have many relationships, The challenge is to extract the relationships and then migrate the applications to run on the new environment.

The question is, what impact does the web have on migrating legacy databases and applications? At this point it does not appear that the web has any significant impact on the migration process itself. Figures 8-21, 8-22, and 8-23 illustrate the steps to migrating a legacy database accessed on the web. As in the case of a non-web environment, the module that is to be migrated may be extracted as objects and then integrated with the new database. Various issues on migrating databases and applications are discussed in [THUR97]. The role of object technology for migration is also addressed in [THUR97]. The impact of the web needs to be investigated.

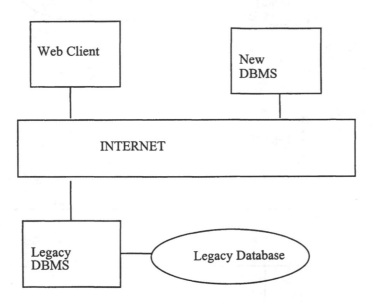

Figure 8-21. Initial Phase of Migration

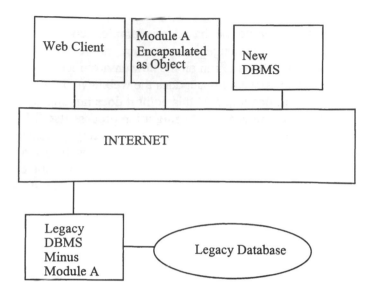

Figure 8-22. Intermediate Phase of Migration

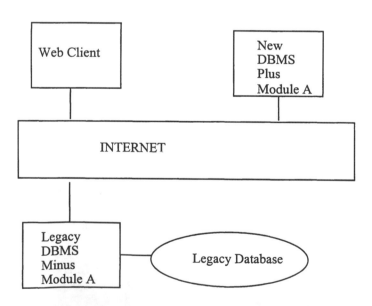

Figure 8-23. Final Phase of Migration

Data modeling will be impacted by the web. For example, how can XML be used to represent the module A that is extracted for the legacy database? Can XML or similar technology be used to access the legacy databases? That is, does one need a mediator that understands XML at the client side and then access the legacy databases as illustrated in Figure 8-24? We are just at the beginning of the migration revolution on the web and we can expect to find answers to some of these questions within the next couple of years. However at this time we feel that legacy migration on the web is still premature.

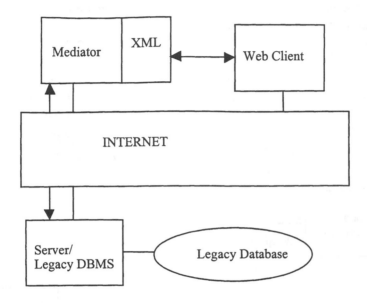

Figure 8-24. Mediator Approach to Migration

8.10 MODELS OF COMMUNICATION

In this section we examine various models for communication on the web. By communication here we do not mean networking. We mean the paradigms for communicating data between the client and the server. Essentially the server here is the producer of the data and the client is the consumer. So the communication is between the producer and the consumer via the web.[24]

In the first model of communication the consumer requests for data. The web agents search for the appropriate producers of the data and get the data for the consumer. This model is illustrated in Figure 8-25. In the second model, also sometimes referred to as the push model, the consumer does not request for the data. As the producer produces the data, it is pushed onto the consumer. This model is illustrated in Figure 8-26. A variation of this model is when the consumer publishes its need

---

[24] I thank Mike Hebert for discussions on push/pull models.

for the data. As the data gets produced, the producers push the data to the consumer. Another variation is when the producer pushes the data to the consumer depending on consumer profiles. In this case the consumer gets personalized services. A third model is a pull model where the consumer pulls the data from the producers. Producers may place the data at a certain repository and the consumers may only pull the data from the repository. This model is illustrated in Figure 8-27. Several variations of these models have been proposed.

While the different models necessitate different processing routines, some of the essential routines are the same. These routines are for processing queries, executing transactions, extracting metadata, as well as accessing complex storage media. As we get to know more about the web, the number of models of communication will also grow

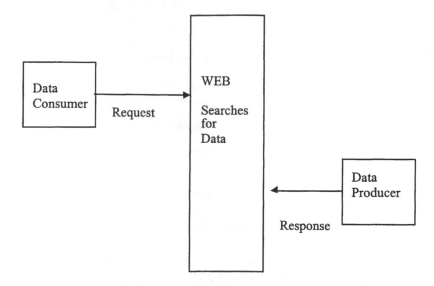

Figure 8-25. Request-Response between Producer and Consumer

8.11 IMPACT OF INTERNET ON CLIENT-SERVER SYSTEMS

One of the major issues faced by the data management community is the impact that the Internet will have on client-server technology. Some argue that with the Internet and languages like Java, one does not need sophisticated clients. That is, all one needs is some sort of terminal to interface to the Internet and all of the application programs and other software can be downloaded and executed.

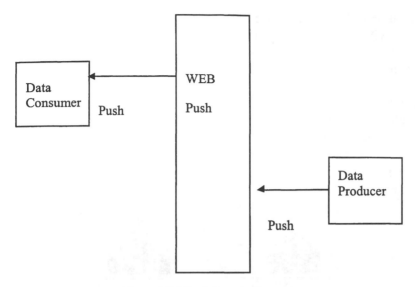

Figure 8-26. Push Data to Consumer

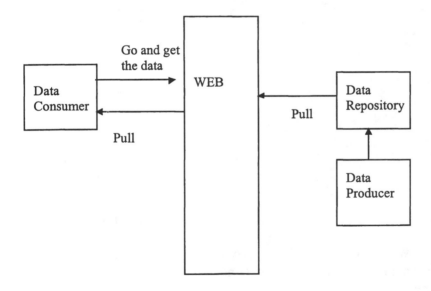

Figure 8-27. Consumer Pulls Data

Others argue that client-server technology will still be alive and well. While much of the software could be downloaded from remote sites and executed, there is still software that is specific to a client's need. Furthermore, there is still work on, say, integrating heterogeneous databases and other data sources that will be specific to a particular client. Especially if the systems form some sort of loose federation, which will likely be the case with so many systems and databases, then there will be a lot of client-dependent software. In summary, while general purpose software development has progressed a great deal, there is still work to do in tailoring the software to a client's need.

Figure 8-28 illustrates how the Internet can be used for communication between the client and the server. A user interfaces to the Internet through the client and accesses the various data servers. In Figure 8-29 we illustrate the concept where the user interfaces to the Internet through a terminal and the client module is on the Internet and invoked by the user as needed. Through this client module, the user can access the data servers.

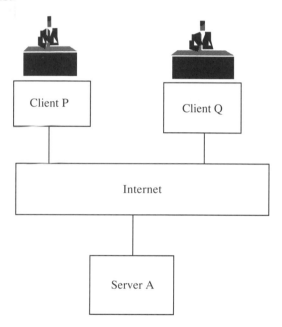

Figure 8-28. Client-Server Communication on the Internet

We feel that it is still too early to forecast the future of client-server technology. The Internet is still not mature, and at present there is a need for client-server technology. The arguments in favor of the existence of client-server technology are rather strong. However, with the maturing of Java and the possible emergence of even newer technologies, we can expect to have major breakthroughs with Internet database access. Therefore, the future of client-server technology will be clearer within the next few years.

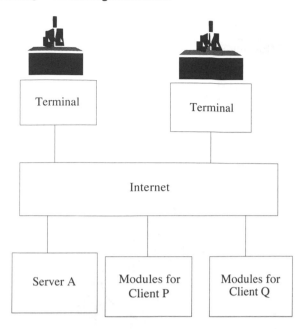

Figure 8-29. Terminal-Client-Server Communication on the Internet

8.12 A NOTE ON FEDERATED COMPUTING

We have discussed models, functions and architectures for web data management. We also described the impact of the web on client-server computing. As mentioned, it is still early to determine whether client-server is dead with the Internet. Three-tier computing is still popular and web is still in its infancy.

Another computing model that is worth mentioning is the federated computing model. In Part I we discussed federated databases. This model for computing is becoming popular for the web. Each group or domain may form its own federation. Various federations have to communicate with each other. As mentioned in Part I, with federated computing one needs to ensure that collaboration and yet autonomy are maintained. Figure 8-30 illustrates federated computing on the web. Many of the techniques and issues discussed in Part I apply. However, the details of the impact of the web on federated computing are not well understood at present. This is an area that needs a lot of research. For example, how can users share data and collaborate with one another? What about security concerns? How can data quality be maintained? Some of the issues are discussed in the chapters on knowledge management and collaboration.

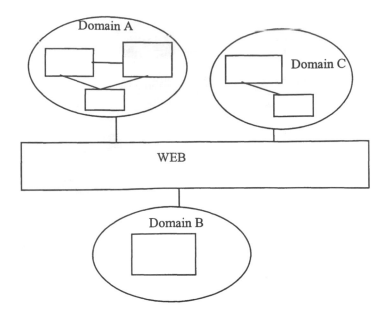

Figure 8-30. Federated Computing on the Web

8.13 SUMMARY

This chapter has provided a broad overview of the developments and challenges on web database management. We first gave an introduction to accessing databases on the web and then gave an overview of JDBC. We also described an example application and that is digital libraries. Next we discussed data modeling for web databases. This was followed by a discussion of the functions. Finally we described architectural aspects. Several issues were addressed including architecture for database access, three-tier computing, interoperability, migration, client-server paradigm, push/pull computing and the federated model.

As we mentioned, this chapter has addressed the three essential components of web data management: models, functions and architectures. These three components could be expanded into a book on web database management as the web evolves. One of the key developments on web database management is the emerging standard XML. We believe that XML and other similar technologies will facilitate data management and interoperability on the web.

CHAPTER 9

DATA MINING AND THE WEB

9.1 OVERVIEW

With information overload on the web, it is highly desirable to mine the data and extract patterns and relevant information to the user. This will make the task of browsing on the Internet so much easier for the user. Therefore, there has been a lot of interest on mining the web, which is also now called web mining. This is essentially mining the databases on the web or mining the usage patterns so that helpful information can be provided to the user.

Data mining and the web developed as independent technology areas in the mid 1990s. While it was felt that mining the data on the web would be useful to help the information overload problem, the extent to which web mining would help key areas like e-commerce was not well understood until recently. It was only about a year or two ago that researchers and practitioners seriously started to think about web mining. The web-mining workshop held during the Knowledge Discovery in Databases conference in 1999 was one of the first [WDM99]. Our initial work on web mining was not until the web-mining panel at the International Conference on Tools in Artificial Intelligence Conference in November 1997 [ICTA97].

Cooley et al. [COOL98] have specified a taxonomy for web mining. They divide web mining into two categories. One is to mine and get patterns from the web data. The other is to mine the URLs and other web links to help the user with various activities on the web. Figure 9-1 illustrates this taxonomy. Closely related to web usage mining is mining to support e-commerce. There are two aspects here. One is to mine and get information about competitors and the other is to mine usage patterns, get customer profiles, and carry out targeted marketing.

The organization of this chapter is as follows. Data mining on the web is the subject of Section 9.2. Web usage mining will be described in Section 9.3. Applications and directions are given in Section 9.4. The chapter is summarized in Section 9.5.

9.2 MINING DATA ON THE WEB

Mining the data on the web is one of the major challenges faced by the data management and mining community as well as those working on web information management and machine learning. There is so much data and information on the web that extracting the useful and relevant information for the user is the real challenge here. When one scans through the web it becomes quite daunting, and soon we get overloaded with data. The question is how do you convert this data into information and subsequently knowledge so that the user only gets what he wants? Furthermore, what are the ways of extracting information previously unknown from the data on the web? In this section we discuss various aspects to web mining.

One simple solution is to integrate the data mining tools with the data on the web. This is illustrated in Figure 9-2. This approach works well especially if the data are in relational databases. Therefore, one needs to mine the data in the relational databases with the data mining tools that are available. These data mining tools have to develop interfaces to the web. For example, if a relational interface is provided as in the Junglee system (see, for example, [JUNG98]), then SQL-based mining tools could be applied to the virtual relational database as illustrated in Figure 9-3.

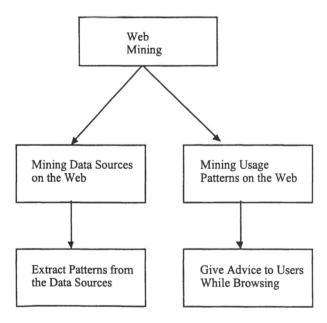

Figure 9-1. Taxonomy for Web Mining

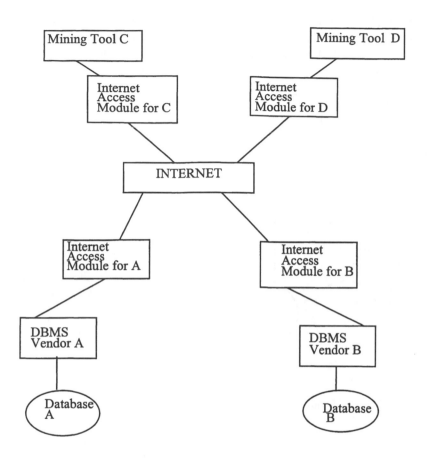

Figure 9-2. Data Mining through the Web

Unfortunately the web world is not so straightforward. Much of the data is unstructured and semistructured. There is a lot of imagery data and video data. Providing a relational interface to all such databases may be complicated. The question is how do you mine such data? In Chapter 11 we discussed various aspects to mining multimedia data. In particular, we focused on mining text, images, video, and audio data. One needs to develop tools first to mine multimedia data and then we can focus on developing tools to mine such data on the web. We illustrate a scenario for multimedia mining on the web in Figure 9-4 where multimedia databases are first integrated and then mined. Much of the previous discussion has focused on integrating data mining tools with the databases on the web. In many cases the data on the web are not in databases. They are on various servers. Therefore, the challenge is to organize the data on these servers. Some form of data warehousing technology may be needed here to organize the data to be mined. A sccnario is illustrated in Figure 9-5. There is little work on developing some sort of data warehousing technology for the web to facilitate mining.

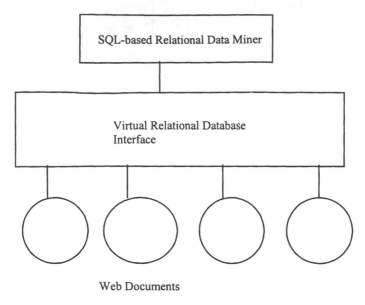

Figure 9-3. Web Mining on Virtual Relational Databases

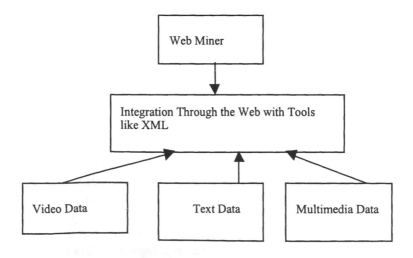

Figure 9-4. Multimedia Web Mining

Another area that really needs attention is visualization of the data on the web [THUR96c]. Much of the data is unorganized and difficult for the user to understand. Furthermore, as discussed in [THUR98a], mining is greatly facilitated by visualization. Therefore, developing appropriate visualization tools for the web will greatly facilitate mining the data. These visualization tools could aid in the mining process as illustrated in Figure 9-6.

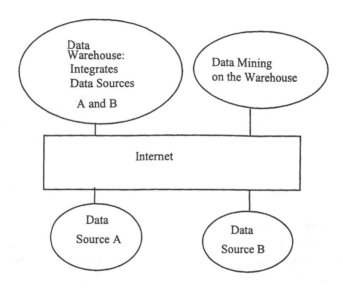

Figure 9-5. Data Warehousing and Mining on the Internet

Recently, various standards have been developed by organizations such as ISO (International Standards Organization), W3C (World Wide Web Consortium), and OMG (Object Management Group) for Internet data access and management. These include models, specification languages, and architectures. One of the developments is XML (Extended Markup Language) for writing what is called a Document Type Definition that allows the document to be interpreted by the person receiving the document (see, for example, [XML1] and [XML2]). Relationships between data mining and standards such as XML are largely unexplored. However, one could expect data mining languages to be developed for the web.

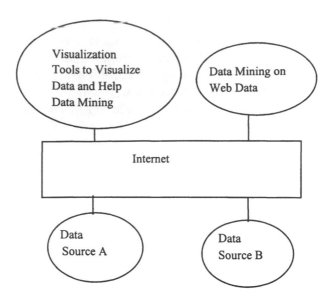

Figure 9-6. Data Mining and Visualization on the Web

In summary, several technologies have to work together to effectively mine the data on the web. These include data mining on multimedia data, mining tools to predict trends and activities on the web, as well as technologies for data management on the web, data warehousing, and visualization. There is active research in web mining and we can expect to see much progress to be made here.

9.3 MINING USAGE PATTERNS

Another aspect to mining on the web is to collect various statistics and determine which web pages are likely to be accessed based on various usage patterns. Research in this direction is being conducted by various groups including by Morey et al. [MORE98a]. Here, based on usage patterns of various users, trends and predictions are made as to the likely web pages a user may want to scan. Therefore, based on this information, a user can have guidance as to the web pages he may want to browse, as illustrated in Figure 9-7. This will facilitate the work a user has to do with respect to scanning various web pages. Note that while the previous paragraphs in this section focused on developing data mining tools to mine the data on the web, here we are focusing on using mining to help with the web browsing process. We can expect to see many results in this area.

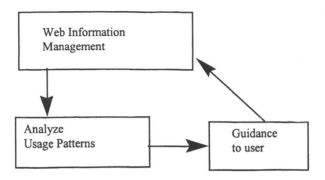

Figure 9-7. Analyzing Usage Patterns and Predicting Trends

Mining can also be used to give only selective information to the user. For example, many of us are flooded with email messages daily. Some of these messages are not relevant for our work. One can develop tools to discard the messages that are not relevant. These tools could be simple filtering tools or sophisticated data mining tools. Similarly, these data mining tools could also be used to display only the web pages in which a user is interested.

9.4 APPLICATIONS AND DIRECTIONS

One of the major applications of web mining is e-commerce. Corporations want to have the competitive edge and are exploring numerous ways to market effectively. Major corporations including retail stores have e-commerce sites now. Customers can order products from books to clothing to toys through these sites. The goal is to provide customized marketing. For example, user group A may prefer literature novels whereas user group B may prefer mystery novels. Therefore, new literature novels have to be marketed to group A and new mystery novels have to be marketed to group B. How does an e-commerce site know about these preferences? The solution is in data mining. The usage patterns have to be mined. In addition, the company may mine various public and private databases to get additional information about these users. That is, both types of data mining described in the taxonomy have to be performed. Figure 9-8 illustrates the application of web mining to e-commerce.

Web mining can also be used to provide entertainment on the web. This is also a variation of e-commerce. Web access and web data may be mined for user preferences on movies and record albums and the corporations can carry out targeted marketing.

As more developments are made on data mining and the web, we can expect better tools to emerge on web mining both to mine the data on the web and to mine the usage patterns. We can expect to hear a lot about web mining in coming years.

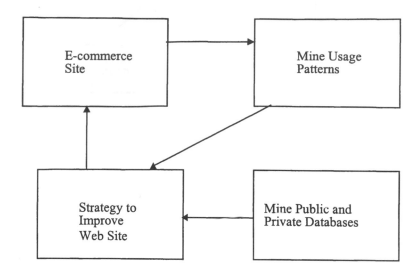

Figure 9-8. Web Mining for E-commerce

Not only can data mining help e-commerce sites data mining can also help the users to find information. For example, one e-commerce site manager mentioned to me that the major problem he has is users finding his e-commerce site. He has advertised in various magazines, but those who do not have access to the magazines find it difficult to access his site. One solution here is to have a third party agent making the connection between the site and the user. Another solution would be to make the search engines more intelligent. Data mining could help here. The data miner could take the requirements of the user and try and match the requirements to what is being offered by the e-commerce sites and connect the user to the right site. Work is beginning in this area and we still have a long way to go. This is illustrated in Figure 9-9.

9.5 SUMMARY

This chapter has discussed the emerging topic of web data mining. First we provided some of the challenges in mining web databases and then we discussed issues on web usage mining. Finally we discussed major applications in electronic commerce.

Web mining is still a relatively new area and there is active research on this topic. Various conferences are now having panels on web mining (see, for example, [ICTA97]). As web technology and data mining technology mature, we can expect good tools to be developed to mine the large quantities of data on the web. As mentioned earlier, at present many of the data mining tools work on relational databases. However, much of the data on the web is semistructured and unstructured. Therefore, we need to focus our attention on mining text and other types of nonrelational databases. Unless advances are made in this area, successful web mining will be difficult to achieve.

As mentioned in [THUR98a], for mining to be effective we need good data. Therefore, to get meaningful results from web mining, we need to have good data on the web. In other words, effective web data management is critical for web mining. There is a lot to be done on web data management. It is only recently that various approaches are being proposed for web data management (see, for example, [IEEE98]). As web data management and data mining technologies mature, we can expect to see good web mining tools emerge.

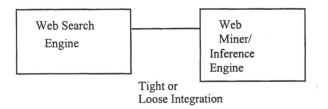

Figure 9-9. Web Mining for Search Engines

CHAPTER 10

SECURITY AND PRIVACY FOR THE WEB

10.1 OVERVIEW

All of our discussions until now have focused on the positive role of the web and technologies such as data mining. Web and data mining can be used to improve efficiency, quality of data, marketing and sales, and have many more benefits. Furthermore, even in the case of security problems, data mining tools could be used to detect abnormal behavior and intrusions in the system. Data mining also has many applications in detecting fraudulent behavior. While all of these applications of the web and data mining can benefit humans, there is also a dangerous side to these technologies, since it could be a serious threat to the security and privacy of individuals. This is the topic addressed in this chapter. While the main focus in this chapter is on privacy issues for the web, we also discuss security measures. However, security is addressed in more detail when we discuss electronic commerce. Furthermore, our discussion here is very much influenced by the threats to security and privacy due to data mining. This is because data mining tools are available on the web and even naive users can apply these tools to extract information from the data stored on the web and consequently violate the privacy of the various individuals.

One of the challenges to securing databases is the inference problem. Inference is the process of users posing queries and deducing unauthorized information from the legitimate responses that they receive. This problem has been discussed quite a lot over the past two decades. However, data mining makes this problem worse. Users now have sophisticated tools that they can use to get data and deduce patterns that could be sensitive. Without these data mining tools, users would have to be fairly sophisticated in their reasoning to be able to deduce information from posing queries to the databases. That is, data mining tools make the inference problem quite dangerous.

Data mining approaches such as web mining also seriously compromise the privacy of the individuals. One can have all kinds of information about various individuals in a short space of time through browsing the web. Security for digital libraries, Internet databases, and electronic commerce is a subject of much research. Data mining and web mining make this problem even more dangerous. Therefore, protecting the privacy of the individuals is also a major consideration.

This chapter discusses both the inference problems through data mining as well as privacy issues. In addition, a general discussion on some security measures for the web is also provided. In Section 10.2, we first provide an overview of the inference problem to give the reader some background. In Section 10.3, we discuss approaches to handling the inference problem that arises through data mining. Since data can be warehoused on the web, we also describe data warehousing, inference, and security in this section. Since inductive logic programming is of interest to us, we discuss inference control through the use of inductive logic programming.[25] Note that there are various efforts to integrate logic programming with programming languages such as Java. Therefore, we can expect such extended logic programming systems to be used to provide security on the web. In Section 10.5, we discuss privacy issues. These privacy issues also depend on policies and procedures enforced. That is, technical, political, as well as social issues play a role here. Then in Section 10.6 we provide an overview of security measures on the web. As mentioned earlier, we discuss security in more detail in Part III as security is a major aspect of e-commerce. Finally the chapter is concluded in Section 10.7.

10.2 BACKGROUND ON THE INFERENCE PROBLEM

Inference is the process of posing queries and deducing unauthorized information from the legitimate responses received. For example, the names and salaries of individuals may be unclassified while taken together they are classified. Therefore, one could retrieve names and employee numbers, and then later retrieve the salaries and employee numbers, and make the associations between names and salaries. The problem that occurs through this inference is called the inference problem.

In the early 1970s, much of the work on the inference problem was on statistical databases. Organizations such as the census bureau were interested in this problem. However, in the mid 1970s and then in the 1980s, the United States Department of Defense started an active research program on multilevel secure databases, and research on the inference problem (see, for example, [AFSB83]) was conducted as part of this effort. The pioneers included Morgenstern [MORG87], Thuraisingham [THUR87], and Hinke [HINK88].

---

[25] For a discussion of inductive logic programming we refer to [ILP97].

We have conducted extensive research on this subject and worked on various aspects. In particular, it was shown that the general inference problem was unsolvable by Thuraisingham [THUR90a], and then approaches were developed to handle various types of inference. These approaches included those based on security constraints as well as those based on conceptual structures (see for example [THUR91b], [THUR93], [THUR95]). These approaches handled the inference problem during database design, query, and update operations (see the scenario in Figure 10-1). Furthermore, logic-based approaches were also developed to handle the inference problem (see, for example, [THUR90b]).

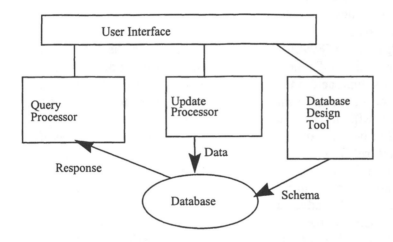

Figure 10-1. Addressing Inference during Query, Update, and Database Design

Much of the earlier research on the inference problem did not take data mining into consideration. With data mining, users now have tools to make deductions and patterns, which could be sensitive. Therefore, in the next section we address inference problems, and data mining. We also add some information on data warehousing and inference.

10.3 MINING, WAREHOUSING AND INFERENCE

First let us give a motivating example where data mining tools are applied to cause security problems. Consider a user who has the ability to apply data mining tools. This user can pose various queries and infer sensitive hypotheses. That is, the inference problem occurs via data mining. This is illustrated in Figure 10-2. There are various ways to handle this problem. Given a database and a particular data-mining tool, one can apply the tool to sec if sensitive information can be deduced from the unclassified information legitimately obtained. If so, then there is an inference problem. There are some issues with this approach. One is that we are applying only one tool. In reality, the user may have several tools available to him. Furthermore, it is impossible to cover all ways that the inference problem could occur. Some of the security implications are discussed in [CLIF96].

Another solution to the inference problem is to build an inference controller that can detect the motives of the user and prevent the inference problem from occurring. Such an inference controller lies between the data mining tool and the data source or database, possibly managed by a DBMS. This is illustrated in Figure 10-3. Discussions of security issues for data warehousing and mining are also given in [THUR96a].

Clifton [CLIF99b] has also conducted some theoretical studies on handling the inference problems that arise through data mining. Clifton's approach is the following. If it is possible to cause doubts in the mind of the adversary that his data mining tool is not a good one, then he will not have confidence in the results. For example, if the classifier built is not a good one for data mining through classification, then the rules produced cannot have sufficient confidence. Therefore, the data mining results also will not have sufficient confidence. Now what are the challenges in making this happen? That is, how can we ensure that the adversary will not have enough confidence in the results? One of the ways is to give only samples of the data to the adversary so that one cannot build a good classifier from these samples (Figure 10-4 illustrates this scenario). The question then is what should the sample be? Clifton has used classification theory to determine the limits of what can be given. This work is still preliminary. There have been some concerns also about this approach, as one could give multiple samples to different groups, and the groups can work together in building a good classifier. But the answer to this is that one needs to keep track of what information is to be given out. At the keynote address on data mining and security (see, for example, [THUR98a]), it was suggested that the only way to handle the inference problem is not to give out any samples. But this could mean denial of service. That is, data could be withheld when it is definitely safe to do so.

Next, let us focus on data warehousing and inference. We have addressed some security issues for warehouses in [THUR96a]. First of all, security policies of the different data sources that form the warehouse have to be integrated to form a policy for the warehouse. This is not a straightforward task, as one has to maintain security rules during the transformations. For example, one cannot give access to an entity in the warehouse, while the same person cannot have access to that entity in the data source. Next, the warehouse security policy has to be enforced. In addition, the warehouse has to be audited. Finally, the inference problem also becomes an issue here. For example, the warehouse may store average salaries. A user can access average salaries and then deduce the individual salaries in the data sources which may be sensitive (see the scenario in Figure 10-5), and, therefore, the inference problem could become an issue for the warehouse. To date, little work has been reported on security for data warehouses as well as the inference problem for the warehouse. This is an area that needs much research.

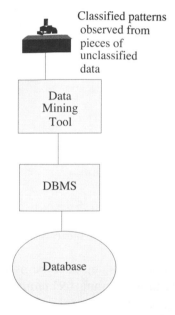

Classified patterns observed from pieces of unclassified data

Figure 10-2. Inference Problem

10.4 INDUCTIVE LOGIC PROGRAMMING AND INFERENCE

In the previous section we discussed data mining and the inference problem. In our research we have used deductive logic programming extensively to handle the inference problem. We have specified what we have called security constraints (see, for example, [THUR93]) and then augmented the database system with an inference engine, which makes deductions and determines if the constraints are violated. That is, the inference engine, by using the constraints, determines if the new information deduced causes security problems. If this is the case, the data are not released.

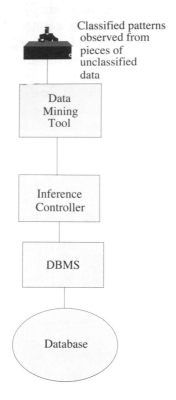

Figure 10-3. Inference Controller

The question is, can this approach be used to control inferences using inductive logic programming techniques? Note that with inductive logic programming one can infer rules from the data. That is, from the various parent-children and grandparent-grandchildren relationships one can infer that the parent of a parent is a grandparent. Figure 10-6 is a possible architecture for such an inference controller based on inductive logic programming. This inference controller is based on inductive logic programming. It queries the database, gets the responses, and induces the rules. Some of these rules may be sensitive or lead to giving out sensitive information. Whether the rule is sensitive or can lead to security problems is specified in the form of constraints. If a rule is sensitive, then the inference controller will inform the security officer that the data has potential security problems and may have to be reclassified.

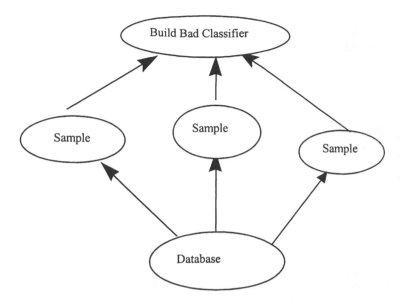

Figure 10-4. Approach to Mining and Inference

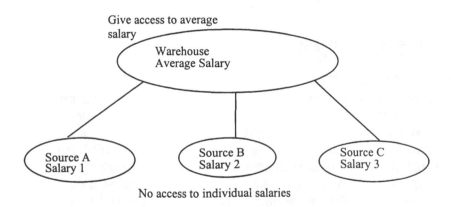

Figure 10-5. Warehousing and Inference

In other words, the inference controller that we have mentioned here does not operate on run time. As we have mentioned, it is very difficult to handle all types of data mining tools and prevent users from getting unauthorized information to queries. What the inference controller does is give advice to the security officer regarding potential problems with the data and safety of the data. Some of the issues on inductive inference, which is essentially the technique used in ILP, to handle the inference problem in secure databases are given in [THUR90c].[26]

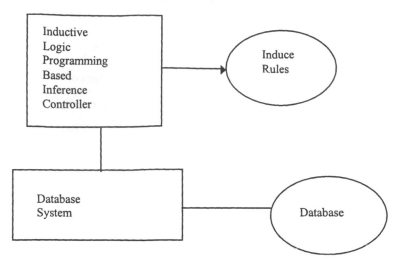

Figure 10-6. Inference Controller Based on ILP

10.5 PRIVACY ISSUES

At the IFIP (International Federation for Information Processing) working conference on database security in 1997, the group began discussions on privacy issues and the role of web, data mining, and data warehousing (see, for example, [IFIP97]). This discussion continued at the IFIP meeting in 1998 and it was felt that the IFIP group should monitor the developments made by the security working group of the World Wide Web Consortium. The discussions included those based on technical, social, and political aspects (see Figure 10-7). In this section we will examine all of these aspects.

First of all, with the World Wide Web, there is now an abundance of information about individuals that one can obtain within seconds. This information could be obtained through mining or just from information retrieval. Therefore, one needs to enforce controls on databases and data mining tools. This is a very difficult problem especially with respect to data mining, as we have seen in the previous section. In summary, one needs to develop techniques to prevent users from mining and extracting information from the data whether they are on the web or on servers. Now this goes against all that we have said about mining in

---

[26] For a discussion of logic programming we refer to [LLOY87].

the previous chapters. That is, we have portrayed mining as something that is critical for users to have so they can get the right information at the right time. Furthermore, they can also extract patterns previously unknown. This is all true. However, we do not want the information to be used in an incorrect manner. For example, based on information about a person, an insurance company could deny insurance or a loan agency could deny loans. In many cases these denials may not be legitimate. Therefore, information providers have to be very careful in what they release. Also, data mining researchers have to ensure that security aspects are addressed.

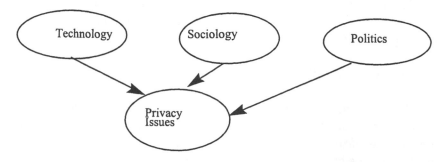

Figure 10-7. Privacy Issues

Next, let us examine the social aspects. In most cultures, privacy of the individuals is important. However, there are certain cultures where it is impossible to ensure privacy. These could be related to political or technological issues or the fact that people have been brought up believing that privacy is not critical. There are places where people divulge their salaries without thinking twice about it, but in many countries, salaries are very private and sensitive. It is not easy to change cultures overnight, and in many cases you do not want to change them, as preserving cultures is very important. So what overall effect does this have on data mining and privacy issues? We do not have an answer to this yet as we are only beginning to look into it.

Next, let us examine the political and legal aspects. We include policies and procedures under this. What sort of security controls should one enforce for the web? Should these security policies be mandated or should they be discretionary? What are the consequences of violating the security policies? Who should be administering these policies and managing and implementing them? How is data mining on the web impacted? Can one control how data are mined on the web? Once we have made technological advances on security and data mining, can we enforce security controls on data mining tools? How is information transferred between countries? Again we have no answers to these questions. We have, however, begun discussions. Note that some of the issues we have discussed are related to privacy and data mining, and some others are related to just privacy in general.

We have raised some interesting questions on privacy issues and data mining as well as privacy in general. As mentioned earlier, data mining is a threat to privacy. The challenge is in protecting the privacy but at the same time not losing all the great benefits of data mining. At the 1998 knowledge discovery in database conference, there was an interesting panel on the privacy issues for web mining. It appears that the data mining as well as the security communities are interested about security and privacy issues. Much of the focus at that panel was on legal issues [KDD98].

10.6 SOME SECURITY MEASURES

So far we have mainly dealt with privacy issues. Security is also a major consideration for the web. The essentials of e-commerce security are web security. For web security there are three components in general: secure client, secure server, and secure network.

We discussed network security issues in Part I. The various network protocols have to be secured. In addition, the basic transmission has to be secure. Encryption provides this type of security. Data is encrypted at the sender's side and decrypted at the receiver's side. The main issue here is how do you maintain the encryption keys? Various techniques such as private key encryption, public key encryption and certification methods have been used and will be discussed in Part III. In addition to network protocol security, the web protocols, such as HTTP, have to be secure.

Traditional client-sever security methods are used to ensure that clients and severs are secure on the web. Furthermore, because of the nature of the web and e-commerce transactions, additional security measures are needed. For example, user A may want to transfer funds from his account to user B's account. There could be a Trojan horse in the system transferring the funds to the account of user C instead. Now, if A and B are multinational corporations millions of dollars could be lost. We hear about such security breaches all the time in the news. Various secure payment protocols and transactions methods have been developed to limit these types of breeches. We will address them in Part III. Figure 10-8 illustrates the security layers for the web.

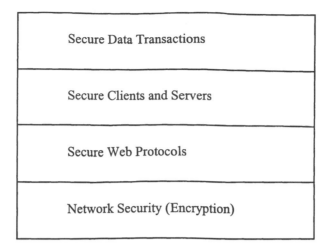

Figure 10-8. Secure Protocols Stack

10.7 SUMMARY

This chapter is devoted to the important area of security and privacy related to the web as well as privacy issues for data mining. While there have been efforts on applying data mining for handling security problems such as intrusion detection (see, for example, [CLIF99b]), in this chapter we focused on the negative effects of data mining. In particular, we discussed the inference problem that can result due to mining as well as ways of compromising privacy especially due to web data access.

First, we gave an overview of the inference problem and then discussed approaches to handle this problem that result from mining. Warehousing and inference issues were also discussed. Then we provided an overview of the privacy issues. Finally we discussed some general security measures for the web. We will elaborate on these measures in Part III.

While little work has been reported on security and privacy issues for web and mining, we are moving in the right direction. There is increasing awareness of the problems, and groups such as the IFIP working group in database security are making this a priority. As research initiatives are started in this area, we can expect some progress to be made. Note that there are also social and political aspects to consider. However, we need the technology first before we can enforce various policies and procedures. In addition, the number of web security conferences is also increasing. However, as the web becomes more and more sophisticated, there is also the potential for more and more threats. Therefore we have to be ever vigilant and continue to investigate, design and implement various security measures for the web.

CHAPTER 11

METADATA, XML, ONTOLOGIES AND THE WEB

11.1 OVERVIEW

Metadata is a term that has been defined rather loosely. It originates from data management. Initially it was called the data dictionary or the catalog that described the data in the databases [DATE90]. As discussed in Chapter 2, in a relational database the data dictionary will have information about the relations and their attributes. Soon data dictionaries included other information such as access control rules, integrity constraints, and information about data distribution. Subsequently, this information came to be known as metadata. With data warehousing, multimedia, and web information management, the definition of metadata started expanding. Finally, with integration of heterogeneous databases, applications, and systems, metadata is now used synonymously with repository technology.

While we could have included metadata as part of the discussion on technologies addressed in Part I of this book, we chose not to do so since metadata is still a new topic for web data management and web data mining, and as the technologies are emerging, the definition of metadata is also expanding. Therefore, we have devoted a chapter on metadata under emerging web data management technologies. This is an area that will change with technological developments.

The role of metadata in mining is now a subject of much research (see, for example, [META96]). There are two aspects here. One is mining the metadata itself to extract patterns, and the other is to use the metadata to guide the mining process. This chapter will also provide a preliminary discussion of metadata mining. First, in Section 11.2, we provide some background information on what metadata is all about for various types of systems. We introduce metadata for the web in Section 11.3. Then, in Section 11.4, we discuss metadata mining and the web is a key part of this. XML, an emerging standard for the web documents, is the subject of Section 11.5. A note on ontologies will be given in Section 11.6. The chapter is summarized in Section 11.7.

11.2 BACKGROUND ON METADATA

Let us revisit the discussion of metadata in Chapter 2. In the example we gave, the database consisted of two relations EMP and DEPT. The metadata includes information about these relations, the number of attributes of each relation, the number of tuples in each relation, and other information such as the creator of the relation. Now metadata also includes information on the three-schema architecture we discussed in Chapter 2. That is, the external, conceptual, and internal views, as well as the mapping between the three layers, are part of the metadata. In addition, metadata includes information such as "John has read access to EMP and write access to DEPT." Metadata also has information on access methods and index strategies.

Next, let us take it one step further and consider the distributed and heterogeneous databases discussed in Chapter 4. Metadata has information on how the data is distributed. For example, EMP relation may have multiple fragments distributed across multiple sites. Metadata also includes information to handle heterogeneity. For example, the fact that at site 1 an object is interpreted as a ship, and at site 2 it is interpreted as a submarine is part of the metadata. The three-schema architecture discussed in Chapter 2 has been extended to multiple layers to handle heterogeneous schema (see the discussion in [THUR97]). Metadata guides the schema transformation and integration process in handling heterogeneity. Metadata is also needed to migrate legacy databases. Information about the legacy databases is stored as part of the metadata. This metadata is used to transform the legacy database systems to new systems.

Multimedia on the web is becoming an important technology area and will be addressed in Part III. Metadata that describes multimedia data could be in different formats. As illustrated in Figure 11-1, in the case of image databases, metadata that describes images could be in text format. Metadata about video and audio data could be in relations or in text. Metadata itself could be multimedia data such as video and audio. Metadata for the web includes information about the various data sources, the locations, the resources on the web, the usage patterns, and the policies and procedures.

Metadata for data warehousing includes data for integrating the heterogeneous data sources as well as metadata to maintain the warehouse. Metadata can also be generated in the mining process. As data mining is performed, metadata could be gathered about the steps involved in mining. Metadata is also collected for visualization, decision support, machine learning, and statistical reasoning.

In summary, whether it be data mining, data management, web information management, data warehousing, visualization, or decision support, metadata is the central component that is common to all technologies. This is illustrated in Figure 11-2.

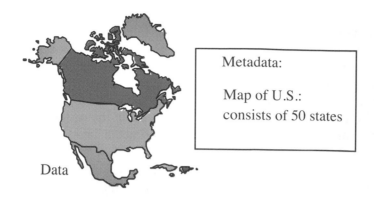

Figure 11-1. Metadata for Image Data

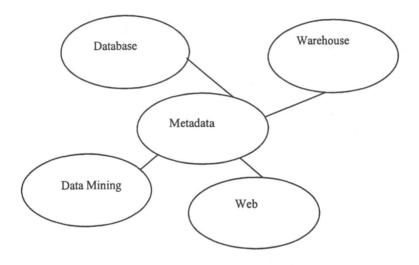

Figure 11-2. Metadata as a Central Component

11.3 METADATA FOR THE WEB

We discussed some of the metadata management issues for Internet database management. Maintaining appropriate metadata is critical for intelligent browsing. As one goes through the Cyberspace, the metadata, which describes the navigation patterns, should get updated. This metadata is consulted periodically so that a user can have some idea as to where he is. Metadata sort of becomes like a map. Furthermore, the Internet metadata manager should continually give advice to the users.

Appropriate techniques are needed to manage the metadata. These include querying and updating the metadata. The Internet environment is very dynamic. This means that the metadata must be updated continually as users browse through the Internet as well as when data sources get updated. Furthermore, as new data sources get added, the changes have to be reflected in the metadata. Metadata may also include various security policies. The metadata must also be available to the users in a timely manner. Finally, appropriate models for the metadata are also needed. These models may be based on the various data models or may utilize the models for text and multimedia data.

Metadata repositories may be included with the various data servers or there may be separate repositories for the metadata. A scenario having multiple data servers and metadata repositories is illustrated in Figure 11-3.

There is a lot of research that is being carried out on metadata management for the Internet (see, for example, [AIPA95], [AIPA96], and [META96]). However, much remains to be done before efficient techniques are developed for metadata representation and management. Defining the metadata is also a major issue.

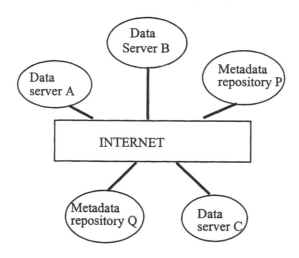

Figure 11-3. Metadata Repositories on the Internet

11.4 MINING AND METADATA

As discussed previously, metadata by itself is becoming a key technology for various tasks such as data management, data warehousing, web searching, multimedia information processing, and now data mining. Because metadata has been so closely aligned with databases in the past, we have included a discussion of the impact of metadata technology on data mining in this book.

Metadata plays an important role in data mining. Metadata could guide the data mining process. That is, the data mining tool could consult the metadatabase and determine the types of queries to pose to the DBMS. Metadata may be updated during the mining process. For example, historical information as well as statistics may be collected during the mining process, and the metadata has to reflect the changes in the environment. The role of metadata in guiding the data mining process is illustrated in Figure 11-4. Extracting metadata from the data and then mining the metadata is illustrated in Figure 11-5.

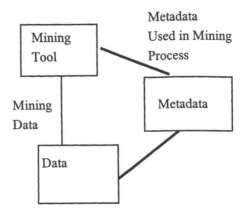

Figure 11-4. Metadata Used in Data Mining

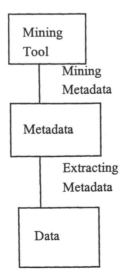

Figure 11-5. Metadata Mining

There has been much discussion recently on the role of metadata for data mining [META96]. There are many challenges here. For example, when is it better to mine the metadata? What are the techniques for metadata mining? How does one structure the metadata to facilitate data mining? Researchers are working on addressing these questions.

Closely associated with the metadata notion is that of a repository. A repository is a database that stores possibly all the metadata, the mappings between various data sources when integrating heterogeneous data sources, information needed to handle semantic heterogeneity such as "ShipX and SubmarineY are the same entity," policies and procedures enforced, as well as information on data quality. So the data mining tool may consult the repository to carry out the mining. On the other hand, the repository itself may be mined. Both these scenarios are illustrated in Figure 11-6.

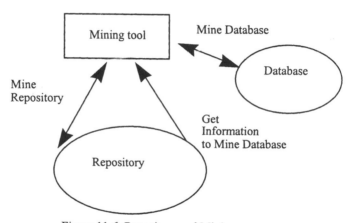

Figure 11-6. Repository and Mining

Metadata plays an important role in various types of mining. For example, in the case of mining multimedia data metadata may be extracted from the multimedia databases and then used to mine the data. For example, as illustrated in Figure 11-7, the metadata may help in extracting the key entities from the text. These entities may be mined using commercial data mining tools. Note that in the case of textual data, metadata may include information such as the type of document, the number of paragraphs, and other information describing the document but not the contents of the document itself.

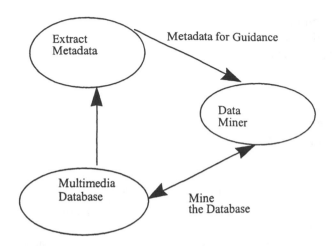

Figure 11-7. Metadata for Multimedia Mining

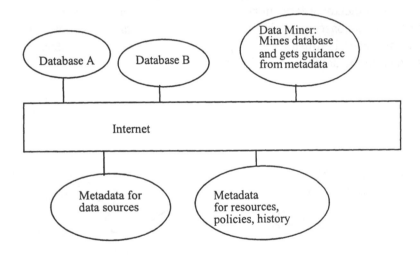

Figure 11-8. Metadata for Web Mining

Metadata is also critical in the case of web mining discussed in Chapter 9. Since there is so much information and data on the web, mining this data directly could become quite challenging. Therefore, we may need to extract metadata from the data, and then either mine this metadata or use this metadata to guide in the mining process. This is illustrated in Figure 11-8. Note that languages such as XML which we will briefly discuss in the next section will play a role in describing metadata for web documents.

In Chapter 10 we addressed security and privacy issues for data mining. We mentioned that policies and procedures will be a key issue for determining the extent to which we want to protect the privacy of individuals. These policies and procedures can be regarded as part of the metadata. Therefore, such metadata will have to guide the process of data mining so that privacy issues are not compromised through mining.

In almost every aspect of mining, metadata plays a crucial role. Even in the case of data warehousing, which we have regarded to be a preliminary step to mining, it is important to collect metadata at various stages. For example, in the case of a data warehouse, data from multiple sources have to be integrated. Metadata will guide the transformation process from layer to layer in building the warehouse (see the discussion in [THUR97]). Metadata will also help in administering the data warehouse. Also, metadata is used in extracting answers to the various queries posed.

Since metadata is key to all kinds of databases including relational databases, object databases, multimedia databases, distributed, heterogeneous, and legacy databases, and web databases, one could envisage building a metadata repository that contains metadata from the different kinds of databases and then mining the metadata to extract patterns. This approach is illustrated in Figure 11-9 and could be an alternative if the data in the databases are difficult to mine directly.

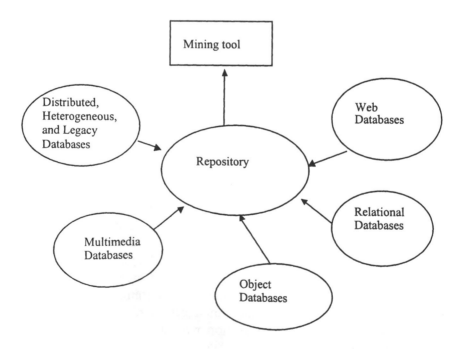

Figure 11-9. Metadata as the Central Repository for Mining

11.5 XML

We have been discussing XML throughout this book and mentioned that it is one of the significant developments in information technology for the 1990s. So what then is XML? It is a data model or is it a meta-data model or is it something else. While different views have been given about XML, it can be viewed as everything. Essentially it specifies a format that you can use to represent documents that can be universally understood. These documents could be text documents, multimedia documents, documents with relational data and documents with financial data. Finally we have some way to specify features in a common way and because the web has millions of users we need this for document representations.

Next let us get into some specifics about XML. XML is a specification by W3C for document representations. Initially it was developed to represent text documents. Text documents could be memos, letters, and papers. As stated in [ROSE99], XML is a semistructured format for data with interesting tags. Tags are defined by tagsets called Domain Type Definitions (DTDs). DTDs can be used to specify memos, letters and other documents. XML is used only for specification. Its counterpart XSL (Extensible Style Language) is used for presenting a document. There are various APIs (Application Programming Interfaces) for accessing XML content. Links between documents are provided by Xlink. It is a form of hyperlinking. Xpointer is used to point within a XML document.

XML evolved from HTML and SGML (Standard Generalized Markup Language). SGML was developed before the web's time and had too many details that were not necessary. HTML was developed for the web and had limitations. For example, HTML has a fixed set of markup tags and these tags do not help to understand the content. They are designed to help a browser know how to display the document. Consequently, what the best search engines can do is to index HTML documents based upon items like frequency of words. HTML cannot do one-to-many linking. Furthermore, it cannot extract pieces of text out of a document, and it cannot link to arbitrary portions of web pages. These are just some of the deficiencies of HTML. XML attempts to overcome these deficiencies (see [ROSE99]).

XML provides the facility for creating one's own set of markup tags. That is, a document can be defined the way you want it. As long the receiver's machine can understand XML tags, then the receiver can look at the document the way it was intended. One can think of XML to be a metalanguage. That is, it is a language describing how to create one's markup language. By changing the tags, an XML document can gct a completely different shape. As mentioned earlier, XSL is used for creating one's own set of presentation rules. Xlink, the XML link language, enables one-to-many linking and also enables bi-directional linking. Xpointer, the XML Pointer Language, enables one to point into a document without putting any anchor tags into the document. XML, XSL, X-Link and X-Pointer are the essential components for document representation for the web. This is illustrated in Figure 11-10.

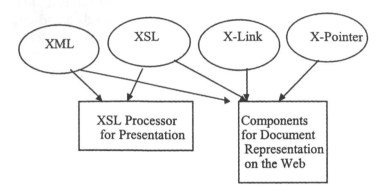

Figure 11-10. XML for the Web

As we mentioned earlier, various groups are proposing XML for representing documents such as financial securities, chemical structures, e-commerce product information, and multimedia data. One specific area of interest to the data management community is XML-QL, which is a query language for XML. As stated by Duetch et al. [DEUT99], XML-QL is a declarative and relationally complete query language. Various proposals have been submitted to W3C for XML-QL. A simple XML-QL query extracts data from an XML document. For example, a query could be to extract the author and title from an XML document. A more complex query can perform joins on contents in XML documents as well as other complex operations. Queries can also be nested. An XML-QL has associated with it a data model, which is usually a graphical model. A thorough discussion of one such XML-QL is given in [DEUT99]. Note that once the standard is adopted by W3C, there will be a common XML-QL.

One of the current limitations of XML is its inability to specify semantics. Some argue that it is not up to XML to specify semantics. Others argue that ontology work has to be integrated into XML. We can see some resolution in the next few years. Ontology, which is an important aspect of metadata, is the subject of the next section. It should be noted that XML specifications are continually evolving like many standards. Therefore we urge the reader to keep track of the developments in www.w3c.org. It should also be noted that XML implementations may not conform entirely to the standards. So users need to be aware of such issues before using an XML product.

11.6 A NOTE ON ONTOLOGIES

During recent years we have been hearing a lot about ontologies. That is, the terms have evolved from data dictionary to metadata and now to ontology. What then is an ontology? Fikes has defined an ontology to be a specification of concepts to be used for expressing knowledge. This would include entities, attributes, reationships and constraints (see the discussion in [ONTO] about this work).

Now, one may argue that we have been talking about entities and relationships for over two decades. So what additional benefits do ontologies give us? Onotologies are essentially an agreed upon way to specify knowledge. Fikes states that ontologies are distinguished not by their form but by the role they play in representing knowledge. One can have ontologies to represent persons, vehicles, animals, and other general entities such as tables, chairs and chemistry. So for example, a group of people could define an ontology for a person and this ontology could be reused by someone else. Another group may want to modify the ontology for a person and have its own ontology for a person. That is, different groups could have different ontologies for the same entity. Once these ontologies are used repeatedly, a standard set of ontologies may evolve. There are efforts to standardize ontologies by different programs. In addition, standards organizations are also attempting to specify ontologies.

Why are ontologies useful? They are needed whenever two or more people have to work together. For example, ontologies are very important for collaboration, agent to agent communication, or knowledge management, and for different database systems to interoperate with each other. Ontologies are also useful for education and training, genetics, as well as modeling and simulation. In summary, many fields require ontologies. A good example is different groups collaborating on a design project. They could define ontologies so that they all speak the same language. If ontologies are previously defined by other design groups they could reuse these ontologies to save time.

We often hear about domain specific ontologies. The question is what are they? Now, one can arbitrarily come up with ontologies for aircraft. But groups working in various airforce organizations may have their own specialization for aircraft. These are domain specific ontologies. One challenge when interoperating heterogeneous databases is whether one can come up with a common set of ontologies for semantic integration of the databases or do you need to take each pair of databases and treat them separately? In order to come up with a common set of ontologies, it is sometimes necessary to examine various pairs and develop ontologies for these pairs and then see if a common set of ontologies can be extracted. The goal for integrating heterogeneous databases is to come up with a common set of ontologies from the domain specific ontologies. This is illustrated in Figure 11-11.

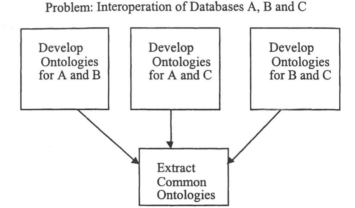

Problem: Interoperation of Databases A, B and C

Figure 11-11. Common Ontologies from Domain Specific Ontologies

E-commerce applications and web data management will define a new set of ontologies. For e-commerce applications, ontologies will include specifications for web pages to set up e-commerce sites as well as ontologies for specifying various goods. There are web sites emerging that specify ontologies. These ontologies can be used for various activities such as collaboration and integration.

One of the questions we are often asked is what is the difference between ontologies and XML. While XML specifies the structure of a document, ontologies specify semantics of various applications. The challenge is to integrate the structure with the semantics to provide a complete set of interoperability mechanisms.

There is extensive research on ontologies by not only computer scientists, but also by logicians and philosophers. Uncertain reasoning, probabilities, and other heuristics are being incorporated into ontology research. As in the case of XML, this is also a very dynamic area and we urge the reader to visit various web sites specifying ontologies and to keep up with the developments.

11.7 SUMMARY

This chapter is devoted to a discussion of web metadata management and mining. We first provided an overview of the various types of metadata, and then discussed metadata management on the web. Since mining metadata is critical for web data management as one can extract, say, usage patterns by mining metadata, we then discussed metadata mining. Metadata is the central component to many kinds of information systems such as decision support systems, database systems, and machine learning systems. We ended this chapter with a discussion of XML and ontologies.

While metadata can be regarded to be a supporting technology for web data management, we have included metadata management as part of the discussion on emerging data management technologies for the web because the notion of metadata is continually changing. Initially metadata was considered to be just the data dictionary. Then it included policies, access control rules, and information about data distribution. Now metadata includes information about the various resources on the web, usage patterns, as well as repositories. We believe that metadata management and mining on the web will become an essential part of all aspects of data management and mining on the web. Finally we can expect developments in both XML and ontologies to explode to benefit effective data management on the web.

CHAPTER 12

COLLABORATION, MULTIMEDIA AND OTHER TECHNOLOGIES FOR THE WEB

12.1 OVERVIEW

Many of the previous technologies deal mainly with data management and data mining for the web. That is, these are the data management technologies. Although this book is about web data management, we cannot separate data with information and knowledge management. Therefore, in this chapter and in the next two we discuss information and knowledge management technologies.

Information management is a broad term and encompasses many areas. Some say that data mining is also part of information management as it extracts information from the databases. We have discussed our views of data, information and knowledge management in Chapter 1. This chapter describes some of the information technologies for the web.

We start with discussions of collaborative computing and in particular data management for collaborative computing. Today users are in different places collaborating on books, articles and designs. Even we have collaborated with our colleagues on writing papers for journals and conferences on the Internet. There are several tools that are emerging for collaboration and these tools have to work on the web. While collaboration in the early 1990s mainly focused on collaborating within an organization, web-based collaboration is becoming a necessity now.

Next we address multimedia computing and in particular multimedia data management for the web. For this we need to understand what multimedia data management is all about. We give special consideration to multimedia data management, as it is an important function for the web. Finally we discuss the impact of the web on multimedia data such as web-based video, broadcasting, films, and training.

Three key technologies for the web are knowledge management, decision support, and agents. Since these are important aspects we discuss them in separate chapters. That is, Chapters 13 and 14 will be devoted to these topics. We end this chapter with a discussion of some other technologies such as real-time processing, training and distance learning, and visualization.

The organization of this chapter is as follows. Section 12.2 describes collaboration. Multimedia computing is the subject of Section

12.3. Other technologies are discussed in Section 12.4. The chapter is concluded in Section 12.5.

12.2 DATA MANAGEMENT FOR COLLABORATION

12.2.1 Overview

Although the notion of computer supported cooperative work (CSCW) was first proposed in the early 1980s, it is only recently that much interest is being shown in this topic. Several research papers have now been published in collaborative computing and prototypes/products have been developed. Collaborative computing enables people, groups of individuals, and organizations to work together with one another in order to accomplish a task or a collection of tasks. These tasks could vary from participating in conferences, solving a specific problem, or working on the design of a system. Specific contributions to collaborative computing include the development of team workstations (where Groupware creates a shared workspace supporting dynamic collaboration in a work group), multimedia communication systems supporting distributed workgroups, and collaborative computing systems supporting cooperation in the design of an entity (such as an electrical or mechanical system).[27] Several technologies including multimedia, artificial intelligence, networking and distributed processing, and database systems as well as disciplines such as organizational behavior and human computer interaction have contributed significantly towards the growth of collaborative computing.

One aspect of collaborative computing of particular interest to the database community is workflow computing. Workflow is defined as the automation of a series of functions that comprise a business process such as data entry, data review, and monitoring performed by one or more people. An example of a process that is well suited for workflow automation is the purchasing process. Applications can range from simple user-defined processes such as document review to complex applications such as manufacturing processes. Original custom-made workflow systems developed over the past twenty years for applications such as factory automation were built using a centralized database. Many commercial workflow system products targeted for office environments are based on a messaging architecture. This architecture supports the distributed nature of current workteams. However, the messaging architecture is usually file based and lacks many of the features supported by database management systems such as data

---

[27] See the discussions in the Communications of the ACM, Special Issue in Collaborative Computing, December 1991 [ACM91b].

representation, consistency management, tracking, and monitoring. Although the emerging products show some promise, they do not provide the functionality of database management systems.

This chapter will identify the database systems technology issues to support collaborative computing in general and workflow computing applications in particular. Many of the ideas discussed here also apply for collaborative computing systems. However, we have limited the scope by focusing mainly on workflow applications. There are two ways to design the data management system for the workflow application. One is to take a top-down approach and design the entire application and then determine the type of data management system that is needed. The other is to focus only on the data management system. The data management system developed under the first approach would be specialized for the particular application whereas the one developed under the second approach would be a more general purpose one. We discuss both approaches here.

This section is organized as follows. First some examples on database support for collaboration will be given in Section 12.2.2. Architectural issues for workflow management systems are discussed in Section 12.2.3. General purpose database management system support for workflow applications is discussed in Section 12.2.4. In particular, data representation and manipulation as well as the role of metadata are discussed. The impact of the web is the subject of Section 12.2.5.

12.2.2 Some Examples

As mentioned in Section 12.2, a collaborative computing system should enable multiple groups and teams from different sites to collaborate on a project. Figure 12-1 illustrates an example where teams A and B are working on a geographical problem such as analyzing and predicting the weather in North America. The two teams must have a global picture of the map as well as any notes that go with it. Any changes made by one team should be instantly visible to the other team and both teams communicate as if they are in the same room.

To enable such transparent communication, data management support is needed. One could utilize a database management system to manage the data or some type of data manager that provides some of the essential features such as data integrity, concurrent access, and retrieval capabilities. In the above example, the database may consist of information describing the problem the teams are working on, the data that is involved, history data, as well as the metadata information. The data manager must provide appropriate concurrency control features so that when both teams simultaneously access the common picture and make changes, these changes are coordinated.

One possible scenario for the data manager is illustrated in Figure 12-2 where each team has its own local data manager and there is a global data manager to maintain any global information, including the data and the metadata. The local data managers communicate with the global data manager. The global data manager illustrated in this figure is at the logical level. At the physical level the global data manager may also be distributed. The data managers coordinate their activities to provide features such as concurrency control, integrity, and retrieval.

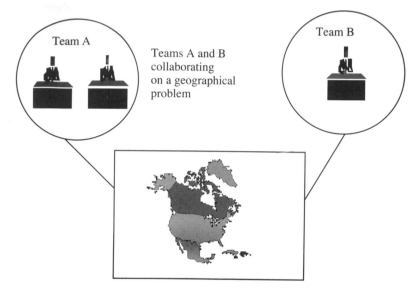

Figure 12-1. Collaboration Example

12.2.3 Architectural Support for Workflow Computing

As stated in Section 12.2, workflow computing is a special case of collaborative computing. This section and the next two discuss various aspects of database support for workflow computing applications.

A database management system for a workflow application manages the database that contains the data required for the application. For a workflow application, the data could be purchase orders, requisitions, and project reports, among others. Like some of the other systems discussed in this book, there are various ways to integrate workflow systems with the database management systems. We discuss two of the approaches. In one approach, there is loose integration between the workflow management system and the database management system. This is illustrated in Figure 12-3. With this approach, one could use a commercial database management system for the workflow application. In the second approach, illustrated in Figure 12-4, there is tight integration between the workflow management system and the database management system. With this approach, often the database management system is a special purpose one.

The database management system could be centralized or distributed. All of the advantages and disadvantages for centralized and distributed database systems discussed in Part I also apply for database management systems designed for workflow applications. In addition, the database management system should provide additional support for special transactions for workflow systems. Some of the database management system issues are discussed in Section 12.3. Note that one could also utilize distributed object management systems to encapsulate the components of the workflow management system.

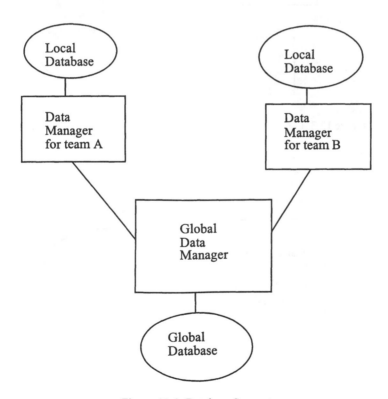

Figure 12-2. Database Support

As mentioned earlier, workflow computing is an aspect of collaborative computing. As illustrated in Figure 12-1, collaborative computing encompasses many more features such as team members collaborating on a project, designing a system, and conducting a meeting. One could build a collaborative application on top of a workflow management system. The relationship between a database management system, a workflow management system, and a collaborative computing system is illustrated in Figure 12-5.

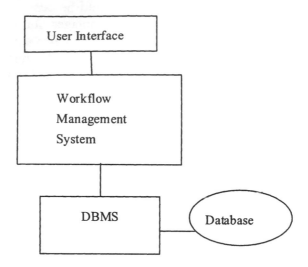

Figure 12-3. Loose Integration between Workflow System and DBMS

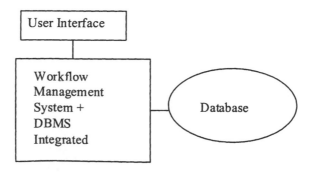

Figure 12-4. Tight Integration between Workflow System and DBMS

12.2.4 Database Support for Workflow Applications

12.2.4.1 Database System Models and Functions

The database management functions for workflow applications will depend on the functionality requirements. These requirements can in general be divided into various categories including data representation and data manipulation. The data representation requirements include support for complex data structures to represent (i) objects like documents, spreadsheets, and mail messages, (ii) the workflow rules which determine the electronic routing of the objects, (iii) tracking data which monitor the status of the objects, (iv) the actions by users, (v) deadlines imposed on the actions, and (vi) security constraints. Special formats for presenting the objects to the users may also be needed. Data manipulation requirements include (i) querying and browsing the database, (ii) managing the metadata, which describes the data in the database, (iii) mechanisms for concurrent access to the data, such as modifying the workflow or the objects, (iv) special view mechanisms for the users, (v) support for remote database access, and (vi) integrating with the databases of other workgroup applications such as project management and document management.

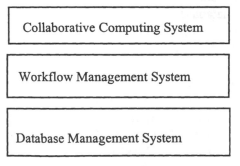

Figure 12-5. Relationship between Systems

The data model for a workflow application should support the data representation requirements. Various types of data models including semantic models such as an object-oriented model as well as simple models which consist of nodes and links are being investigated for this purpose. Also, a data model which accommodates different representation schemes may be needed for the different types of data. For example, the workflow rules may be represented in rule bases and the documents, spreadsheets, and messages may be represented as complex objects. The data model should also provide the support to enforce integrity and security constraints, maintain different versions and configurations, and also represent the changes that an object goes through within a transaction. Also, if the objects are to be represented to the user in a different scheme, then mappings between the different schemes have to be stored. The data model should also be flexible to support ad hoc changes and schema evolution. The use of temporal constructs may be needed to represent historical and/or time-dependent data objects.

Since workflow applications are distributed in nature, both centralized as well as distributed architectures need to be examined for the data management systems. For example, should all of the data such as workflow rules and objects be stored in a centralized location or should the data be distributed across the different workstations? If the architecture is distributed, then should it support a heterogeneous environment? From the discussion of the functionality requirements of workflow applications described by Marshak in the March 1992 issue of the Office Computing Report [MARS92], it appears that the database should be fully integrated with the application. This means that the environment is most likely to be homogeneous. Note that if the workflow application has to be integrated with other applications such as project management, then there may be a need to integrate the heterogeneous databases. Another issue here is whether to store all of the data in the database. For example, changes that an object goes through during a transaction may be transient and need to be stored only until the duration of the transaction. In this case, the changes could be stored in temporary storage. If the changes have to be stored for historical purposes, then the database could be used.

The functions of the data management system should provide support for the data manipulation requirements. One of the main issues here is developing a suitable model of concurrency control (see, for example, [ALON96] and [SHET93]). Since the goal is to enable the collaborators to share as much data as possible, a fine-grained granularity locking approach seems more appropriate than a coarse-grained one. Furthermore, alternatives to locking as a concurrency control mechanism as well as variations to the locking technique are being explored by researchers. In general, the model should be flexible so that a user can lock one part of an object while his peers could work with other parts of an object. Furthermore, it is also desirable for the collaborators to be notified almost instantly if any part of an object is being modeled by a user, and if so by whom. If this feature is not provided, then it will be difficult to maintain the consistency of the objects. Concurrency control support is also needed for updating the workflow rules. In addition to developing suitable concurrency control algorithms, appropriate recovery mechanisms need to be developed to handle system failures and transaction aborts. Workflow transaction management is an active research area. This research is also being transferred into commercial products. Other functions of the system include querying and browsing, managing the metadata, enforcing appropriate access control policies, managing different versions and configurations, and monitoring the changes to an object within a transaction. In addition, the system must manage the links between the different users' shared objects. Since metadata plays an important role in collaborative computing, a discussion of this role is given separately.

In summary, workflow applications will require efficient support for managing the database which may possibly be distributed. This section has identified some of the issues that need to be investigated. In particular, approaches to developing a data management system as well as issues on developing a data model, architecture, and modules for such a system which satisfy the functionality requirements were discussed. While the developments in database systems technology have contributed significantly to support new generation applications, applying these developments as well as generating new developments for collaborative computing applications in general, and workflow computing applications in particular, is the next challenge. Database system vendors are integrating their products with workflow systems. We can expect significant developments to be made in workflow-based database management systems.

12.2.4.2 The Role of Metadata

Metadata plays a major role for collaborative computing and workflow applications. Metadata not only describes the data in the database such as the schemas, it also contains other information such as access control rules, links between different objects, policies, information about the various teams collaborating, information about the various versions, and other historical information. For workflow computing applications, metadata includes information about projects, schedules, and other activities. Metadata should be used by the various teams to support their collaboration and also help in providing a global synchronized picture of the problem being handled.

An appropriate model for the metadata is needed. Again this model could be closely linked with the models used by the data managers or it could be completely independent. Various schema transformations between different representations are also included in the metadata. The metadata manager should provide support for querying and updating the metadata as well as giving advice to the various collaborating teams and guide the decision making process.

The metadata manager could be centralized or distributed. This design may depend on the architecture selected for the environment. If the database is distributed, say each team having its own local database, then there could be a metadata manager for each database. The various metadata managers have to communicate with each other.

Metadata research for workflow computing as well as collaborative applications is just beginning. However, with the recent emphasis on metadata for various applications including digital libraries, one can expect more results on metadata issues for collaborative computing.

12.2.5 Impact of the Web on Collaboration

The web has increased the need for collaboration even further. Users now share documents on the web and work on papers and designs on the web. Corporate information infrastructures promote collaboration and sharing of information and documents. Therefore, the collaborative tools have to work effectively on the web. While the web promotes collaboration, collaboration also benefits the web. That is, it is a key information technology to enhance the web. Therefore the two technologies can benefit from each other.

The challenge is to use these tools to work effectively on the web. In the simple case you build web interfaces. However, many of the tools were developed not with the web in mind. For example this was the case with the database systems and building web access is the easy part. There are many challenges such as data formats, transactions, and metadata management on the web. Such challenges are present for collaboration also. Some of the collaborative tools work with the understanding that the people are located in the same building. While for corporate Intranets this may not be a problem, with the Internet this could pose some major problems. Scalability of the tools is also an important issue. Typically the tools have been developed for tens of users. With the web, these tools have to work for tens of thousands of users. Such requirements have to be taken into consideration. Figure 12-6 uses the same example discussed earlier in this section and shows collaboration on the Internet.

We believe that collaboration and the web will go hand in hand. In the future collaboration tools will have to work with multimedia data. Therefore, we address multimedia data in the next section. In recent years there have been some interesting articles published on collaboration and the impact of the web on the collaboration tools [IEEE99].

12.3 MULTIMEDIA DATA MANAGEMET

12.3.1 Overview

A multimedia database system includes a multimedia database management system and a multimedia database. A multimedia database management system (MM-DBMS) manages the multimedia database. A multimedia database is a database, which contains multimedia data. Multimedia data may include structured data as well as semi-structured and unstructured data such as audio, video, text, and images. An MM-DBMS provides support for storing, manipulating, and retrieving multimedia data from a multimedia database. In a sense, a multimedia database system is a type of heterogeneous database system, as it manages heterogeneous data types. Heterogeneity is due to the media of the data such as text, video, and audio.

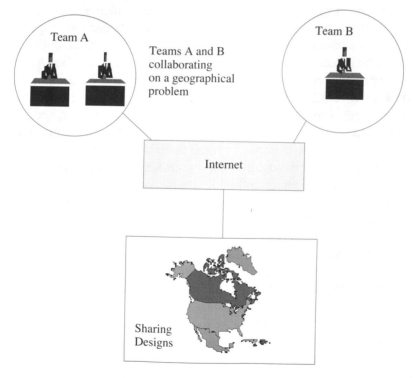

Figure 12-6. Collaboration on the Web

An MM-DBMS must provide support for typical database management system functions. These include query processing, update processing, transaction management, storage management, metadata management, security, and integrity. In addition, in many cases, the various types of data such as voice and video have to be synchronized for display, and, therefore, real-time processing is also a major issue in an MM-DBMS.

Recently there has been much interest on mining multimedia databases such as text, images, and video. As mentioned, many of the data mining tools work on relational databases. However, a considerable amount of data is now in multimedia format. There is lots of text and image data on the web. News services provide lots of video and audio data. This data has to be mined so that useful information can be extracted. One solution is to extract structured data from the multimedia databases and then mine the structured data using traditional data mining tools. Another solution is to develop mining tools to operate on the multimedia data directly. Multimedia data mining is the subject of this chapter. Note that to mine multimedia data, we must mine combinations of two or more data types, such as text and video, or text, video, and audio. However, in this book we deal mainly with one data type at a time. This is because we need techniques to mine the data belonging to the individual data types first before mining multimedia data. In the future we can expect tools for multimedia data mining to be developed.

In Section 12.3.2, we first provide some useful information on multimedia databases so that the reader can understand the mining and web concepts better. In particular, architectures, modeling, and multimedia database functions are discussed. Then in Section 12.3.3 we discuss multimedia mining including text mining, image mining, video mining, and audio mining. We also briefly address the issues on mining combinations of data types. Mining multimedia is a key function for multimedia data management on the web. Therefore, we give considerable attention to this topic. Developments and challenges on multimedia for the web is the subject of Section 12.3.4.

12.3.2 Multimedia Databases: Architectures, Models and Functions

12.3.2.1 Architectures for an MM-DBMS

Various architectures are being examined to design and develop an MM-DBMS. In one approach, the DBMS is used just to manage the metadata, and a multimedia file manager is used to manage the multimedia data. Then there is a module for integrating the DBMS and the multimedia file manager. This architecture is based on the loose-coupling approach and is illustrated in Figure 12-7. In this case, the MM-DBMS consists of the three modules: the DBMS managing the metadata, the multimedia file manager, and the module for integrating the two.

The second architecture, illustrated in Figure 12-8, is the tight coupling approach. In this architecture, the DBMS manages both the multimedia database as well as the metadata. That is, the DBMS is an MM-DBMS. The tight coupling architecture has an advantage because all of the DBMS functions could be applied on the multimedia database. This includes query processing, transaction management, metadata management, storage management, and security and integrity management. Note that with the loose coupling approach, unless the file manager performs the DBMS functions, the DBMS only manages the metadata for the multimedia data. Functional architecture is illustrated in Figure 12-9.

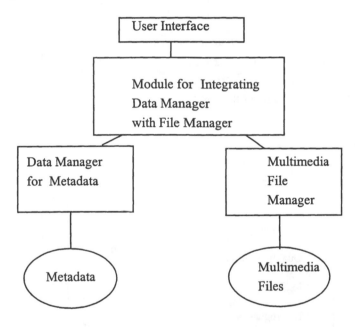

Figure 12-7. Loose Coupling Architecture

There are also other aspects to architectures as discussed in [THUR97]. For example, a multimedia database system could use a commercial database system such as an object-oriented database system to manage multimedia objects. However, relationships between objects and the representation of temporal relationships may involve extensions to the database management system. That is, a DBMS together with an extension layer provide complete support to manage multimedia data. In

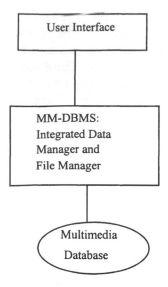

Figure 12-8. Tight Coupling Approach

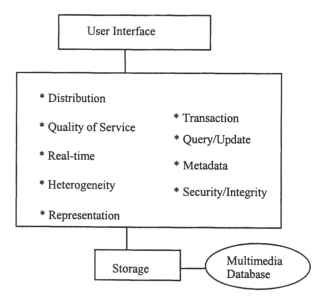

Figure 12-9. Functional Architecture

the alternative case, both the extensions and the database management functions are integrated so that there is one database management system to manage multimedia objects as well as the relationships between the objects. These two types of architectures are illustrated in

Figure 12-10 and Figure 12-11. Multimedia databases could also be distributed. In this case, we assume that each MM-DBMS is augmented with a Multimedia Distributed Processor (MDP) as illustrated in Figure 12-12.

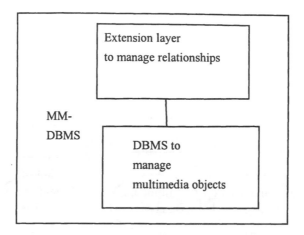

Figure 12-10. DBMS + Extension Layer

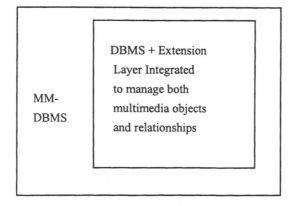

Figure 12-11. DBMS and Extension Layer Integrated

12.3.2.2 Data Modeling

In representing multimedia data, several features have to be supported. First of all, there has to be a way to capture the complex data types and all the relationships between the data. Various temporal constructs such as play-before, play-after, play-together, etc., have to be captured (see, for example, the discussion in [PRAB97]). Figure 12-13 illustrates a representation of a multimedia database. In this example, there are two objects: A and B. A consists of 2000 frames and B consists of 3000 frames. A consists of a time interval between 4/95 and 8/95 and B consists of a time interval between 5/95 and 10/95.

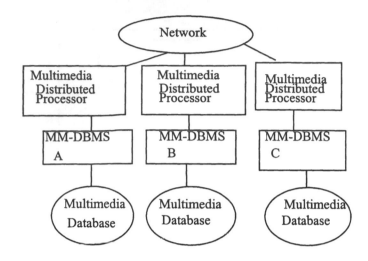

Figure 12-12. Distributed Multimedia DBMS

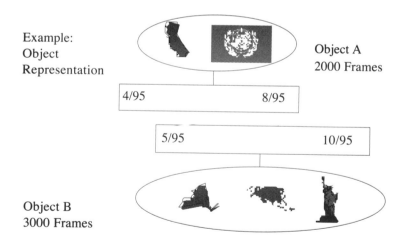

Figure 12-13. Data Representation

An appropriate data model is critical to represent an MM-DBMS. Relational, object-oriented, as well as object-relational data models have been examined to represent multimedia data. Some argue that relational models are better since they can capture relationships, while others argue that object models are better as they represent complex structures. In the example of Figure 12-13, with an object-oriented data model, each object in the figure would correspond to an object in the object model. The attributes of an object may be represented as instance variables and will include time interval, frames, and content description. With the relational model, the object would correspond to an instance of a relation. However with atomic values, it will be difficult to capture the attributes of the instance. In the case of the object-relational model, the attribute value of an instance could be an object. That is, for the instance that represents object A, the attribute value time interval would be the pair (4/95, 8/95). Representing object A with an object model is illustrated in Figure 12-14. Representing the same object with an object-relational model is illustrated in Figure 12-15. Note that one could build extensions to an existing data model to support complex relationships for multimedia data. These relationships may include temporal relationships between objects such as play together, play before, and play after.

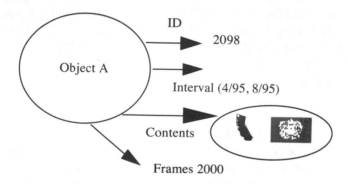

Figure 12-14. Data Representation with Object Model

ID	Interval	Contents	Frame
2098	(4/95, 8/95)		2000

Figure 12-15. Data Representation with Object-Relational Model

Languages such as SQL are being extended for MM-DBMS (see, for example, [SQL3]). Others argue that object-oriented models are better as they can represent complex data types. It appears that both types of models have to be extended to capture the temporal constructs and other special features. Associated with a data model is a query language. The language should support the constructs needed to manipulate the multimedia database. For example, one may need to query to play frames 500 to 1000 of a video script.

In summary, several efforts are under way to develop appropriate data models for MM-DBMSs. Standards are also being developed. This is an area that has matured within the past couple of years.

12.3.2.3 Functions of an MM-DBMS[28]

Overview

An MM-DBMS must support the basic DBMS functions. These include data manipulation, which includes query/update processing, transaction management, metadata management, storage management, and maintaining security and integrity. All of these functions are more complex since the data may be structured as well as unstructured. Furthermore, handling various data types such as audio and video is quite complex. In addition to these basic DBMS functions, an MM-DBMS must also support real-time processing to synchronize multimedia data types such as audio and video. Quality of service is an important aspect for MM-DBMS. For example, in certain cases, high quality resolution for images may not always be necessary. Special user interfaces are also needed to support different media.

This section provides an overview of the various functions. These include data manipulation such as query/update processing, browsing, and editing, transaction management, metadata management, data distribution, storage management, security, and integrity.

Data Manipulation

Data manipulation involves various aspects. Support for querying, browsing, and filtering the data is essential. Appropriate query languages are needed for this purpose. As discussed earlier, SQL extensions show much promise. In addition to just querying the data, one also may want to edit the data. That is, two objects may be merged to form a third object. One could project an object to form a smaller object. As an

---

[28] We discuss the functions briefly in this chapter. For more details and illustrations on MM-DBMS functions we refer to [THUR97]. A text devoted entirely to MM-DBMS is [PRAB97]. Other useful references are [NWOS96], [CHOR94], and [WOEL86].

example, objects may be merged based on time intervals, and an object may be projected based on time intervals. Objects may also be updated in whole or in part. Much of the focus on MM-DBMS has been on data representation and data manipulation. Various algorithms have been proposed. Some of these algorithms have also been implemented in various systems [TKDE93].

Transaction Management

There has been some discussion as to whether transaction management is needed in MM-DBMS [ACM94]. We feel this is important, as in many cases annotations may be associated with multimedia objects. For example, if one updates an image, then its annotation must also be updated. Therefore, the two operations have to be carried out as part of a transaction. Unlike data representation and data manipulation, transaction management in an MM-DBMS is still a new area. Associated with transaction management are concurrency control and recovery. The issue is what are the transaction models? Are there special concurrency control and recovery mechanisms? Much research is needed in this area.

Metadata Management

Many of the metadata issues discussed for DBMSs also apply to MM-DBMSs. What is a model for metadata? What are the techniques for metadata management? In addition, there may be large quantities of metadata to describe, say, audio and video data. For example, in the case of video data, one may need to maintain information about the various frames. This information is usually stored in the metadata.

There are several other considerations. Metadata plays a crucial role in pattern matching. To do data analysis on multimedia data, one needs to have some idea as to what one is searching for. For example, in a video clip, if various images are to be recognized, then there must be some patterns already stored to facilitate pattern matching. Information about these patterns has to be stored in the metadata.

In summary, metadata management in an MM-DBMS is still a challenge. Some ideas were presented in [META96]. The emergence of Internet technologies makes this even more complex.

Storage Management

The major issues in storage management include developing special index methods and access strategies for multimedia data types. Content-based data access is important for many multimedia applications. However, efficient techniques for content-based data access are still a challenge. Other storage issues include caching data. How often should the data be cached? Are there any special considerations for multimedia data? Are there special algorithms? Also, storage techniques for integrating different data types are needed. For example, a multimedia database may contain video, audio, and text databases instead of just one data type. The display of these different data types has to be synchronized. Appropriate storage mechanisms are needed so that there is continuous display of the data.

Storage management for multimedia databases is also an area that has been given considerable attention. Several advances have been made during recent years [MDDS94].

Maintaining Data Integrity and Security

Maintaining data integrity will include support for data quality, integrity constraint processing, concurrency control, and recovery for multi-user updates, and accuracy of the data on output. The issues on integrity for database management systems in Chapter 2 are present for MM-DBMSs. However, enforcing integrity constraints remains a challenge. For example, what kinds of integrity constraints can be enforced on voice and video data? There is little research to address these issues.

Security mechanisms include supporting access rights and authorization. All of the security issues discussed in Chapter 2 also apply to MM-DBMSs. There are also additional concerns. For example, in the case of video data, should access control rules be enforced on entire scripts or frames? Again, little research has been done here.

Other Functions

Other functions for an MM-DBMS include quality of service processing, real-time processing, and user interface management. For example, with respect to quality of service, in some instances one may need continuous display of data, and in some instances one could tolerate breaks of service. One has to come up with appropriate primitives to specify quality of service. Real-time processing plays a major role since appropriate scheduling techniques are needed to display various types of media such as the voice with the video. Finally, appropriate multimodal interfaces are needed for inputting and displaying multimedia data.

12.3.3 Multimedia Data Mining

12.3.3.1 Overview

Now that we have provided a brief overview of multimedia databases and discussed some of the essential concepts in terms of architectures, data models, and functions, in this section we will discuss the issues involved in mining and extracting information from these multimedia databases.

As stated earlier, multimedia data include text, images, video, and audio. Text and images are still media, while audio and video are continuous media. The issues surrounding still and continuous media are somewhat different and have been explained in various texts and papers such as [PRAB97]. In this section we will consider text, image, video, and audio and consider how such data can be mined. First of all, what are the differences between mining multimedia data and topics such as text, image, and video retrieval? What is meant by mining such data? What are the developments and challenges?

Data mining has an impact on the functions of multimedia database systems discussed in the previous section. For example, the query processing strategies have to be adapted to handle mining queries if a tight integration between the data miner and the database system is the approach taken. This will then have an impact on the storage strategies. Furthermore, the data model will also have an impact. At present, many of the mining tools work on relational databases. However, if object-relational databases are to be used for multimedia modeling, then data mining tools have to be developed to handle such databases.

Sections 12.3.3.2, 12.3.3.3, 12.3.3.4, and 12.3.3.5 will discuss text, image, video, and audio mining, respectively. In particular, the definition of mining, the developments, challenges, and directions are given. Then, in Section 12.3.3.6, we will briefly discuss the issues of mining combinations of data types.

12.3.3.2 Text Mining

Much of the information is now in textual form. This could be data on the web or library data or electronic books, among others. One of the problems with text data is that it is not structured as relational data. In many cases it is unstructured and in some cases it is semistructured. Semistructured data, for example, is an article that has a title, author, abstract, and paragraphs. The paragraphs are not structured, while the format is structured.

Information retrieval systems and text processing systems have been developed for more than a few decades. Some of these systems are quite sophisticated and can retrieve documents by specifying attributes or key words. There are also text processing systems that can retrieve associations between documents. So we are often asked what the difference between information retrieval systems and text mining systems is?

We define text mining to be data mining on text data. Text mining is all about extracting patterns and associations previously unknown from large text databases. The difference between text mining and information retrieval is analogous to the difference between data mining and database management. There is really no clear difference. Some of the recent information retrieval and text processing systems do discover associations between words and paragraphs, and therefore can be regarded as text mining systems.

Next, let us examine the approaches to text mining. Note that many of the current tools and techniques for data mining work for relational databases. Even for data in object-oriented databases, rarely do we hear about data mining tools for such data. Therefore, current data mining tools cannot be directly applied to text data. Some of the current directions in mining unstructured data include the following.

- Extract data and/or metadata from the unstructured databases possibly by using tagging techniques, store the extracted data in structured databases, and apply data mining tools on the structured databases. This is illustrated in Figure 12-16.

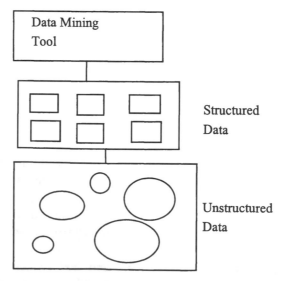

Figure 12-16. Converting Unstructured Data to Structured Data for Mining

- Integrate data mining techniques with information retrieval tools so that appropriate data mining tools can be developed for unstructured databases. This is illustrated in Figure 12-17.

- Develop data mining tools to operate directly on unstructured databases. This is illustrated in Figure 12-18.

Now, while converting text data into relational databases, one has to be careful so that there is no loss of key information. As we have stated before, unless you have good data you cannot mine the data effectively and expect to get useful results. One needs to create a sort of a warehouse first before mining the converted database. This warehouse is essentially a relational database that has the essential data from the text data. In other words, one needs a transformer that takes a text corpus as input and outputs tables that have, for example, the keywords from the text.

Clifton et al. [CLIF97] have been conducting extensive research on text mining. Their approach is to use natural language tagging tools to tag text data and place them in relational databases such as Oracle. Then they use various commercial tools and research prototypes to mine for associations. More recently Clifton and others have developed a database query optimizer called Queryflocks to carry out data mining [TSUR98] of queries and make associations with the data.

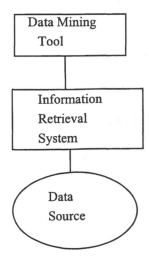

Figure 12-17. Augmenting an Information Retrieval System

As an example, in a text database that has several journal articles, one could create a warehouse with tables containing the following attributes: author, date, publisher, title, and keywords. From the key-words, one can form associations. The keywords in one article could be "Belgium, nuclear weapons" and the keywords in another article could be "Spain, nuclear weapons." The data miner could make the associa-tion that authors from Belgium and Spain write articles on nuclear weapons.

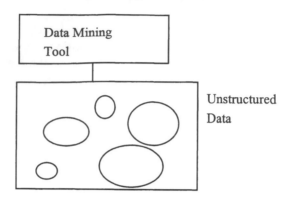

Figure 12-18. Mining Directly on Unstructured Data

Note that we are only in the beginning of text mining. In the longer-term approach we would want to develop tools directly to mine text data. These tools have to read the text, understand the text, put out pertinent information about the text, and then make associations between different documents. We are far from developing such sophis-ticated text mining tools. However, the work reported by Tsur, Ullman, and Clifton et al. (see, for example, [TSUR98]) is the first step in the right direction toward text mining. Some interesting early work on text mining was reported in [FELD95].

12.3.3.3 Image Mining

If text mining is still in the early research stages, image mining is an even more immature technology. In this section, we will examine this area and discuss the current status and challenges.

Image processing has been around for quite a while. We have image processing applications in various domains including medical imaging for cancer detection, processing satellite images for space and intelli-gence applications, and also handling hyperspectral images. Images include maps, geological structures, biological structures, and many other entities. Image processing has dealt with areas such as detecting abnormal patterns which deviate from the norm, retrieving images by content, and pattern matching.

The main question here is what is image mining? How does it differ from image processing? Again we do not have clear cut answers. One can say that while image processing is focusing on detecting abnormal patterns as well as retrieving images, image mining is all about finding unusual patterns. Therefore, one can say that image mining deals with making associations between different images from large image databases.

Clifton et al. [CLIF98] have begun work in image mining. Initially their plan was to extract metadata from images and then carry out mining on the metadata. This would essentially be mining the metadata in relational databases. However, after some consideration it was felt that images could be mined directly. The challenge then is to determine what type of mining outcome is most suitable. One could mine for associations between images, cluster images, classify images, as well as detect unusual patterns. One area of research being pursued by Clifton et al. is to mine images and find out whether there is anything unusual. So the approach is to develop templates that generate several rules about the images, and from there, apply the data mining tools to see if unusual patterns can be obtained. However, the mining tools will not tell us why these patterns are unusual. Figure 12-19 shows an image with some unusual patterns.

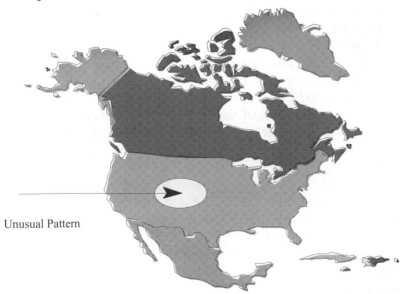

Unusual Pattern

Figure 12-19. Image Mining

Note that detecting unusual patterns is not the only outcome of image mining. However, this is just the beginning. We need to conduct more research on image mining to see if data mining techniques could be used to classify, cluster, and associate images. Image mining is an area with applications in numerous domains including space images, medical images, and geological images.

12.3.3.4 Video Mining

Mining video data is even more complicated than mining image data. One can regard video to be a collection of moving images, much like animation. Video data management has been the subject of much research. The important areas include developing query and retrieval techniques for video databases, including video indexing, query languages, and optimization strategies. The first question one asks yet again is what is the difference between video information retrieval and video mining? Unlike image and text mining, we do not have any clear idea of what is meant by video mining. For example, one could examine video clips and find associations between different clips. Another example would be to find unusual patterns in video clips. But how is this different from finding unusual patterns in images? So, the first step to successful video mining is to have a good handle on image mining.

Let us examine pattern matching in video databases. Should one have predefined images and then match these images with the video data? Is there any way one can do pattern recognition in video data by specifying what one is looking for and then try to do feature extraction for the video data? If this is video information retrieval what then is mining video data? To be consistent with our terminology we can say that finding correlations and patterns previously unknown from large video databases is video mining. So by analyzing a video clip or multiple video clips, one comes to conclusions about some unusual behavior. People in the video who are unlikely to be there, yet have occurred two or three times could mean something significant. Another way to look at the problem is to capture the text in video format and try and make the associations one would carry out with text but this time use the video data instead.

Unlike text and image mining where our ideas have been less vague, the discussion here on video mining is quite preliminary. This is mainly because there is so little known on video mining. Even the word video mining is something very new, and to date we do not have any concrete results reported on this. We do have a lot of information on analyzing video data and producing summaries. Now one could mine these summaries, which would amount to mining text as shown in

Figure 12-20. One good example of this effort is the work by Merlino et al. on summarizing video news [MERL97]. Converting the video mining problem to a text mining problem is reasonably well understood. However, the challenge is mining video data directly, and, more importantly, knowing what we want to mine. With the emergence of the web, video mining becomes even more important. An example of direct video mining is illustrated in Figure 12-21.

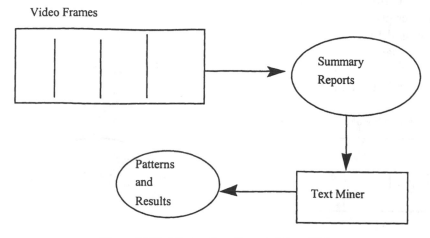

Figure 12-20. Mining Text Extracted from Video

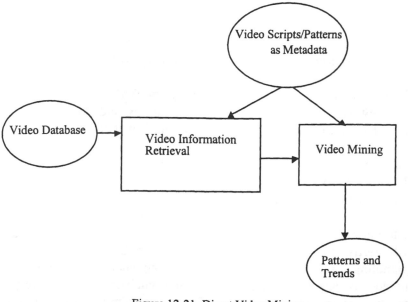

Figure 12-21. Direct Video Mining

12.3.3.5 Audio Mining

Since audio is a continuous media type like video, the techniques for audio information processing and mining are similar to video information retrieval and mining. Audio data could be in the form of radio, speech, or spoken language. Even television news has audio data, and in this case audio may have to be integrated with video and possibly text to capture the annotations and captions.

To mine audio data, one could convert it into text using speech transcription techniques and other techniques such as keyword extraction and then mine the text data as illustrated in Figure 12-22. On the other hand, audio data could also be mined directly by using audio information processing techniques and then mining selected audio data. This is illustrated in Figure 12-23.

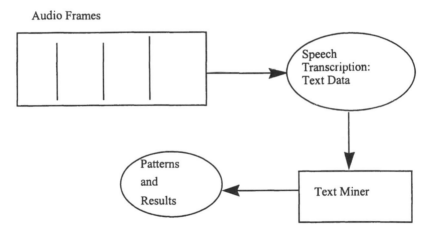

Figure 12-22. Mining Text Extracted from Audio

In general, audio mining is even more primitive than video mining. While a few papers have appeared on text mining and even fewer on image and video mining, work on audio mining is just beginning.

12.3.3.6 Mining Combinations of Data Types

The previous section discussed mining on individual data types such as text, images, video, and audio. If we are to mine multimedia data, then we need to mine combinations of two or more data types such as text and images, text and video, or text, audio, and video. In this section we will briefly discuss some of the issues on multimedia data mining.

Handling combinations of data types is very much like dealing with heterogeneous databases. For example, each database in the heterogeneous environment could contain data belonging to multiple data types.

These heterogeneous databases could be first integrated and then mined or one could apply mining tools on the individual databases and then combine the results of the various data miners. These two scenarios are illustrated in Figures 12-24 and 12-25. In both cases the Multimedia Distributed Processor (MDP) plays a role. If the data are to be integrated before being mined, then this integration is carried out via the MDPs. If the data are to be mined first, the data miner augments the corresponding MM-DBMS and the results of the data miners are integrated via the MDPs.

Since there is much to be done on mining individual data types such as text, images, video, and audio, mining combinations of data types is still a challenge. Once we have a better handle on mining individual data types, we can then focus on mining combinations of data types.

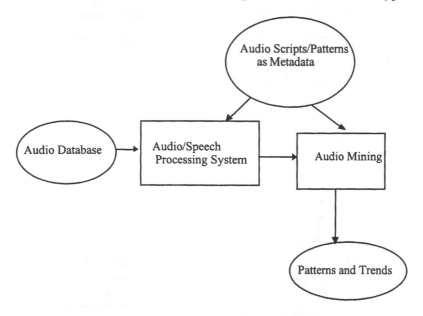

Figure 12-23. Direct Audio Mining

12.3.4 Impact of the Web on Multimedia Computing

There is news all over the world from British Broadcasting Corporation to American Broadcasting Corporation to Financial Times of London to Wall Street Journal to Cable News Network. Many of the organizations that are producers of such multimedia information now want to put their information on the web. But there is so much data that it is almost impossible to get quality presentations of multimedia data on the web. This is especially true with continuous media such as video and audio.

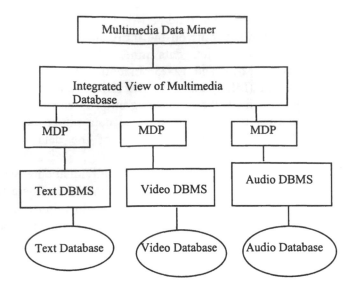

Figure 12-24. Integration and Then Mining

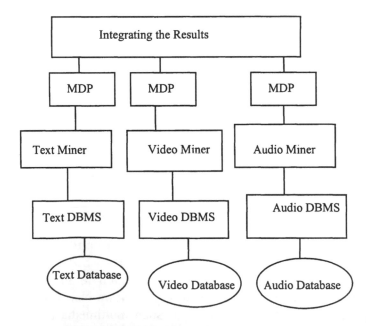

Figure 12-25. Integration and Then Mining

There are network communication problems that have to be overcome. While there is progress and hardware is becoming less expensive,

developing good software to ensure quality of service and timely access and presentation of this data remains the challenge. We have come a long way over the past few years in implementing delayed broadcast services. For example, important speeches by heads of countries are posted on the Internet within minutes. But we still are a long way from live video broadcast as well as live movies on the web. This does not mean live entertainment is not yet possible. The service we get today is not of good quality.

The biggest consumer of multimedia data on the web is the entertainment, broadcasting, and journalism industries. There is a huge market for this and these organizations have tapped into only a small portion of it. As technology becomes more mature we can expect major players in the entertainment industry to be very active. In a way this is all part of e-commerce. Although this does not deal with buying and selling music and video on the Internet, it deals with playing video and music on the Internet. Some of the technical challenges for data management include synchronizing presentation with storage and security, and ensuring that quality of service is maintained. Figure 12-26 illustrates multimedia on the web with a three-tier approach where the middle tier does all the web-based multimedia data processing. Another application area for multimedia on the web is training and distance learning. We will discuss this application in the next section.

12.4 SOME OTHER TECHNOLOGIES FOR THE WEB

12.4.1 Overview

This section describes a collection of other important technologies for web data management. These include training and distance learning, real-time processing and high performance computing, visualization, quality of service, and some other technologies such as knowledge management, decision support and agents. Since the last three technologies are becoming very important for the web we give special consideration for these technologies in Chapters 13 and 14.

The organization of this section is as follows. Training and distance learning, which are becoming important technologies for the web, will be the subject of Section 12.4.2. Real-time processing, where traders have to get stock information within prescribed time limits, is the subject of Section 12.4.3. High performance computing issues are also addressed here. Visualization is the subject of Section 12.4.4. The data on the web has to be visualized for better understanding. Quality of service, which makes tradeoffs between features like security and real-time processing, is the subject of Section 12.4.5. Section 12.4.6 describes some other technologies.

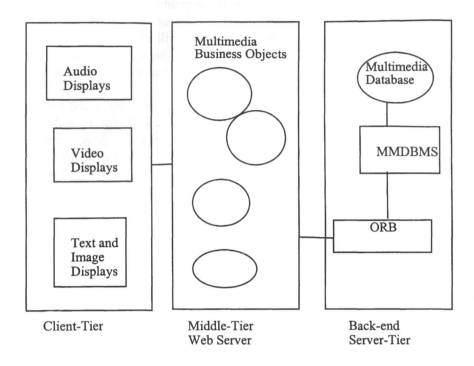

Figure 12-26. Three-Tier Multimedia Computing on the Web

12.4.2 Training and Distance Learning

Computer-based training is a hot topic these days. It is more popularly known as CBT. CBT is all about preparing course materials and placing it electronically so that trainees can learn at their own pace. Since the instructor is often not present, there are several user interface issues and human computer interaction aspects come into play here. The challenges are how do you provide a personalized service to the trainees. For example, in a course on data management, financial workers may want additions on e-commerce while defense workers may want information on data management for government applications. Instructors have to interview users and gather requirements and prepare the material according to the requirements.

Closely related to CBT is CBT on the web. This is also a form of distance learning. We now see various universities offering degrees on the web based on distance learning. The challenge here is not only preparing the material to satisfy the users but also to deliver the material in a timely manner. Multimedia on the web is an important technology for this application, as live teaching may be desired at times. That is, while CBT is extremely useful, from time to time students may want contact with the instructor who may be thousands of miles away. Distance learning is not restricted to within a country. It is now being implemented across continents. Figure 12-27 illustrates CBT on the web. Several technologies have to work together, not just CBT but also multimedia, real-time processing and all of the technologies for web data management. We can expect to hear a lot about CBT on the web and distance learning over the next several years.

12.4.3 Real-time Processing and High Performance Computing

Real-time computing is all about meeting timing constraints and deadlines. That is, transactions and queries have to meet timing constraints. Although fast computing is important to meet the constraints, it is not sufficient. For many applications, say, in e-commerce, the traders may want the answers of stocks within five seconds, else it will be too late. Essentially these are hard real-time constraints. There are also soft real-time constraints where it is desirable to meet the timing constraints for as many transactions as possible.

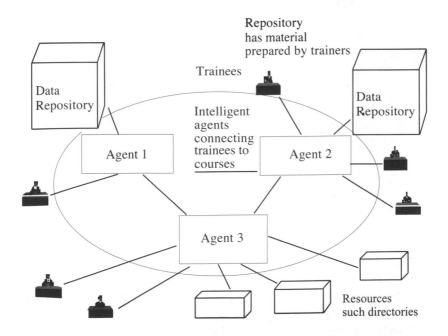

Figure 12-27. Computer-Based Training on the Web

We discussed the need for real-time scheduling for multimedia applications in the previous section. For example, it may be important to
display voice and video together synchronously. Real-time operating
systems, networks, and databases have to work together to meet the
constraints. More recently there is a lot of work on real-time middleware and especially object-oriented real-time middleware [WOLF00].
These real-time technologies now have to be effectively integrated into
the web. One promising development is the specifications for Real-time
Java. The idea is to develop technology to take the Java scheduling
mechanisms to meet the real-time constraints [JENS00]. This will be a
key direction for e-commerce where the timing constraints of transactions have to be met and many of the transactions may be written in
Java. Integrating real-time and e-commerce technologies is in its
infancy. We can expect to see much progress here. Figure 12-28
illustrates real-time processing on the web.

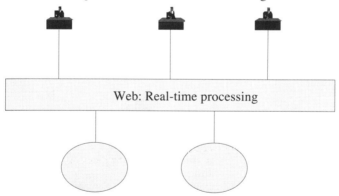

Figure 12-28. Real-time Processing on the Web

Closely related to real-time computing is high performance computing. While real-time computing is concerned about meeting deadlines, high performance computing is concerned about fast processing.
Parallel processing technology is key to high performance computing.

Parallel processing is a subject that has been around for a while. The
area has developed significantly from single processor systems to
multiprocessor systems. Multiprocessor systems could be distributed

systems or they could be centralized systems with shared memory multiprocessors or with shared-nothing multiprocessors. There has been a lot of work on using parallel architectures for database processing (see, for example, [IEEE89]). While considerable work was carried out, these systems did not take off commercially until the development of data warehousing. Many of the data warehouses employ parallel processors to speed up query processing.

In a parallel database system, the various operations and functions are executed in parallel. While research on parallel database systems began in the 1970s, it is only recently that we are seeing these systems being used for commercial applications. This is partly due to the explosion of data warehousing and data mining technologies where performance of query algorithms is critical.

Let us consider a query operation which involves a join operation between two relations. If these relations are to be sorted first before the join, then the sorting can be done in parallel. We can take it a step further and execute a single join operation with multiple processors. Note that multiple tuples are involved in a join operation from both relations. Join operations between the tuples may be executed in parallel.

Many of the commercial database system vendors are now marketing parallel database management technology. This is an area we can expect to grow significantly over the next decade. One of the major challenges here is the scalability of various algorithms for functions such as data warehousing and data mining.

Recently parallel processing techniques are being examined for data mining. Many of the data mining techniques are computationally intensive. Appropriate hardware and software are needed to scale the data mining techniques. Database vendors are using parallel processing machines to carry out data mining. The data mining algorithms are parallelized using various parallel processing techniques. This is illustrated in Figure 12-29.

Vendors of workstations are also interested in developing appropriate machines to facilitate data mining. This is an area of active research and development, and corporations such as Silicon Graphics and Thinking Machines (now part of Oracle Corporation) have developed products. We can expect to see a lot of progress in this area during the next few years. With the advent of the web, these various high performance computing tools have to work on the Internet. There are two aspects here. One is that functions like mining have to be carried out on the Internet and therefore parallel processing tools are needed to interface to the web. Secondly tools are also needed to make the web more efficient and fast.

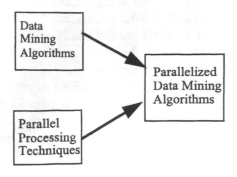

Figure 12-29. Parallel Data Mining

12.4.4 Visualization

Visualization technologies graphically display the data in the databases. Much research has been conducted on visualization and the field has advanced a great deal especially with the advent of multimedia computing. For example, the data in the databases could be rows and rows of numerical values. Visualization tools take the data and plot them in some form of a graph. The visualization models could be 2-dimensional, 3-dimensional or even higher. Recently, several visualization tools have been developed to integrate with databases, and workshops are devoted to this topic [VIS95]. An example illustration of integration of a visualization package with a database system is shown in Figure 12-30.

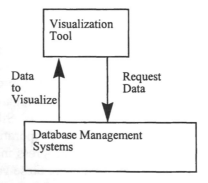

Figure 12-30. Database and Visualization

More recently there has been a lot of discussion on using visualization for data mining. There has also been some discussion on using data mining to help the visualization process. However, when considering visualization as a supporting technology, it is the former approach that is getting considerable attention (see, for example, [GRIN95]). As data mining techniques mature, it will be important to integrate them with visualization techniques. Figure 12-31 illustrates interactive data mining. Here, the database management system, visualization tool, and machine learning tool all interact with each other for data mining.

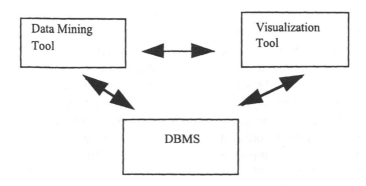

Figure 12-31. Interactive Data Mining

Let us re-examine some of the issues on integrating data mining with visualization. There are four possible approaches here. One is to use visualization techniques to present the results that are obtained from mining the data in the databases. These results may be in the form of clusters or they could specify correlations between the data in the databases. The second approach applies data mining techniques to visualization. The assumption here is that it is easier to apply data mining tools to data in the visual form. Therefore, rather than applying the data mining tools to large and complex databases, one captures some of the essential semantics visually, and then applies the data mining tools. The third approach is to use visualization techniques to comple- ment the data mining techniques. For example, one may use data mining techniques to obtain correlations between data or detect patterns. However, visualization techniques may still be needed to obtain a better understanding of the data in the database. The fourth approach uses visualization techniques to steer the mining process.

The various data visualization tools now have to work on the web. For example, these tools need to access the various data sources on the web and visualize them to help understand the data. This is illustrated in Figure 12-32.

12.4.5 Quality-of-Service Aspects

We have introduced so many web data management technologies such as database management, security, fault tolerance, multimedia, integrity, and real-time processing that it will be a challenge to make all of them work together effectively. For example, how can we guarantee that the stock information meets the timing constraints for delivery to the trader and yet maintain one hundred percent security? This will be very difficult. If we add the task of ensuring integrity of the data and techniques for recovering from faults, and presenting multimedia data in a timely manner, the problem becomes nearly impossible to solve. So the question is what do we do? This is when quality of service, popularly known as QoS comes in. It is almost impossible to satisfy all of the requirements all of the time. So, QoS specifies policies for tradeoffs. For example, if security and real-time are both constraints that have to be met, then perhaps at some instances it is not absolutely necessary to meet all the timing constraints and we need to focus on security. At other instances, meeting timing constraints may be crucial. As another example, consider multimedia presentation. At some instances we can live with low resolution while some other times we may need perfect pictures.

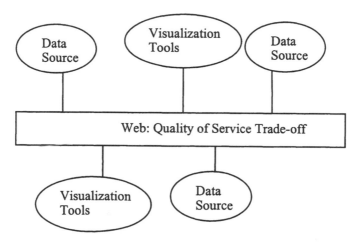

Figure 12-32. Visualization on the Web

Recently there has been a lot of work on QoS. But we are yet to find a model that takes into consideration all factors for quality of service. This is a difficult problem and with so many research efforts under way we can expect to see progress. Essentially the user specifies what he wants and the user requirements get mapped down to the database system, operating system, and the networking requirements. Figure 12-3 illustrates an approach to QoS on the web. The ideas are rather preliminary and a lot needs to be done.

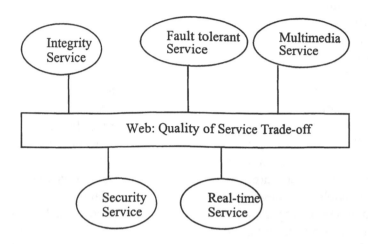

Figure 12-33. Quality of Service Tradeoffs

12.4.6 Some Directions

This chapter has discussed various technologies and services for the web. Much of our discussion was focused on collaboration and multimedia technologies and services. We also briefly addressed training and distance learning, real-time processing and high performance technologies and visualization aspects.

Note that in Chapter 1 we provided an overview of data, information, and knowledge management. Many of the technologies we have discussed so far are about data and information management for the web. Another critical technology is knowledge management. One could argue that the whole area of knowledge management came about as a result of the web. Knowledge management is all about capturing, storing, accessing, sharing, and even reusing the knowledge of organizations. A considerable amount of work on knowledge management has been about sharing knowledge on the web. As we mentioned earlier, many corporations are using their internal information infrastructures as precious resources for knowledge management. In summary knowledge management is a key technology for web data management. Therefore we give it special consideration in the next chapter.

Many of the technologies such as data, information and knowledge management are being used ultimately for managers, policymakers and other people in authority to make effective decisions. Therefore decision support is an important technology area for the web as in the future we can expect these managers and policy makers to access the web and based on the information they get make effective decisions. Since decision support is also an important technology we give it special consideration in the next chapter.

Finally technologies for accessing the resources on the web as well as processing these resources are critical for effective data management on the web. The technology that is vital for these services is agent technology. There are different types of agents. Some agents locate resources, some carry out mediation, and some are mobile and execute in different environments. A Java applet can be regarded to be a simple agent. Since agents are critical for web data and information management, we discuss them in Chapter 14.

Therefore, in addition to data, information and knowledge management technologies, other technologies for web data management and electronic commerce include security, collaboration, visualization real-time processing, training and multimedia. There are several other technologies we have not addressed in this book. These include data quality, fault tolerance, mass storage, fuzzy systems and soft computing, and data administration. All of these technologies and services have to work together to make web information management a success. Figure 12-34 illustrates how a distributed object management system can integrate the various technologies and services to provide effective web data and information management

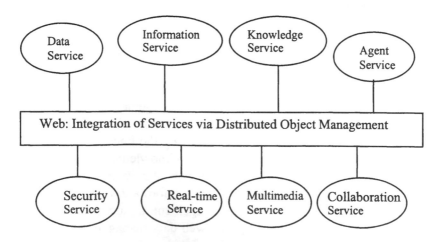

Figure 12-34. Integration of Services on the Web

12.5 SUMMARY

We have described numerous technologies in this section for web data management. First we provided a fairly detailed discussion of collaboration and multimedia. With respect to collaboration we gave examples, discussed the data management needs, focused on a specific type of collaborative application and that is workflow and then described the impact of the web on collaboration. Essentially we need tools that can be used by various groups on the web.

Our discussion on multimedia focused on multimedia data management architectures, data models and functions. Then we paid some attention to multimedia data mining, as this will be an important function for the web. Finally we discussed the impact of the web and described the need for multimedia on the web for applications such as entertainment and training.

Then we provided an overview of a number of technologies for the web. We started with a discussion of computer based training and distance learning. As we mentioned, various universities and colleges are now offering degree programs on the web. Therefore web-based CBT will be a very important area for the future. We also elaborated on the need for multimedia on the web for training. Even elementary and high schools are now using CBT and distance learning and multimedia will be an important aspect.

Next we discussed real-time processing and high performance computing. For many applications such as financial trading not only do we need the information fast but we also need the information within a certain time. If the timing constraints are not met then the information may be useless.

Visualization on the web was the next subject. We discussed issues on integrating visualization tools with databases and data mining systems to better understand the results. Such tools now have to be integrated with the web to better understand the large quantities of data on the web.

Next we focused on Quality of Service. Since several technologies have to work together to provide effective web data management and e-commerce, it will be almost impossible to meet all of the requirements. So QoS specifies the various tradeoffs and will be driven by user requirements. This is an important area that will receive much attention over the next several years.

Finally we discussed various other technologies such as knowledge management, decision support and agents. Since they are important technologies we will devote separate chapters to these areas.

The technologies we have discussed are critical for web data management and e-commerce. The challenge is to make them work together with the web. Web data management is still in its infancy. There is a lot to do and a lot to learn.

CHAPTER 13

KNOWLEDGE MANAGEMENT, DECISION SUPPORT AND THE WEB

13.1 OVERVIEW

We have discussed various technologies for data and information management for the web. We started with database systems technology and went on to discuss data mining, metadata management, security, collaboration, multimedia, visualization and training. Some other technologies that are emerging for the web are knowledge management and decision support.

Knowledge management is a relatively new technology. However some say that knowledge management is essentially a re-packaging of business process reengineering. In one view, knowledge management is all about using knowledge as a resource in an organization. In another view knowledge management is about creating a knowledge organization with knowledge workers. Yet in a third view knowledge management is about installing and using a corporate Intranet. That is, there is no standard definition of knowledge management. It is a multi-disciplinary area. Business professionals, organizational behavior experts as well as psychologists have studied it in the past. However, information technology has made knowledge management into a technology area. That is, information technology has enabled the development of tools for knowledge management. The web has enhanced knowledge management a great deal.

Another technology that is gaining popularity is decision support. Unlike knowledge management, decision support has existed for quite a while. Even in the 1970s people were talking about decision support and tools for decision support have been around for many years. However, it is only during the past decade that decision support has emerged as part of information technology. Decision support systems are essentially systems that help managers and analysts make decisions. They could be as simple as relational database systems or as complex as data mining systems. The web has also enhanced decision support capabilities. Managers now have information at their fingertips through the web. However, the decision support systems have to make this information intelligible to the managers so that they can make effective decisions.

This chapter describes knowledge management and decision support technologies. While we could have made them part of Chapter 12, we decided to give special consideration to these two technologies due to their increasing importance. We will be hearing more and more about knowledge management and decision support and therefore we feel that these topics warrant special consideration. Section 13.2 discusses concepts and technologies for knowledge management while Section 13.3 discusses concepts and technologies for decision support. For both these technologies we discuss the impact of the web. The chapter is summarized in Section 13.4.

13.2 KNOWLEDGE MANAGEMENT

13.2.1 Knowledge Management Concepts and Technologies

Knowledge management is the process of using knowledge as a resource to manage an organization. It could mean sharing expertise, developing a learning organization, teaching the staff, learning from experiences, as well as collaboration. Essentially knowledge management will include data management and information management. However this is not a view shared by everyone. Various definitions of knowledge management have been proposed. A good text on knowledge management is that by Davenport [DAVE97]. Knowledge management is a discipline invented mainly by business schools. The concepts have been around for a long time. But the word knowledge management was coined as a result of information technology and the web.

In the collection of papers on knowledge management by Morey et al. [MORE00], knowledge management is divided into three areas as shown in Figure 13-1. These are strategies such as building a knowledge company and making the staff knowledge workers; processes such as techniques for knowledge management including developing a method to share documents and tools; and metrics that measure the effectiveness of knowledge management. In the Harvard Business Review on knowledge management there is an excellent collection of articles describing a knowledge creating company, building a learning organization, and teaching people how to learn [HARV96]. Organizational behavior and team dynamics play major roles in knowledge management.

Knowledge management essentially changes the way an organization functions. Instead of competition it promotes collaboration. This means managers have to motivate the employees for sharing ideas and collaborating by giving awards and other incentives. Team spirit is essential for knowledge management. People often get threatened with imparting knowledge as their jobs may be on the line. They are reluctant to share expertise. This type of behavior could vary from culture to culture. It is critical that managers eliminate this kind of behavior not by forcing the issue but by motivating the staff and educating them of all the benefits that can occur to everyone with good knowledge management practices.

Teaching and learning are two important aspects of knowledge management. Both the teacher and the student have to be given incentives. Teachers can benefit by getting thank you notes and write-ups in the company newsletter. Students may be rewarded by certificates, monetary awards and other similar gestures. Knowledge management also includes areas such as protecting the company's intellectual properties, job sharing, changing jobs within the company, and encouraging change in an organization. Effective knowledge management eliminates dictatorial management style and promotes more collaborative management style. Knowledge management follows a cycle of creating knowledge, sharing the knowledge, integrating the knowledge, evaluating the performance with metrics, and then giving feedback to create more knowledge. This is illustrated in Figure 13-2. Variations of this cycle have been proposed in the literature [MORE98b].

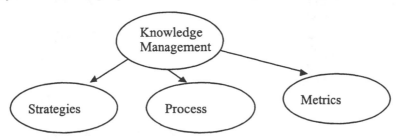

Figure 13-1 Knowledge Management Components

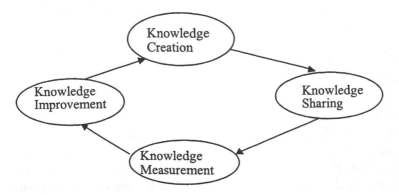

Figure 13-2. Knowledge Management Cycle

The major question is what are knowledge management technologies? This is where information technology comes in. Artificial Intelligence researchers have carried out a considerable amount of research on knowledge acquisition. They have also developed expert systems. These are also knowledge management technologies. Other knowledge management technologies include collaboration tools, tools for organizing information on the web as well as tools for measuring the effectiveness of the knowledge gained such as collecting various metrics. Knowledge management technologies essentially include data management and information management technologies. Figure 13-3 illustrates some of the knowledge management technologies. As can be seen, web technologies play a major role in knowledge management. The impact of the web will be the subject of the next subsection.

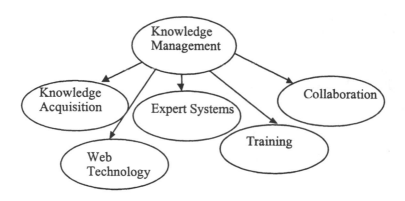

Figure 13-3. Knowledge Management Technologies

13.2.2 Knowledge Management and the Web

Knowledge management and the web are closely related. While knowledge management practices have existed for many years it is the web that has promoted knowledge management. Remember knowledge management is essentially building a knowledge organization. No technology is better than the web for sharing information. You can travel around the world in seconds with the web. As a result so much knowledge can be gained by browsing the web.

Many corporations now have Intranets and this is the single most powerful knowledge management tool. Thousands of employees are connected through the web in an organization. Large corporations have sites all over the world and the employees are becoming well connected with one another. Email can be regarded to be one of the early knowledge management tools. Now there are many tools such as search engines and e-commerce tools.

With the proliferation of web data management and e-commerce tools, knowledge management will become an essential part of the web and e-commerce. Figure 13-4 illustrates the knowledge management activities on the web such as creating web pages, building e-commerce sites, sending email, and collecting metrics on web usage.

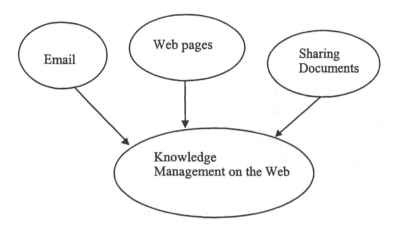

Figure 13-4. Knowledge Management on the Web

13.3 DECISION SUPPORT

13.3.1 Decision Support Concepts and Technologies

While data mining deals with discovering patterns from the data, machine learning deals with learning from experiences to do predictions as well as analysis; knowledge management deals with developing a learning organization; and decision support systems are tools that managers use to make effective decisions. There is a well-defined theory and principles developed for decision support systems. Such theories are known as decision theories. However in practice the decision support techniques encompass various types of data, information and knowledge management systems. For example, one can consider data mining tools to be special kinds of decision support tools. So are the tools based on machine learning, as well as tools for extracting data from data warehouses. In fact data warehouses are often referred to as systems used by managers to make effective decisions. In summary, decision support tools belong to a broad category (see, for example, [DECI]).

Decision support tools could also be tools that remove unnecessary and irrelevant results obtained from data mining. These pruning tools could also be decision support tools. They could also be tools such as spread sheets, expert systems, hypertext systems, web information management systems, and any other system that helps analysts and managers to effectively manage the large quantities of data and information. One can also regard knowledge management to be a kind of decision support system [MORE98b]. This includes storing the information, managing it, as well as developing tools to extract useful information. Some of the knowledge management tools also help in decision support. Collaboration tools are also special kinds of decision support tools. Various user modeling tools as well as human computer interaction tools also help analysts make decisions. An excellent introduction to decision support is given in the book by [TURB97]. In this text essentially a decision support system is viewed as any tool that can be used to get any data, information or knowledge.

In summary, we believe that decision support is a technology that overlaps with data mining, data warehousing, knowledge management, machine learning, statistics, and other technologies that help to manage an organization's knowledge and data. We illustrate this in Figure 13-5. Figure 13-6 illustrates the relationship between data warehousing, database management, mining and decision support.

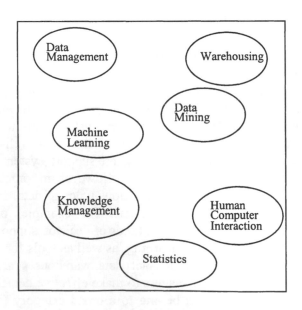

Figure 13-5. Decision Support Technologies

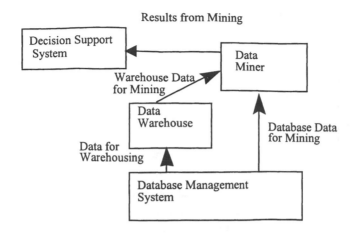

Figure 13-6. Decision Support and Data Mining

In Part I we discussed various technologies for data mining and the web. One needs architectural support for integrating these technologies. Figure 13-7 shows a pyramid-like structure as to how the various technologies fit with one another. As shown in Figure 13-7, we have communications and system level support at the lowest level. Then we have middleware support. Database management and data warehousing follow this. Then we have the various data mining technologies. Finally, we have the decision support systems that take the results of data mining and help the users to effectively make decisions. These users could be managers, analysts, programmers, and any other user of information systems.

When one builds systems, the various technologies involved may not fit the pyramid identically as we have shown. For example, we could skip the warehousing stage and go straight to mining. One of the key issues here is the interface between the various systems. At present we do not have any well-defined standard interfaces except some of the standards and interface definition languages emerging from various groups such as the Object Management Group. However, as these technologies mature, one can expect standards to be developed for the interfaces.

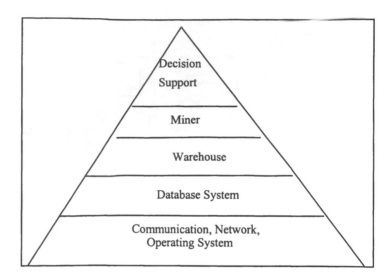

Figure 13-7. Pyramid for Data Mining and Decision Support

Various other diagrams have been illustrated throughout Chapters 1 through 12, as to how the different technologies work together. For example, one possibility is the one shown in Figure 13-8 where multiple databases are integrated through some middleware and subsequently form a data warehouse which is then mined. The data mining component is also integrated into this setting so that the databases are mined directly. Some of these issues will be discussed in the section on system architecture.

Figure 13-9 illustrates a three-dimensional view of decision support technologies. Central to this is the technology for integration. This is the middleware technology such as distributed object management and also web technology for integration and access through the web. On the one plane we have all the basic data technologies such as multimedia, relational and object databases, and distributed, heterogeneous and legacy databases. On another plane we have what we call the technologies for decision support. We have included warehousing as well as data mining and statistical reasoning here. The third plane has technologies such as parallel processing, visualization, metadata management, and secure access which are important to carry out decision support. The various chapters in this book have discussed the technologies of Figure 13-9 in more detail.

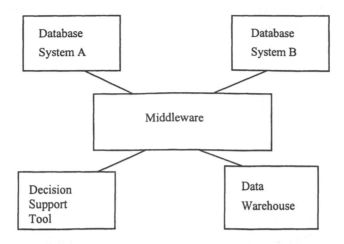

Figure 13-8. A Decision Support Architecture

Central to decision support is data management. Without good data, one cannot get information and knowledge and therefore effective decision support. In Chapter 2 we discussed the functional components of a database management system. A question is, should a decision support tool augment a database management system or should it be embedded into a database system? This is similar to the tight and loose integration between a data miner and a database management system. Figure 13-8 illustrates a form of loose integration. A tight integration where the decision support tool is part of, say, a query processor is illustrated in Figure 13-10. That is, the query processor modules such as the query optimizer could be extended to handle decision support. Note that in this diagram we have omitted the transaction manager, as decision support is used mostly for on-line analytical processing.

Figure 13-9 illustrates a three-dimensional view of decision support technologies. Central to this is the technology for integration. This is the middleware technology such as distributed object management and also web technology for integration and access through the web. On the one plane we have all the basic data technologies such as multimedia, relational and object databases, and distributed, heterogeneous and legacy databases. On another plane we have what we call the technologies for decision support. We have included warehousing as well as data mining and statistical reasoning here. The third plane has technologies such as parallel processing, visualization, metadata management, and secure access which are important to carry out decision support.

The various chapters in this book have discussed the technologies of Figure 13-9 in more detail.

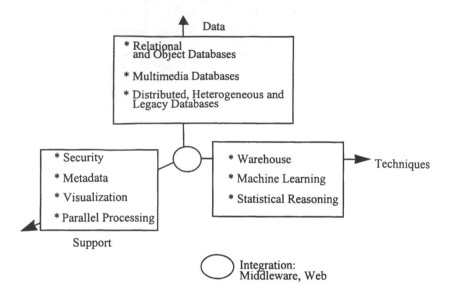

Figure 13-9. Three-dimensional View

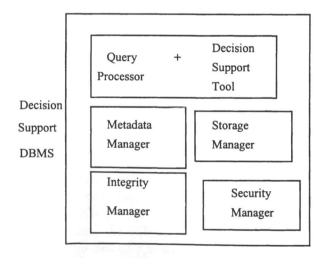

Figure 13-10. Decision Support as Part of Query Processor

13.3.2 Impact of the Web

Now that we have discussed some of the essential points in decision support, the question is how is the web impacting it? The answer is a great deal. While the principles of decision support have not changed, the way decisions are made has changed. No longer do managers and analysts have to go through the laborious process of getting the data ready so that the decision support tools can be applied. There are now lots of data available and more and more tools are available to organize the data. Therefore, within a short space of time the decision support tools can be applied to the data and we can get answers. That is, effective data, information and knowledge management on the web is key to effective decision support.

With the web, the distinction between data management, information management and knowledge management is becoming rather vague. The problem is there is lots and lots of data and the challenges are to extract useful information to make decisions. Therefore, the various decision support tools have to be interfaced to the web and we are seeing progress in this area. Essentially web decision support can be described with the pyramid in Figure 13-11. What we have done here is added the term web to the pyramid in Figure 13-6. Web data management, web warehousing, web mining and many other web technologies such as web knowledge management and web collaboration play a role in making decisions utilizing the web. Because the infrastructure is already there with the web, one can then keep on adding the various tools. The challenges will be the scalability of the tools as well as making sense out of the data out there.

At present decision support on the web is still premature. With the emphasis on e-commerce and various knowledge management and collaboration technologies we can expect significant developments in this area.

13.4 SUMMARY

This chapter has described two key technologies for the web; they are knowledge management and decision support. Knowledge management is a newly coined term and is all about building a knowledge organization and enabling each employee to be a knowledge worker. The decision support tool enables managers to make effective decisions. Both these technologies rely on data and information management. Furthermore, the web has had a major impact on them.

Tools for knowledge management and decision support on the web are emerging. The challenge is to make sense out of the data so that an organization can improve its knowledge and make decisions. That is, data is key to both knowledge management and decision support. This means that web data management is essential.

With e-commerce we can expect both knowledge management and decision support technologies to grow tremendously. We can expect better tools to emerge. This all means increased productivity and growth for organizations.

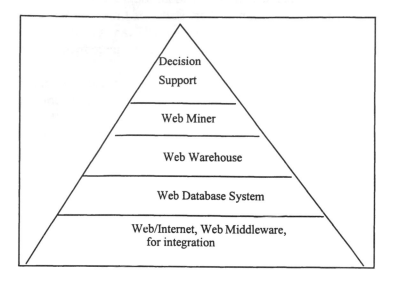

Figure 13-11. Web and Decision Support

CHAPTER 14

AGENTS FOR THE WEB

14.1 OVERVIEW

Ever since the development of the web in the early 1990s, we have heard the term agents. The problem is, it has been very difficult for people to agree with what agents mean. Some say agents are simply processes and some others say agents are Java applets. Yet a third group says that agents are processes that can jump from machine to machine and can execute everywhere. A fourth group says that agents are processes that have to communicate according to some well-defined protocol. In fact all of these definitions are correct. That is, agents are essentially processes that function on behalf of other processes and users. But they have to satisfy some agreed upon method of communication.

Agents carry out many functions. These include locating resources on the web or otherwise, retrieving data, filtering data for security purposes, as well as executing code. Agents also may be self-describing, they may be decentralized and autonomous, or they may be distributed and heterogeneous. Various agent architectures have been proposed. These architectures essentially describe frameworks for agent communication. Commutation also occurs based on well defined protocols and languages. While agents carry out security features like performing access controls and filtering, the agents themselves have to be secure. Furthermore, recent research investigates real-time and fault tolerant aspects of agents. That is, agents have to react in a timely manner and recover from failures gracefully.

This chapter describes various aspects of agents. In Section 14.2 we start with a definition of agents and then describe the various types of agents and their functions. Architectures and communication for agents are described in Section 14.3. Features like security, real-time and fault tolerance are also addressed here. Mobile agents are discussed in Section 14.4. Since agents play a major role in information dissemination, we will address this topic in Section 14.5. The chapter is summarized in Section 14.6. Various books and articles have been published on agents. There are also annual conferences conducted on mobile agents as well as on intelligent agents. Some references are given in [MOBI97]. IEEE Computer magazine as well as Communications of the Association of Computing Machinery have published special issues on agents since the mid-1990s.

14.2 AGENTS: DEFINITION, TYPES AND FUNCTIONS

As mentioned in Section 14.1, various views of agents have been proposed. That is, some say agents are simply processes and some others say agents are Java applets. Yet a third group says that agents are processes that can jump from machine to machine and can execute everywhere. A fourth group says that agents are processes that have to communicate according to some well-defined protocol. After examining the various definitions of agents, DiPipio et al. give the following definition in [DIPI99].

An agent is "a computer system, situated in some environment, that is capable of flexible autonomous action in order to meet its design objectives."

DiPippo et al. also define agents to have three major characteristics as illustrated in Figure 14-1. They are:

* responsive - react to environment
* proactive - opportunistic, goal-directed, take initiative
* social - interact with other agents (and users)

For example, agents have to take certain actions when a certain situation occurs like getting data to the right users when it becomes available as described in the push model in Chapter 8.

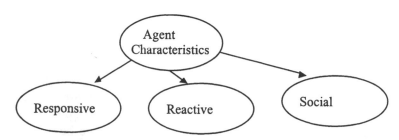

Figure 14-1. Agent Characteristics

Various types of agents have been proposed. These include the following:

• Data retrieval agent: Retrieves data and knows when a user (or other agent) requires certain data; autonomously retrieves it on behalf of the user (or agent)

- Data filtering agent: Sorts incoming data - email, news, etc.; determines relevance place in appropriate location

- Resource locating agent: locates various resources such as databases and files

- Situation monitoring agent: Monitors a situation and when an event occurs executes triggers

- Mobile agent: Migrates from machine to machine and executes code in different environments

- Database management agent: Executes various functions such as query and transactions

- Mining agent: Carries out data mining

- E-commerce agent: Performs various e-commerce activities.

Note that the first five types can be regarded to be basic agents and may carry out activities for database management, data mining and e-commerce. So we have separated the two in Figures 14-2 and 14-3. Note that agents do not necessarily have to function on the web. However, the web has really expanded agent technology. Agents now perform web mining, web database management and e-commerce. Relationship between agents and the web was illustrated in Figures 8-6 and 8-7. We also give some additional information about this in Figure 14-4.

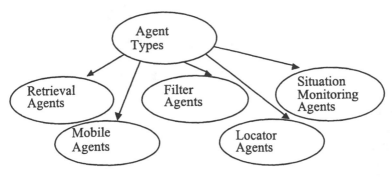

Figure 14-2. Agent Types

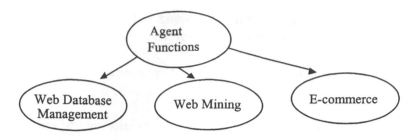

Figure 14-3. Agent Functions

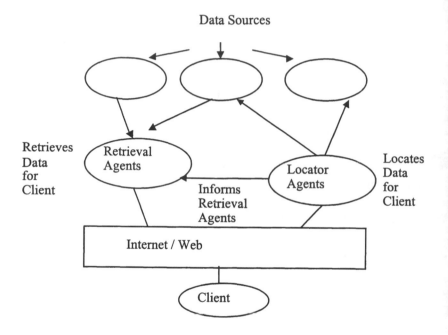

Figure 14-4. Agents and the Web

14.3 AGENT ARCHITECTURE AND COMMUNICATION

Previous section defined agents and also described various types of agents. In this section we discuss agent architectures and also describe communication between agents.

DiPippio et al. have defined an agent architecture to be a framework in which agents cooperate to meet common objectives as well as negotiate to come to an acceptable result when objectives conflict. This is illustrated in Figure 14-5 where agents communicate via a language

such as KQML (Knowledge Query Manipulation Language). A key
component of agent architecture is an agent facilitator. Essentially
agents register with the facilitator, advertise its capabilities and the
facilitator determines which agents to invoke for a task in a multi-agent
system. Agent facilitator is illustrated in Figure 14-6.

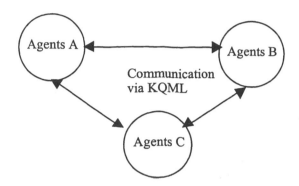

Figure 14-5. Agent Interaction

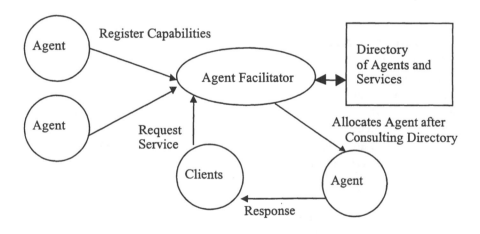

Figure 14-6. Agent Facilitator

Closely associated with agent architectures is communication. A
standard language is needed for communication between agents. KQML
is one such approach. It is a widely used agent communication language. Its constructs include the following and are illustrated in Figure
14-7.

- ask-one - request an agent to perform a task
- tell - provide other agent(s) with certain information
- advertise - register capabilities with facilitator
- monitor - watch another agent for a particular condition

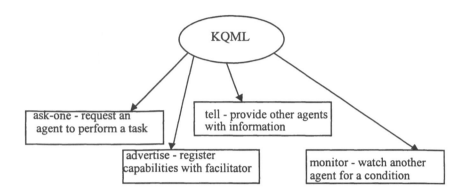

Figure 14-7. KQML Constructs

There are various ways to build agent services. One is to examine existing architectures and extend them to provide the service you want. The second approach is to build an architecture from scratch. Since various agent architectures have been proposed (see for example the survey in [DIPI99]), the more efficient approach will be to examine the various architectures before developing a new one; that is, extend existing agent architectures. This is because of the emphasis placed on reuse and not reinventing the wheel. Below we describe some of the agent architectures in the literature.[29]

- DECAF: This is developed at the University of Delaware. It provides a toolkit for building agents. It removes low-level details from development and provides some real-time scheduling.

- FIPA_SMART: This is a system developed by the United States Department of the Navy (SPAWAR) and is a tool for building FIPA-based agent software. It is Java-based.

---

[29] DiPippo et al. have given several references to the agent architectures in their paper [DIPI99]. These include [FINI94], [GRAH99], [FIPA98], and [MART99].

- Open Agent Architecture (OAA): This is developed by SRI International and is an architecture for collections of autonomous agents. It is CORBA-like and is Java-based.

- JAFMAS: This is developed at the University of Cincinnati and is a Java-based Agent Framework for Multi-Agent Systems. It provides a framework to guide development of multiagent systems and is essentially a set of classes for agent deployment in Java.

- COBALT: This is an agent communication toolkit based on KQML and CORBA. It provides a mapping from KQML to CORBA/IDL. Consists of both KQML parser (client) and KQML generator (server).

- Agent Services Layer (ASL): This is by Broadcom and allows agents to find each other and communicate. It defines an agent as anything which supports an asynchronous KQML interface defined in CORBA's IDL. It has an authority construct that handles routing among agents.

- AGLETS: These are agents for the web developed at IBM Research Laboratory in Tokyo. Various aspects such as security have been examined for AGLETS in IBM's Zurich Research Laboratory (see[IBM]).

University of Rhode Island and SPAWAR are jointly developing architectures for real-time agents. They have examined various architectures and proposed extensions. In [DIPI99] it is stated that such agents work together on behalf of collaborating users to meet goals within timing constraints. QoS scheduling is a major function of such environments. They have applications in e-commerce such as programmed stock trading, real-time auctions, and business-to-business coordination of services within timing constraints. It also has applications in military training simulations where agents work together to represent enemy forces.

In addition to real-time agents, security is very important for agents. Security for agents has been investigated extensively at the University of Zurich by Gunter et al. There is some work on secure agents carried out at the MITRE Corporation by Swarup et al. While agents perform security functions, the agents also have to be secure. The issues include trusting agents as well as proposing extensions to KQML for secure communication.

Finally agents have to be fault tolerant. They have to recover from failure in a graceful manner. Integrating security, real-time and fault tolerance are areas that needs further investigation. That is, QoS features for agents need to be examined. This is illustrated in Figure 14-8. (See also [THUR99b].)

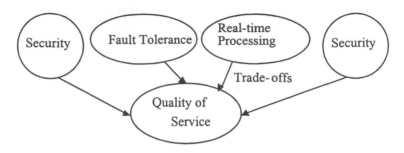

Figure 14-8. Quality of Service Agents

14.4 MOBILE AGENTS

While the previous sections focused on agents such as retrieval agents and locator agents, this section discusses mobile agents. Mobile agents are essentially agents on the web that execute at different locations and sites. These are processes that migrate from one environment to another and execute in a new environment.

Example of a simple mobile agent is a Java Applet. As we stated in Part I, an applet is a piece of code that resides in the server. It is brought into the browser environment when requested by a web page and executes in the browser environment. Another alternative is a servlet, which executes in the server environment and the results are brought to the client.

An applet is a mobile agent since it migrates to the client environment from a server environment and executes in the client environment. Security is a major consideration for applet execution. An applet may be untrusted and therefore could corrupt the client resources. This is why in general applets execute in what is called a sandbox and cannot corrupt the client's resources.

Mobile code is not just restricted to applet. It is essentially any process that exists on any of the machines, either client or server, and executes in any environment. The advantages with this approach are that you need to execute processes in the server environment and bring the results to the client. This could have a performance impact. By bringing the process into the client environment, speed may be enhanced especially if the server environment is slow. Also, a server may execute many requests and priority may not be given to a client's request. By bringing the process into the client, this problem is avoided. Mobile code can execute between servers. For example, mobile agents can move from one server to another.

Various aspects of mobile code are being examined. Most important we believe is security for the reasons mentioned earlier. In addition to trusting mobile code, other security issues include access control and execute permissions. That is, appropriate access control and execution rules have to be enforced. The challenge is, who is to enforce these rules in a web environment? When code migrates from system to system, what privileges does it have? Does it use the privileges originally granted to it or does it modify the privileges depending on the execution environment? A good discussion of secure mobile agents is given in [CORR99]. They focus on not only securing the agents, but also ensuring that untrusted hosts do not corrupt the agents or spy on the agents. That is, protecting the agents is also an issue. Other research issues for mobile agents include real-time computing where these agents have to migrate, execute and give results within a certain time. Fault tolerance is also a major consideration, as the mobile agents have to recover from faults.

Ultimately we feel that whether an agent is a mobile agent or another type of agent such as a retrieval agent, there is little difference. For example, a mobile agent can perform retrieval facilities. Retrieval agents can migrate to different environments. We expect that research and practice on mobile agents and code will continue to explode. Java and similar developments are just the beginning. Figure 14-9 illustrates an example of mobile agents.

14.5 AGENTS FOR INFORMATION DISSEMINATION

The ideal goal is to get the right information at the right time to the users. This could be achieved either through the push model where information is pushed to the user or a pull model where the user goes out and gets the data or a combination of both push and pull. In Chapter 8 we discussed various models for communications including the push and pull models. Essentially it all comes down to information dissemination. That is, producers produce all kinds of information. This information has to be disseminated to the users in an appropriate manner. Now that we have examined various aspects of agents, we discuss the role of agents in information dissemination.

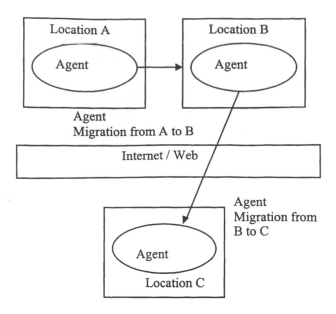

Figure 14-9. Mobile Agents

As stated earlier, agents could be locator agents that locate the resources, retrieval agents that retrieve data either by monitoring or when requested, situation monitoring agents that monitor for events and filtering agents that filter unwanted information. All of these agents play a role in information dissemination. Figure 14-10 illustrates a situation where situation agents monitor for information production and this information is retrieved and filtered and then given to the consumer. Figure 14-11 illustrates the case where the consumer requests information, the locator agent locates the producers and then the retrieval agent retrieves the information.

Information dissemination technologies have expanded due to the web. The challenge is to get the information to the user without overloading the user. Since this is such a big challenge we cannot expect this problem to be solved completely. However, technologies being developed show much promise so that information dissemination is enhanced.

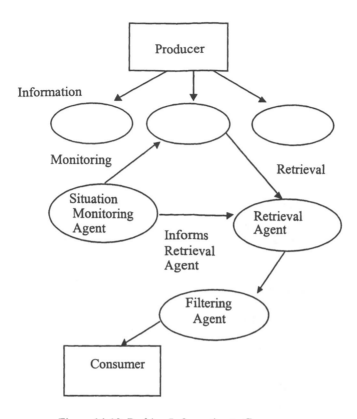

Figure 14-10. Pushing Information to Consumer

14.6 SUMMARY

This chapter has provided a brief overview of agents and discussed how they operate on the web. We first defined an agent and then discussed various types of agents and their functions. Agent architecture and communication aspects were described next. Finally we provided an overview of mobile agents and ended with a discussion of information dissemination.

As the web develops and e-commerce expands, agents will continue to play a critical role. Agents will be developed to carry out numerous functions including data mining and e-commerce. Agents will also be used for training, collaboration and knowledge management. One can also expect various agents to be reused. We have provided only a brief overview of this critical topic. We urge the reader to keep up with the agent literature.

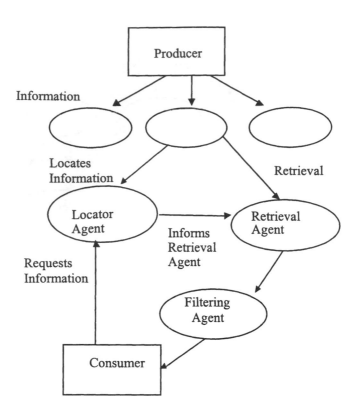

Figure 14-11. Pulling Information from Producer

CHAPTER 15

DATA AND INFORMATION MANAGEMENT TOOLS FOR THE WEB

15.1 OVERVIEW

This chapter describes some examples of commercial web data and information management products. We group them into various categories such as database systems, data mining, and knowledge management. As stated earlier, all of the information on these products has been obtained from published material as well as from vendor product literature. Since commercial technology is advancing rapidly, the status of these products as described here may not be current. Again, our purpose is to give an overview of what has been out there recently and not the details of these products.

We discuss only some of the key features of the commercial products. Note that various web data management conferences including data management/mining magazines, books, and trade shows such as Database Programming and Design (Miller Freeman Publishers), Data Management Handbook Series (Auerbach Publications), and DCI's Database Client Server Computing Conferences have several articles and presentations discussing the commercial products. We urge the reader to take advantage of the information presented in these magazines, books, and conferences and keep up with the latest developments with the vendor products. Furthermore, in areas relating to the web we can expect the developments to be changing very rapidly. The various web pages are also a useful source of information.

It should also be noted that we are not endorsing any of these products or prototypes. We have chosen a particular product or prototype only to explain a specific technology. We would have liked to have included discussions of many more products and prototypes. But such a discussion is beyond the scope of this book. In recent years various documents have provided a detailed survey of various web data management products. As an example, for data mining, the Two Crows Corporation puts out a manual describing details of the products and compares them. We encourage the reader to take advantage of such up-to-date information.

The organization of this chapter is as follows: In Section 15.2 we discuss the web database system tools. In Section 15.3 we discuss web data mining tools. Web application server tools are discussed in Section 15.4. Web knowledge management tools are given in Section 15.5. Web metadata tools and in particular XML-based tools are discussed in Section 15.6. An overview of some other tools such as web security tools, collaboration tools, and agent tools are given in Section 15.7. The chapter is summarized in Section 15.8. Figure 15-1 provides an overview of the various web data and information management tools. Figure 15-2 illustrates graphically the tools we have discussed in this chapter.

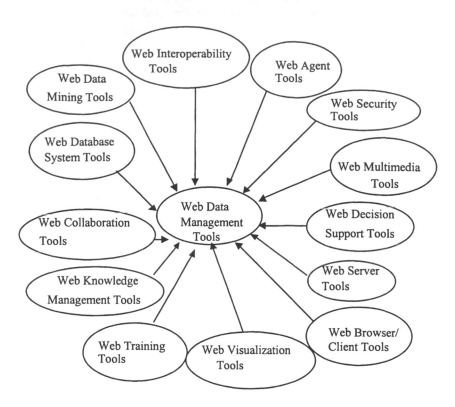

Figure 15-1. Data and Information Management Tools for the Web

15.2 WEB DATABASE SYSTEMS TOOLS

Web databases are a key part of web data management. We discussed web database systems in Chapter 8. Current trends include accessing relational databases on the web through JDBC. Application servers and data servers (i.e., web servers) also access database systems and format data in a way that can be understood by the web clients.

Almost every major database system vendor now has access to the web. That is, relational, object-oriented as well as object relational systems have web access. Web clients can now access these databases.

XML is becoming a standard language for formatting the responses from database systems so that the web clients can understand the results. With XML, one can eliminate the various gateways discussed in Chapter 8.

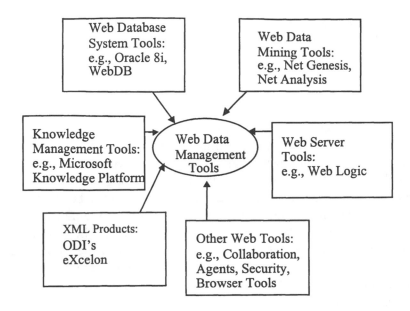

Figure 15-2. Tools Discussed in this Chapter

This section describes an example database system and discusses how it can be interfaced to the web. The database system that we have selected is Oracle Corporation's recent web database system product. As mentioned earlier, we selected this product only because we are more familiar with this product than some of the other products. This does not mean that this is the best product or we are endorsing this product. As we stated, every major database system vendor including Oracle, Sybase, Informix, and Object Design have designed their products in such a way that they have web interfaces. We are most familiar with Oracle's product and will therefore discuss it in this section. There are also other good products. For example, recently there have been write-ups about Sybase's *ASE* product for the web and enterprise information management [INFO2].

Let us examine the features of Oracle's products called *Oracle 8i* and *Oracle WebDB*. Oracle 8i (as described in [ORAC1]) combines Internet database capabilities with traditional warehousing and transaction processing capabilities. The Internet File System feature of Oracle

8i enables users to move their data into Oracle's database. In addition, the interMedia module supports the management of multimedia data. WebDB (to be described later) is a tool to build HTML-based web pages with data from Oracle databases. Oracle 8i integrates the Java Virtual Machine into its server and this way can deploy Java programs at various tiers (such as client and middle tiers).

In addition to supporting web data management, Oracle 8i also supports various database management functions. It has enhanced features for transaction processing and warehouse management, database administration, indexing, parallel server management, replication, caching, fine-grained access control as well as support for objects. Oracle 8i also provides rich support for enterprise data management.

Oracle WebDB (see the description in [ORAC2]) is essentially a web browser that builds web pages from various types of data in the Oracle databases. For example, Oracle 8i supports the management of multimedia data such as video and text. With the web browser, the multimedia data can be viewed efficiently. Essentially WebDB enables the visualization of the data in the database via the web. The web pages can be personalized and can provide multiple views of the same data. For example, some users may want to see graphs while others may want to see just numbers. WebDB provides the support for both views.

Oracle 8i, Oracle WebDB and many of the other tools that are emerging make web data management a reality. As we have stressed, we have chosen products in this book mainly due to our familiarity with them. It should be noted that various database vendors such as Sybase, Microsoft, Informix, and Object Design have developed various web database management products. This is one of the fastest growing areas in web information management.

15.3 WEB MINING TOOLS

In the web page of KDD Nuggets [KDDN] numerous resources to data mining are given. These include references to web mining products. Some of the recent web mining products include *Easy Miner for Web* by MINEit Software that carries out cross section analysis, *HiLis* by Accrue Software that carries out server log analysis, *e.Analysis* by Genesis that carries out e-business intelligence analysis, and *NetTracker* by Sane Solutions that is an Internet usage tracking program. In addition to products, there is also free software such as AltavistaDiscovery that one can attach to the browser to search the web and The Kensington Open Infrastructure for Enterprise Data Mining by Guo et al. at Imperial College in London (see [GUO00]).

Since this book has a strong interest in e-commerce, we will discuss the Net Genesis products. These products attempt to provide customer intelligence to the e-business enterprise so that customers can be retained. For example different segments of shoppers are evaluated and analyzed so that the e-business organization can carry out customized marketing. These products also enable the enterprise to identify the key drivers of the business and how it can provide a competitive advantage. It also helps the organization to understand the nature of the different shoppers and why they behave the way they do and gives reasons as to why they purchase certain products.

The web mining products such as the ones described here are still in their infancy and many of them have been around less than a year. As we learn more about e-commerce and e-business we will see more and more tools applying data mining to e-business. Some of the aspects are discussed in Part III of this book.

15.4 WEB APPLICATION SERVER TOOLS

Various server tools have emerged over the years since the mid 1990s. These server tools perform various functions including access to database management systems as well as legacy databases. As described in Chapter 8, the application servers are often based on EJB technology. There are also data servers that access the database systems.

Many application server tools are in the market and an overview is given in [INFO1]. We illustrate some of the concepts with the tool called *WebLogic*, a product of BEA systems (see for example [BEA]). BEA states that its e-commerce application server products include WebLogic and BEA's *Tuxedo*. They are used to build rapid e-commerce applications and transactions. They use the latest distributed technologies including Enterprise Java and ORB. BEA's *eLink* integrates new and existing applications for office systems. BEA's products are based on multi-tier client-sever computing with business logic for e-commerce applications in the middle-tier.

BEA's WebLogic application server is essentially based on component technology. Its goals are to provide a complete set of tools for enterprise applications and ensure scalability and security. It interfaces to web applications on the one side and server technologies on the other side. That is, through products like WebLogic client applications to legacy databases are made less complex. Associated with Web Logic is BEA's WebLogic Enterprise and it provides support for manipulating business logic across to multiple servers and multiple heterogeneous databases.

15.5 WEB KNOWLEDGE MANAGEMENT TOOLS

Numerous tools for knowledge management are emerging. These include collaboration and decision support tools as well as web information management tools. Note that the term knowledge management is still rather vague and therefore various types of tools have been grouped together and called knowledge management tools.

We describe a suite of tools for knowledge management by Microsoft Corporation and their industry partners. These tools are called the *Knowledge Management Platform* (see for example [MICR]. This platform has five components; they are Knowledge Desktop, Knowledge Services, System, Connected Devices, and Partner Solutions. We briefly describe these components below.

Knowledge Desktop is essentially a collection of tools to seamlessly access and use Microsoft Corporation's knowledge assets. Products such as Office 2000 enable this. Knowledge Services include collaboration services such as meeting facilities, content management services that capture and manage various experiences and ideas, analysis services that turn data into knowledge, and tracking and workflow services that capture best practices.

The system component essentially consists of a Microsoft Server that provides a complete set of services to the user. Connected Devices component supports knowledge workers through partnerships, say, with telecommunications companies. Partner Solutions components enable Microsoft to team with various industry partners to produce various tools such as digital dashboards.

Essentially what we have described here is a collection of tools by Microsoft to support the various knowledge management, collaboration and decision support functions that we have described in earlier chapters. There are also several smaller companies specializing entirely on knowledge management products. This is an area in which we can expect numerous products to be developed within the next few years. Furthermore, as definitions of knowledge management become clearer we can also decide which of these products really perform knowledge management.

15.6 WEB METADATA/XML TOOLS

Various XML tools have emerged during the past year or so. One of the prominent tools is *eXcelon* by Object Design Inc. Much of the information about this tool is obtained from [ODI]. eXcelon is an application development environment for integrating structured, unstructured as well as semi-structured data. The goal of eXcelon is to support a variety of e-business web information management activities for the enterprise. Towards achieving its goal, the company is providing a toolbox to support various XML tools.[30]

One of the key components of this product is eXcelon Stylus, a visual XSL editor for XML. eXcelon's Data Server stores and manages XML documents. Therefore, Object Design provides a complete solution to XML and that is the server to manage the data and tools to edit and manipulate the XML data.

Object Design has discussed various applications for eXcelon. These include web commerce, knowledge management, business-to-business and enterprise application integration. Web e-commerce is about carrying out transactions on the web. Typically one has to advertise the company's products. Object Design's eXcelon enables the specification of the company's products whose descriptions may be structured, unstructured or semi-structured. Knowledge management is enhanced by eXcelon by capturing the knowledge assets of the corporation in various data formats. Business-to-business applications are enhanced by eXcelon by its support for XML extensions. Traditional EDI type information exchange is rather limiting for such applications and one needs richer representation schemes. The data server component facilitates enterprise application integration. That is, one needs to efficiently integrate the data of the corporation and be able to query the data effectively for enterprise application management. Object Design's eXcelon provides this support.

In summary XML tools such as eXcelon are in their infancy. Although they provide many critical capabilities for e-business, there is so much to be done. As progress is made on XML, we can expect these tools to advance also.

15.7 OTHER WEB INFORMATION MANAGEMENT TOOLS

We have briefly discussed various web data management tools in this chapter. There are numerous other tools that we have not mentioned. We name some of these tools.

Several tools for web security have emerged. Some of them are discussed in Part III when we discuss e-commerce security. These tools include firewall products as well as secure Java and Microsoft's ActiveX. In addition, various secure transaction systems have also emerged for the web. These include the secure payment protocols. Encryption products are also a type of web security products.

---

[30] Some of the e-commerce terms will be made clearer in Part III of this book.

Other web tools include tools for collaboration. We discussed knowledge management tools, which included collaboration. Corporations such as Lotus have developed various collaboration tools and these tools enable users to share information and collaborate with one another. Another example of a prototype collaborative system is given in [JONE99]. We discussed web browser tools such as Oracle's WebDB. This is only one such tool where database data are transformed into web pages. There are numerous other tools such as Netscape's browsers[31] and other browser tools which also perform visualization. Web agent tools include the various types of web crawlers and know-bots that locate various resources as well as enable information sharing and collaboration.

Other web tools include tools for distance learning, multimedia information processing and decision support. Some of these functions are already provided by the tools we have discussed. For example, Oracle 8i supports multimedia information management. Microsoft's knowledge platform provides support for collaboration, decision support, and training. In addition to these large corporations, many smaller corporations are all specializing in collaboration, multimedia, decision support and training. Distance learning and training will become key components of e-business and, therefore, we can expect to see many tools emerge in this area.

In addition to the data management tools for the web we can also see various components and infrastructures to emerge for the web. We can expect plug and play tool-based component technology as well as specialized framework and infrastructures to emerge for the web. OMG's ORB based tools are the first step toward such infrastructures.

In summary, during the past two years or so the number of web data management tools has grown almost exponentially. We cannot expect to see a slow down in the near future. In fact we believe that this exponential growth will continue well into the twenty-first century.

15.8 SUMMARY

This chapter has provided a brief overview of the various web data and information management tools. In particular, tools for web database management, web mining, web server management, and knowledge management tools are discussed. First a general discussion of the tools is given and this is followed by the description of an example tool. We also described some other classes of tools. We have selected the tools only because of our knowledge about them. As mentioned earlier, we

---

[31] Netscape is now part of AOL.

are not endorsing any of the products. A description of all of the tools is beyond the scope of the book. Furthermore, due to the rapid developments in the field, the information about these products may soon be outdated. Therefore, we urge the reader to take advantage of the various commercial and research material available on these products.

The developments in web data and information management over the last few years have shown a lot of promise. Although some of the tools have been around for a while, like database system products, they are now being integrated with the web. As mentioned previously, we need the integration of multiple technologies to make web data management work. Therefore in the future we will see more and more tools being integrated with each other to provide effective web data and information management.

Conclusion to Part II

Part II, consisting of eight chapters, has described various data and information management technologies for the web. Chapter 8 discussed database systems for the web. It also included a discussion of web architectures as well as digital libraries. Chapter 9 described web data mining. Both mining data as well as mining usage patterns were discussed. Chapter 10 provided an overview of security and privacy issues. The focus was mainly on privacy violations due to web mining. Chapter 11 discussed metadata management for the web. We also included a discussion of ontologies and the emerging standard XML. Chapter 12 provided an overview of multimedia for the web as well as collaboration. It also discussed other technologies such as training, real-time processing and visualization. Chapter 13 discussed knowledge management and decision support for the web. Agents for the web were the subject of Chapter 14. Finally, Chapter 15 described some tools for web data and information management.

As we mentioned earlier, our original plan was to divide this part into two parts. We had planned to group Chapters 8, 9, 10 and 11 into web data management and the rest into web information management. However, since the distinction between data and information management was not clear, we decided to combine them into one part.

The technologies discussed in this part form the foundation for e-commerce. That is, while the supporting technologies in Part I prepared us for Part II, the technologies of Part II have prepared us for Part III. We are now in a position to address one of the significant developments in computing as well as for society, and that is e-commerce.

Part III

ELECTRONIC COMMERCE

Introduction to Part III

Part III, consisting of four chapters, describes electronic commerce (also known as e-commerce). Chapter 16 provides an overview of e-commerce. In particular, a definition of e-commerce as well as a discussion of process and models for e-commerce will be given.

Chapter 17 examines how the data and information management technologies can be applied for e-commerce. It examines databases, data mining, agents, knowledge management, and other technologies such as collaboration and shows how e-commerce can benefit from these technologies.

Chapter 18 provides an overview of e-commerce security. Essentially web security issues as well as their application to e-commerce will be discussed.

Finally, Chapter 19 discusses transaction for commerce. We provide an overview of data transactions and will then discuss database transactions for e-commerce.

The four chapters in this part only provide some preliminary information for e-commerce. E-commerce is a new area and still not much is known about it. Policy makers and technologists have to work together. For example, a challenge is to determine which laws apply for e-commerce. Is it those of the country of the seller or the country of the buyer? What about export controls? As progress is made, we can expect answers to such difficult questions.

CHAPTER 16

INTRODUCTION TO E-COMMERCE:
MODELS, ARCHITECTURES AND FUNCTIONS

16.1 OVERVIEW

We are now ready to embark on what is now referred to as the killer application for the web and that is e-commerce. The question is what is e-commerce? Simply stated, e-commerce is all about carrying out commerce on the web. Essentially it is about carrying out transactions on the web which is essentially buying and selling products on the web. Earlier in this book we mentioned that e-commerce could be as simple as putting up a web page or as complicated as merging two corporations on the web. More recently we have heard the term e-business which is much broader than e-commerce and that is doing any business on the web. Therefore, e-commerce has come to be known as carrying out transactions on the web and tasks like putting up web pages and other activities are part of e-business. Figure 16-1 illustrates how one does a normal transaction (that is, a non-web transaction) and Figure 16-2 illustrates how one carries out a business transaction on the web.

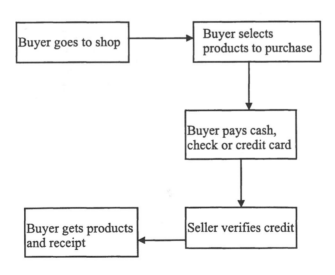

Figure 16-1. Process of Commerce

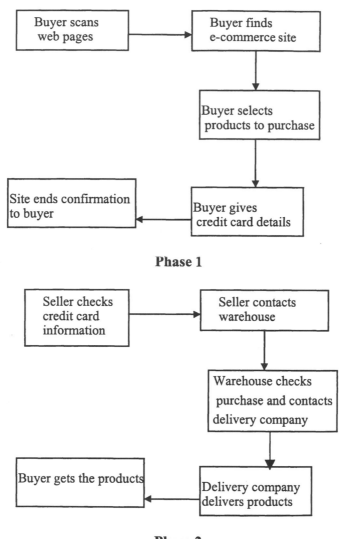

Phase 1

Phase 2

Figure 16-2. Process of E-commerce

This chapter provides a broad overview of e-commerce. More specialized topics will be addressed in the next three chapters. We first discuss e-business and its relationship to e-commerce. This will give the reader some idea about the latest buzzwords in e-commerce. Then we discuss some models for e-commerce. In particular, business-to-business e-commerce as well as business-to-consumer e-commerce models will be discussed.[32] It should be noted that models for e-commerce are rather immature and as we know more about e-commerce various models will emerge. Next we discuss architectures for e-commerce. These include centralized as well as distributed architectures and architectures for interoperability. E-commerce functions will be discussed next. This will be followed by a discussion of how Java is being used for e-commerce. Then we provide a note on the role of telecommunications in e-commerce. Note that this book has focused mainly on data and information management for the web, and we discuss the application of these technologies in Chapter 17. Telecommunications as well as Java will also have a significant impact for the web. However, since Java and telecommunications are not strictly part of information management, we add them in this chapter. Networking is also critical for e-commerce and we do provide some background on networking in Appendix B. However, telecommunication technology will be very visible to web users and this aspect will be discussed in this chapter. Finally some other considerations such as legal issues and political considerations will be given in this chapter.

The organization of this chapter is as follows. Section 16. 2 discusses e-business and its relationship to e-commerce. Models of e-commerce are the subject of Section 16.3. Architectures will be described in Section 16.4. E-commerce functions will be discussed in Section 16.5. Java for e-commerce will be the subject of Section 16.6. Telecommunication aspects will be given in Section 16.7. Legal and other considerations will be described in Section 16.8. The chapter will be concluded in Section 16.9.

16.2 E-BUSINESS AND E-COMMERCE

We often hear the term e-business these days. Many companies prefer to be doing e-business rather than e-commerce as e-commerce they feel may be too narrow and e-business encompasses e-commerce. As far as we are concerned, e-commerce can be considered to be broad such as putting up a web page or listening to music on the web or conducting transactions on the web. However to be consistent with the terminology that is emerging let us explain the differences between e-business and e-commerce. However we have often used these two terms interchangeably.

Those who differentiate between e-business and e-commerce state that e-commerce is all about carrying out transactions on the web. But

---

[32] Note that business-to-business e-commerce is popularly called B-to-B and business-to-consumer e-commerce is popularly called B-to-C.

e-business is much broader and includes learning and training on the web, entertainment on the web, putting up web pages and hosting web sites, conducting procurement on the web, carrying out supply chain management on the web, handling help on the web for telephone repairs or other services, and almost anything that can be conducted on the web. E-business and some of its various components are illustrated in Figure 16-3.

Various types of corporations are now in e-business. One group consists of corporations that simply have web pages. A second group consists of corporations that carry out e-commerce. A third group consists of corporations that help other corporations formulate e-business strategies. A fourth group consists of corporations that provide solutions and products for e-business. Other groups include those that carry out e-learning and e-training, e-procurement, and provide e-helpdesks. It is stated in [BUSI99] that with e-helpdesks the time it takes to handle a customer problem is greatly reduced and also elimi-nates the need for too many human operators. Corporations that provide consulting as well as solutions and products include Fortune 100 corporations like IBM or smaller corporations such as the Dot-Com companies. For example, some of these smaller corporations can connect consumers with healthcare providers, lawyers, real estate agents and others who provide services. Consulting companies come in and assess the state of a corporation, its business practices and advise the corporation on how to develop e-business solutions. One of the latest trends is to provide fully integrated enterprise resource management and business process reengineering on the web. Corporations such as SAP-AG are active in this area.[33]

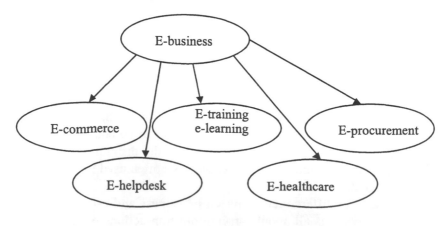

Figure 16-3. E-business and its Components

---

[33] We discuss these business processes in Appendix C.

Figure 16-4 illustrates the building blocks of e-business. For example, in Figure 16-4(a), the building blocks are the web, information management technologies, and business processes (such as the business processes supported by the SAP product). These building blocks support e-commerce. Figure 16-4(b) illustrates the building blocks for e-music (i.e. entertainment on the web). These include the web, information management technologies and the music business. Figure 16-4(c) illustrates building blocks for universities and schools. These include web, information management, and school/university business activities. We will stress in this book that to carry out good e-commerce not only do we need technologies to be described in the next chapter we also need good business practices. We have approached the subject from a technology point of view since we are technologists and not business specialists. Nevertheless we need business specialists to build an e-commerce organization. In Chapter 17 we briefly discuss issues on building an e-commerce organization. Also, in Appendix C we discuss some aspects of business processes such as those supported by products like SAP. Note that many organizations are well into e-business with functions such as time card reporting, project management, logistics and purchasing.

In summary, we will be hearing quite a lot about e-business in the future. Often the terms e-business and e-commerce will be used interchangeably. There are some debates as to whether e-business is mainly about business or is to do with information technology. After reading more about this subject and thinking about it, a strong business component is essential for e-business. Technology will provide only the tools to make e-business more efficient. One can draw an analogy to healthcare. Good medical practices and policies are essential for good healthcare. Technology only makes the management of healthcare more efficient.

16.3 MODELS FOR E-COMMERCE

As mentioned earlier, there are no well-defined models for e-commerce. However, two paradigms, which we can consider to be models are emerging. They are business-to-business e-commerce and business-to-consumer e-commerce. In this section we will discuss both these models with examples.

As its name implies, business-to-business e-commerce is all about two businesses conducting transactions on the web. We give some examples. Suppose corporation A is an automobile manufacturer and needs microprocessors to be installed in its automobiles. It will then purchase the microprocessors from corporation B who manufactures the microprocessors. Another example is when an individual purchases some goods such as toys from a toy manufacturer. This manufacturer then contacts a packaging company via the web to deliver the toys to the

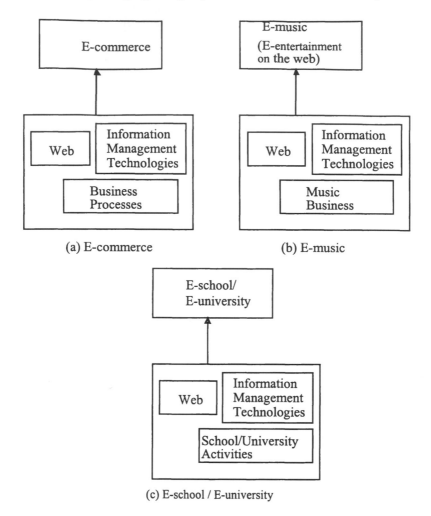

(a) E-commerce   (b) E-music

(c) E-school / E-university

Figure 16-4. Building Blocks for E-business

individual. The transaction between the manufacturer and the packaging company is a business-to-business transaction. Business-to-business e-commerce also involves one business purchasing a unit of another business or two businesses merging. The main point is that such transactions have to be carried out on the web.

Business-to-consumer e-commerce is when a consumer such as a member of the mass population makes purchases on the web. In the toy manufacturer example, the purchase between the individual and the toy manufacturer is a business-to-consumer transaction. It is reported in [INFO1] and [INFO2] that business-to-consumer e-commerce has grown tremendously during the past year. While computer hardware purchases is still the leading e-commerce transaction, purchasing toys, apparel, software, and even groceries via the web has also increased. But many feel that the real future will be in business-to-business transactions, as this will involve millions of dollars.

The major difference between the two models is the a business is carried out. This is similar to the real word. In a business-to-consumer transaction, people can give credit cards, cash or checks to make a purchase. In the web world, credit cards are used most often. However, the use of e-cash and checks are also being investigated. In business-to-business transactions, corporations have company accounts that are maintained and the corporations are billed at certain times. This is the approach being taken in the e-commerce world also. That is, corporations have accounts with one another and these accounts are billed to when purchases are made. Figures 16-5 and 16-6 illustrate examples of business-to-business and business-to-consumer transactions, respectively.

Regardless of the type of model, one of the major goals of e-commerce is to complete the transaction on time. For example, in the case of business-to-consumer e-commerce, the seller has to minimize the time between the time of purchase and the time the buyer gets his goods. The seller may have to depend on third parties such as packaging and trucking companies to achieve this goal. It should also be noted that with e-commerce the consumer has numerous choices for products. In a typical shop, the consumer does not have access to all of the products that are available. He cannot see the products displayed at the shop. However, in an e-commerce world, the consumer has access to all the products that are available to the seller.

Another key point to note is the issue of trust. How can the consumer trust the seller and how can the seller trust the consumer? For example, the consumer may give his credit card number to a seller who is a fraud. The consumer may himself be a fraud and not send a check when he gets the goods. The best known model is the business/consumer relationships. But this is not always the case in the e-commerce world. Some of the challenges here are not very different from the mail order and the catalog world. If the goods do not arrive, the consumer could write to his credit card company. But this could be a lengthy and possibly a legal process. Another solution is for the seller to establish an account with a credit card company and this way the seller

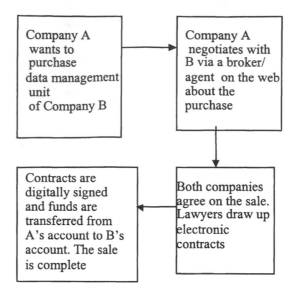

Figure 16-5. Business-to-Business E-commerce

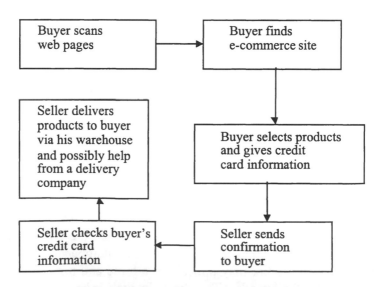

Figure 16-6. Business-to-Consumer E-commerce

would have some credibility established. That is, a vendor from some unknown company called XXX may not be able to establish a relationship with a credit card company and therefore the buyer may not be in danger. In the e-commerce world there are several additional security measures such as secure wallets and cards and these aspects will be discussed under the chapter on security for e-commerce. We also discuss some aspects under the section on Java for e-commerce later in this chapter.

16.4 ARCHITECTURES FOR E-COMMERCE

In the previous sections we discussed the process and models for e-commerce. In particular, in Section 16.1 we illustrated a process for e-commerce and then in Section 16.3 we discussed two models for e-commerce. In Section 16.2 we discussed the relationship between e-commerce and e-business. In this section we discuss architectures for e-commerce. There are two ways to view architectures. One is centralized vs distributed architecture and the other is client-server vs federated architecture. We also discuss our views of the architectures suitable for the models we have described. Then we provide an overview of interoperability issues and the role of ORBs for e-commerce as well as a discussion of three-tier computing for e-commerce.

In the centralized architecture, illustrated in Figure 16-7, we assume that all of the information at the e-commerce site is centralized. Many of the issues discussed for centralized data management would apply here. The challenges include maintaining all of the data, which could be in databases, web pages, and files. Data mining components may also be

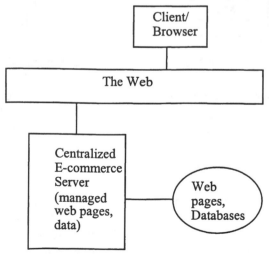

Figure 16-7. Centralized Architecture for E-commerce

part of the central e-commerce server. The functions of a central e-commerce manager are illustrated in Figure 16-8. Note that in this case we assume that the e-commerce business functions as well as data management functions are carried out by the e-commerce server. We will illustrate an alternative in the three-tier computing architecture later on.

In a distributed architecture, the information managed by the e-commerce server is distributed. This could be because the corporation's assets may be distributed across multiple sites. For example, major corporations have sites all over the world and each site may host components of the e-commerce server. The servers may be connected by a distributed processor which we call EDP (e-distributed processor). Figure 16-9 illustrates a distributed architecture.

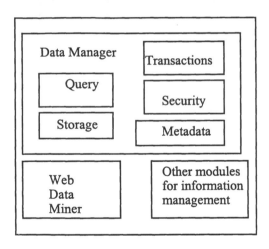

Figure 16-8. Modules of an E-commerce Server

Currently e-commerce is carried out in a client-server environment. Typically browsers run in the client environment. We use browsers to access the commerce sites and specify the items we want to purchase. This is typically a client-server environment and is illustrated in Figure 16-10. Note that this is a 2-tier client-server system where the server is responsible for data as well as web page management. As we have mentioned in the previous chapters, a current trend is to move toward a 3-tier environment. Here the client is responsible for presentation, the database server for managing databases and the middle tier which is the e-commerce server will be responsible for managing business objects that will implement the business functions of e-commerce such as brokering and mediation. This is illustrated in Figure 16-11.

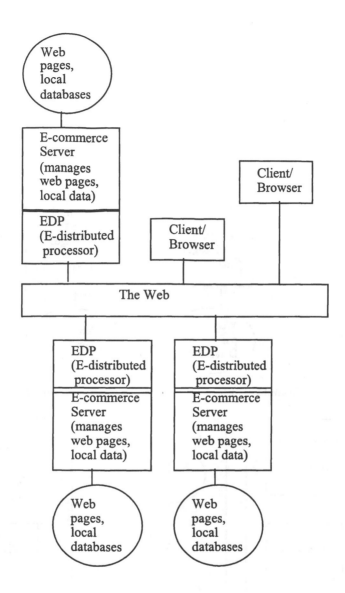

Figure 16-9. Distributed Architecture for E-commerce

While client-server is the current trend, in a business-to-business e-commerce environment, many corporations may have to collaborate with each other. That is, a federated environment may be needed. This is illustrated in Figure 16-12 where the e-commerce sites are connected through an EFDP (e-federated distributed processor). The various e-commerce servers form a federation and have to cooperate with one another. They also have to maintain some kind of autonomy. The issues,

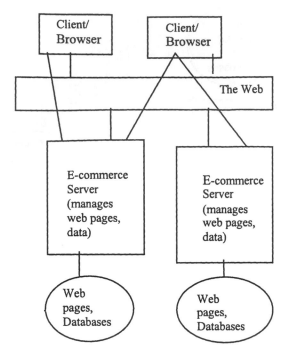

Figure 16-10. Client-Server Architecture for E-commerce

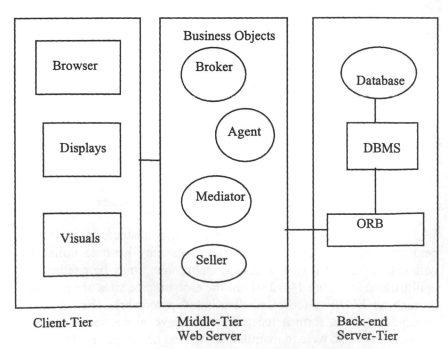

Figure 16-11. Three-Tier Computing for E-commerce

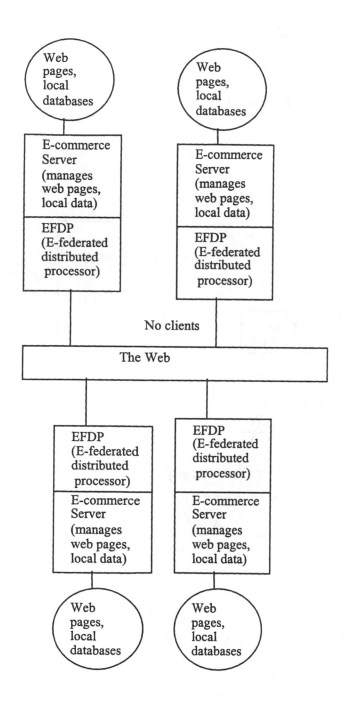

Figure 16-12. Federated Architecture for E-commerce

problems and solutions for federated architectures are still unknown. As we conduct more research on e-commerce and get practical experience, some of the architectural issues will be clearer.

Next let us look at interoperability aspects for e-commerce. OMG has a SIG focussing on services for e-commerce. The idea here is for any e-commerce client to talk to any e-commerce server. That is, heterogeneous applications and systems have to interoperate on the web for carrying out e-commerce. Figure 16-13 illustrate an example where ORB services such as mediation and brokering help clients to communicate with servers.

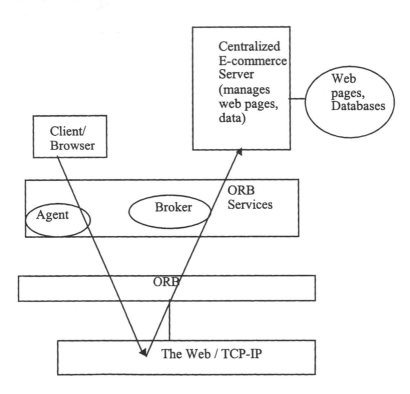

Figure 16-13. ORB Services for E-commerce

16.5 E-COMMERCE FUNCTIONS

There are three aspects to discussing e-commerce functions as illustrated in Figure 16-14. One is e-commerce client/server functions, which are essentially the information management functions; the other is the business functions for commerce, and the third is the distribution functions. We will look at all aspects.

E-commerce server functions are also illustrated in Figure 16-14. The modules of the e-commerce server may include modules for managing the data and web pages, mining customer information, security enforcement, as well as transaction management. E-commerce client functions may include presentation management, user interface as well as caching data and hosting browsers. There could also be a middle tier, which may implement the business objects to carry out the business functions of e-commerce. These business functions may include brokering, mediation, negotiations, purchasing, sales, marketing, and other e-commerce functions.

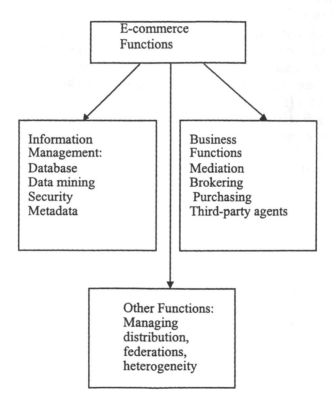

Figure 16-14. E-commerce Functions

The business functions are essentially the functions that are carried out in business transactions. Additional issues for e-commerce include the legal, ethical and political considerations to be discussed later in this chapter. The e-commerce server functions are impacted by the information management technologies for the web. These technologies are discussed in detail in the next chapter. In addition to the data management functions and the business functions the e-commerce functions also include those for managing distribution, heterogeneity, and federations.

16.6 JAVA FOR E-COMMERCE

Java, just within these past few years, has emerged as the programming language for the Internet. We do not know what the future holds as everything is changing so rapidly. However, we can safely say that some form of Java will be out there for a very long time. We can also expect the JINI architecture essentially based on Java and RMI to form the backbone for e-commerce transactions.

This section briefly examines the application of Java both for clients and servers for e-commerce transactions. Learning Tree International is teaching an excellent class on Java for E-commerce and Security and since we have taken this class, many of our ideas are influenced by the tutorial notes [LEAR99].

Javasoft started a project called the Java Commerce Project back in 1996 and many of the ideas in this project are now being used in e-commerce. As illustrated in Figure 16-15, the main modules of this project are the Java Commerce Client and Java Commerce Messages,

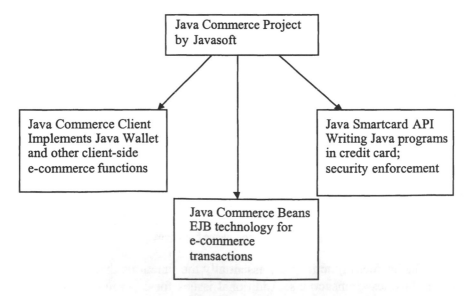

Figure 16-15. Java for E-commerce

Java Commerce Beans and Java Smartcard API. The Java Commerce Client essentially is launched within the web browser and is responsible for client functions of an e-commerce transaction. The Java Commerce Beans is a type of EJB technology and is used to perform the e-commerce transactions. Note that these are the business functions described in our three-tiered architecture. The Java Smartcard API (application programming interface) enables the use of Java programs in credit cards and provides security features to be described in Chapter 18. One of the interesting features implemented by the Java Commerce Client is the Java Wallet and operates in many ways similar to the real-world wallet. That is, users of e-commerce transactions may have their own wallets and use the cash from the wallets to pay for the transactions. Note that electronic cash is stored for each user. Transferring cash from the user's bank account may accumulate this cash. Some of these features will be explained in Chapter 19. Various payment protocols have been implemented by the Java Commerce Project.

While the previous paragraph discussed Java for client functions, Java is also being used for server functions. One option is to use Java programs to act as servlets. These servlets extend web server functions. They execute in the server environment unlike the applets that are brought into the client environment. Another option is to implement application-based logic into the server and make the server a rich server. The problem with this approach is that the various application logics are embedded into the server making the server quite complex. Various Java plug-in modules are also being used to carry out e-commerce functions on the server side. Since this technology is so new, at present, there is no correct way to carry out e-commerce transactions. As the technology matures we can expect specialized approaches and perhaps even standard approaches to be developed.

16.7 TELECOMMUNICATIONS FOR E-COMMERCE

Telephones, one of the basics of telecommunications, have played a major role in networking, the web and now e-commerce. Currently much of the commerce is being carried out in text format. There is a lot of push to move toward voice portals for e-commerce. In this section we will examine how e-commerce has evolved over the years with the help of telecommunications.

Laptops and personal computers are being used extensively now for e-commerce. All we need is a telephone connection from our computer to the ISP (Internet Service Provider) and we are fully networked. However, even with laptops, it is cumbersome to carry them around. The trend is to make them lighter and cheaper. The fashion now is carrying palm pilots and wireless phones. Palm pilots are essentially palm size computers that we can carry in our pocket. Here again you connect one end of the cord to your palm pilot and the other end to an ISP connection. When you are in your office you connect it to the office network and may get all your messages which you can then read when you are on travel. The latest trend is to get all your mail and carry out other electronic functions with your wireless phone. The phone is all you need to dial into your company's network and get all your messages via voice. You also send messages via voice. Eventually this will transform into voice-based e-commerce. That is, all you need is your wireless phone to carry out major transactions on the Internet. Figures 16-16 and 16-17 illustrate the current trends.

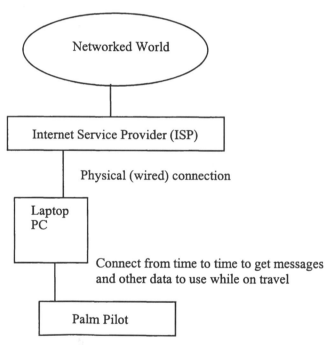

Figure 16-16. Laptop/Palm Pilot Connections to ISP

All these facilities do not come for free. You need to have excellent telecommunications and networking facilities. More importantly you need strong security mechanisms, as it will not be difficult to intercept messages and to eavesdrop on electronic conversations. We hear so often of eavesdropping of conversations carried out on mobile phones by well-known people. Carrying out major transactions this way makes it even more dangerous. In addition to security, we also need to ensure that the communication is reliable and safe and the system can recover from faults in a timely manner.

This chapter has only briefly discussed the need for secure tele-communications for e-commerce. The good news is that the various SIGs and task forces at OMG are working together to provide reliable services for e-commerce. For example, the e-commerce, security, and real-time SIGs are working together with the telecommunications task force to provide secure timely services for e-commerce transactions. We have a long way to go before the issues are resolved and a complete set of services are specified and formulated. Nevertheless we are proceeding in the right direction. Since this book is focussing on information management for the web, a description of networking and telecommunications is beyond the scope of this book. However, we provide some background in Appendix B.

16.8 FURTHER CONSIDERATIONS FOR E-COMMERCE

This section examines some of the other pressing issues with e-commerce. Figure 16-18 provides a high level overview of these issues. These include legal and ethical considerations. It has to be pointed out that we are still in the early stages of e-commerce. Therefore, the issues discussed here are rather preliminary.

Legal issues are a major challenge. For example consider the case of a buyer purchasing a product from a seller. If the buyer is from country X and the seller from country Y which laws apply? Can we treat it as in the case of the real world? That is, is it the same as the buyer going to country Y and purchasing the product? What about the taxes? Which tax laws apply since the tax laws vary a great deal from country to country and even from state to state? In many cases, the company may not exist in a country and could be a virtual corporation. That is, the seller may not have a country. Also, what happens if the buyer is purchasing a product while he is traveling over the ocean? Which laws apply for such a situation since he is not in either country? In the real world, we cannot take goods from country to country without declaring it through customs. In the e-commerce world the situation is different as the buyer may not take the goods out of a country. Also, while the buyer may be in country X when purchasing the goods, he may not be a resident of X. Furthermore, the goods may be in a completely different country, say country Z. There are so many permutations and combinations for which we do not have appropriate answers. We need lawyers and policy makers specializing in e-commerce.

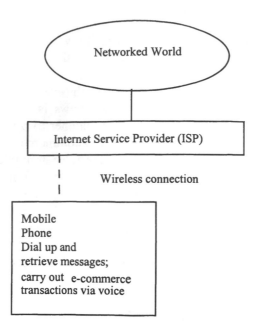

Figure 16-17. Wireless Connections

Another challenge is protecting intellectual property. For example, countries are very particular about protecting encryption algorithms and there are strict export controls. The question is, is it the same in the e-commerce world? How can you protect the intellectual assets of a country? What happens if a company has different branches in different countries? Are the issues for protecting intellectual property in the e-commerce world the same as in the real world?[34]

Other considerations include ethical ones. Consider the case of e-commerce sites mining the usage patterns and getting information about buyers so that they can carry out customized marketing. While this may be legal is this ethical? Should the buyer be informed that information about him is being extracted? What about privacy considerations? In Chapter 10 we discussed privacy problems that can occur through data mining. This problem could become quite severe with e-commerce. There are also cases where the seller may sell information about the buyer to other organizations. For example, a pharmacy could sell information about buyers to drug companies. Drug companies could in turn sell this information to marketing organizations. This could result in a chain of events and cause serious privacy problems. This situation also occurs in the real world. However, with electronic media it is a lot easier to gather information about buyers and transmit the information

---

[34] By real world we mean the non-e-commerce world

in various media to others. Security considerations are also major for e-commerce transactions and we will address security in Chapter 18.

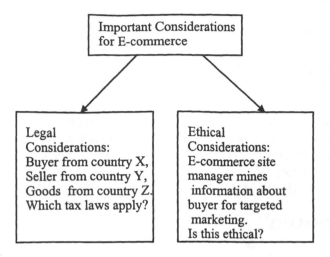

Figure 16-18. Legal and Ethical Considerations

Another dangerous problem is when people buy drugs without prescriptions from e-commerce sites. In some cases this is now possible. This could cause serious health problems as people are taking medications without the supervision of a physician. This may not only be an ethical problem but also a legal one. Recently we have heard about children committing crimes after seeing inappropriate material on the web. This is a very sensitive issue and we do not have any good solutions to handle such situations.

Some other considerations include handling the different cultures in the world. Since we believe that e-commerce is partly technology and partly business, the heterogeneous nature of the business aspects will have a major impact. Different countries have different ways of conducting business. Even within the states of the same country the business practices may be different. Reconciling these differences may become a major challenge. Note that the business schools in each country mainly focus on businesses within that country. However there is an increasing emphasis on international business these days. Therefore, we need to establish international business practices for e-commerce.

Other minor challenges include handling different languages and different currencies. That is, the client may speak English and carry out transactions in British Pound Sterling and the seller may speak French and carry out transactions in French Francs. The introduction of the

Euro may make this easier. However, if Europe is to carry out transactions with the United States, the translators between the different currencies are needed. This is not different from the way transactions are carried out in the real world today. However we need to explore the additional considerations for e-commerce.

The discussion in this section shows that building e-commerce solutions are not straightforward. Even if we have the technology there are so many other factors that come into play. To ensure that e-commerce is successful we need technologists, business experts, economists, lawyers, policy makers, and perhaps psychologists and sociologists to work closely together. It will not be easy to get experts with such diverse backgrounds to work together. But it is imperative that organizations do this. Else e-commerce cannot progress further and may even be disallowed if dangerous situations arise.

16.9 SUMMARY

This chapter has given a broad overview of e-commerce. We started with a discussion of the e-commerce process, which was followed by a discussion of the differences between e-business and e-commerce. Then we described models, architectures and functions for e-commerce. We also discussed the application of Java as well as the communications for e-commerce. Finally we provided an overview of some of the legal and ethical considerations for e-commerce.

In the next three chapters we will give more details about e-commerce. Chapter 17 will show how the various information management technologies discussed in Part II may be applied for e-commerce. That is, this chapter makes the connection between the different parts of this book. Chapter 18 provides an overview of e-commerce security while Chapter 19 discusses e-commerce transactions.

It should be noted that many of the tools that we discussed in Chapter 15 for web information management were related to e-commerce. For example, the data mining tool focused on gathering intelligence to help e-commerce sites. Oracle 8i and WebDB are both data management tools for the web. The Knowledge Management Platform's goal was to develop tools to manage the corporation's knowledge assets and this will be important for e-commerce. The Web Logic tool by BEA supports application development for e-commerce. In particular, the solutions provided by BEA for e-commerce includes the integration of application servers and transaction processing monitors so that enterprise data in heterogeneous databases can be integrated and managed efficiently. Ultimately we expect e-commerce and web information management to merge into e-business. Directions for e-commerce, web information management and e-business will be discussed in Chapter 20. Various book are being published on e-commerce. An example is [FING00].

CHAPTER 17

E-COMMERCE AND INFORMATION MANAGEMENT

17.1 OVERVIEW

Chapter 16 provided an introduction to e-commerce. In particular, the definition of e-commerce, its relationship to e-business, the process of e-commerce, models for e-commerce, architectures for e-commerce, and further considerations such as the role of information technology, security, transactions and some other aspects were discussed. Now that we have some understanding of what e-commerce is all about, let us take a look at the various information technologies discussed in Part II and determine how they can be applied to e-commerce. Since data mining is of special interest to us, we explore the application of web mining further.

Without the various data and information management technologies, e-commerce cannot be a reality. That is, the technologies discussed in Part II are essentially technologies for e-commerce. E-commerce also includes nontechnological aspects such as policies, laws, social and psychological impacts. We are now doing business in an entirely different way and therefore we need a paradigm shift. We cannot do successful e-commerce if we still want the traditional way of buying and selling products. We have to be more efficient and rely on the technologies a lot more to gain a competitive edge.

Universities that have had strong reputations in information technology and computer science are now offering special programs in e-commerce. To our knowledge, Carnegie Mellon University (CMU) is one of the first to start a graduate program specializing in e-commerce. It will not be long before other universities do the same. Examining the course offered by CMU, there is heavy emphasis on information technology applied to e-commerce. There is also some focus on policy aspects. That is, it gives a good balance between technology and policy. As we have stressed in Chapter 16, both are important for successful e-commerce.

The organization of this chapter is as follows. Section 17.2 examines each technology discussed in Part II and shows how it can be applied to e-commerce. It should be noted that since e-commerce is still a new area, many of the ideas expressed on the application of the technologies are those of the author and do not reflect the policies of any government or business organization carrying out e-commerce. That is there is really no standard way of conducting e-commerce. As the area matures we can expect policies and regulations to determine how technology may be applied. Section 17.3 pays special emphasis on data mining application to e-commerce. Essentially we have elaborated on what we have discussed in Section 17.2, as data mining is an area of interest to us. Now that we have an understanding of the information technologies for e-commerce, we then discuss how to build an effective e-commerce organization in Section 17.3. The chapter is summarized in Section 17.4.

17.2 APPLICATIONS OF INFORMATION MANAGEMENT TECHNOLOGIES

17.2.1 Overview
Chapter 16 discussed models, architectures, and functions for e-commerce. Both centralized and distributed architectures as well as functions of an e-commerce web server were elaborated. Some of these functions include data management, data mining, security management, and transaction management. In addition we also discussed some other technologies such as Java and telecommunications for e-commerce. This section not only reexamines the information management functions as they are applications of information technologies to e-commerce, it also examines many of the other information management technologies discussed in Part II such as multimedia, collaboration, and knowledge management and shows how they can be applied to e-commerce.[35] Figure 17-1 illustrates the overall picture of the technologies that may be applied to e-commerce.

Now we will examine each of the technologies discussed in Part II. We will list them one by one and give a description of its applications or potential applications with illustrations if possible. Sections 17.2.2 to 17.2.16 will be devoted to a discussion of the application of information management technologies to e-commerce.

17.2.2 Web Database Systems
Web database systems management was the topic of Chapter 8. Data management module may be part of the e-commerce server or it may have an interface to the database system residing elsewhere. In any case, the information to be managed by the e-commerce site may be large quantities and therefore efficient data management techniques are necessary. A database system may even have to be part of the e-commerce server. Database system functions of interest include transac-

---

[35] As mentioned earlier, many of the ideas are those of the author since there are no standards and policies for applying these technologies.

tion processing, security management, integrity management and query processing. In addition, metadata has to be extracted and maintained. Also, efficient storage management techniques are necessary. We will revisit transaction management and security in Chapters 18 and 19, respectively. Security will also be briefly addressed in this section. Figure 17-2 gives an illustration of database systems and e-commerce.

17.2.3 Web Data Mining

Data mining will have a great impact on improving e-commerce sites as well as carrying out targeted marketing. The data miner which may be part of the e-commerce server tracks the usage pattern, and based on information already available in the web databases, may develop patterns, associations and correlations. We will revisit data mining in Section 17.3.

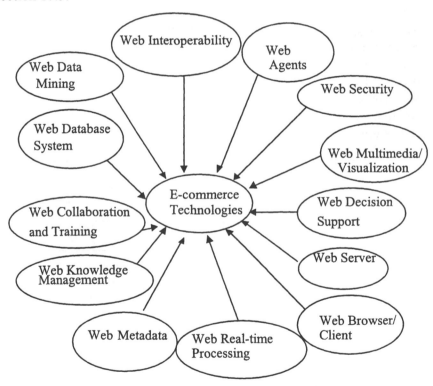

Figure 17-1. Information Technologies for E-commerce

17.2.4 Web Security

Security for e-commerce is critical. Security has to be end-to-end. That is, the servers, network and clients have to be secure. The threats include access control violations, sabotage, and fraud. Various encryption technologies, digital certificates as well as authentication mechanisms have been developed. Security threats as well as solutions will be elaborated in Chapter 18.

17.2.5 Web Metadata

Metadata is another critical technology for e-commerce. Metadata includes information about the e-commerce site itself. That is, the internal information such as how the site is structured is part of the metadata. Metadata also includes information about the users of the site. Various ontologies are being developed for e-commerce. These ontologies are common definitions for various e-commerce terms. Finally, XML is being examined for ecommece. XML specification for e-commerce would include information about specifying e-commerce site specific data, information about the process for e-commerce, and domain specific data such as say securities information for financial transactions. With XML, both the clients and servers specify documents with common notations and that is the domain type definitions. Figure 17-3 illustrates an example of XML for carrying out web transactions.

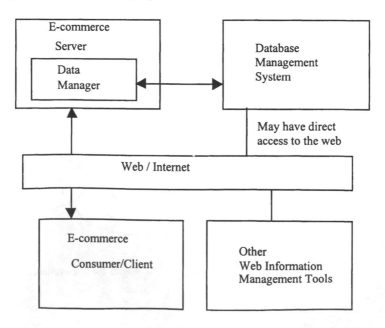

Figure 17-2. Database Systems and E-commerce

17.2.6 Web Collaboration

Web collaboration is an important technology for e-business. Various groups of, say, designers have to collaborate with one another to come up with a design. In certain cases such collaborations could occur in e-commerce; where businesses have to collaborate with one another especially with joint ventures. In the case of distributed architectures discussed in Chapter 16, various e-commerce sites may have to collaborate even within an organization and work toward a common goal. Figure 17-4 illustrates collaboration and e-commerce.

17.2.7 Web Training

This is an important technology for e-business, especially for learning. Various e-universities and e-campuses have been instituted and therefore e-learning will be a critical part. Although we have made elearning part of e-business to which e-commerce also belongs, e-learning can also be used in e-commerce to educate various organizations about e-commerce. Figure 17-5 illustrates training and e-commerce.

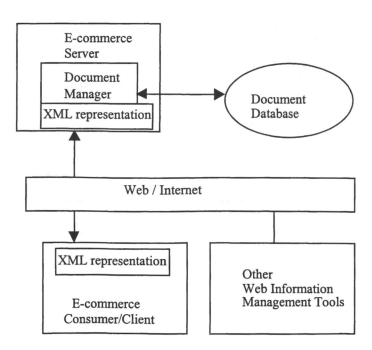

Figure 17-3. XML and E-commerce

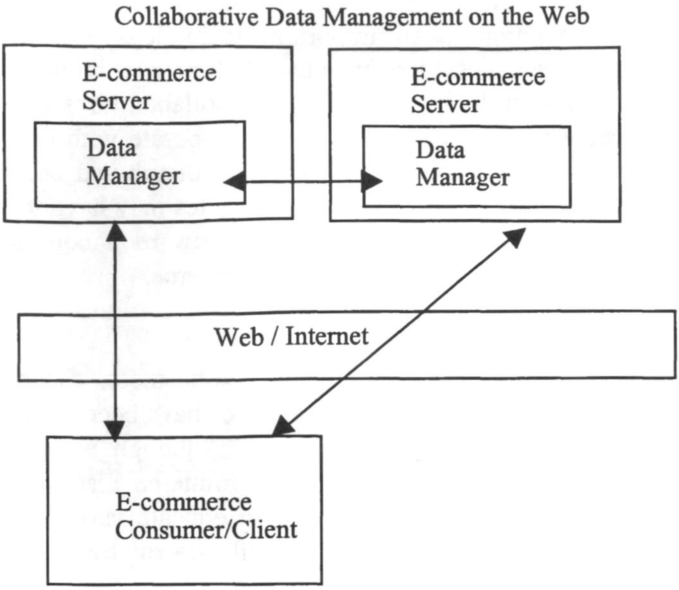

Collaborative Data Management on the Web

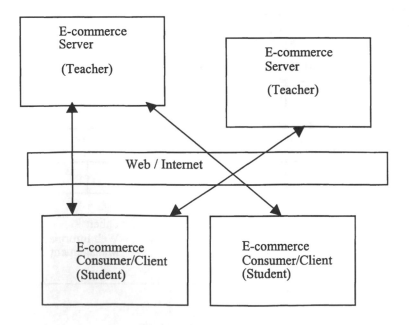

Figure 17-4. Web Collaboration and E-commerce

Figure 17-5. Web Training and E-commerce

17.2.8 Web Multimedia

Chapter 12 discussed multimedia information management for the web. Multimedia technology had numerous applications, say, in training and therefore in e-learning. Multimedia is also an important aspect of e-entertainment. While e-learning and e-entertainment are part of e-business and not strictly e-commerce, one can use e-learning and e-entertainment for e-commerce purposes. That is, one could listen to parts of a video or audio tapes and then place orders via the web. Multimedia for e-commerce is illustrated in Figure 17-6. Multimedia technology also has another critical application for e-commerce and that is with voice portals. Instead of filling out forms in text, one only has to place a call via the mobile phone or personal digital assistants. This facility is almost here and will be dominant in a few years.

17.2.9 Web Visualization

Visualization tools on the web are important to help the users to picture the large quantities of data out there. Visualization also helps to guide the user in the data mining process. That is, like multimedia, visualization tools help with e-learning and as we have argued earlier it helps e-commerce also. Essentially, Figure17-6 illustrates the use of visualization tools also for e-commerce.

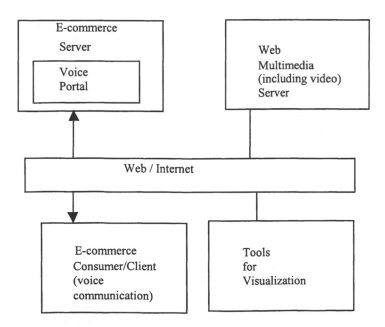

Figure 17-6. Multimedia/Visualization for E-commerce

17.2.10 Web Real-time Processing

Real-time processing is important especially for carrying out financial transactions on the web. One would need price quotes within, say, five seconds else the answers may not be of much use. Essentially queries and transactions have to meet timing constraints. The challenge is how to schedule the transactions on the web. We will revisit real-time transactions in Chapter 19.

17.2.11 Web Knowledge Management

We mentioned in Chapter 14 that knowledge management emerged as an area mainly due to the web. Although the ideas behind knowledge management have been around for a while and taught in business schools, it is as a result of the web that millions of people are able to share and impart knowledge with the use of technology. The question is how does knowledge management support e-commerce? Since training is part of knowledge management, knowledge management helps e-learning and eventually would help e-commerce. One needs to learn from experiences and from experts in creating and managing e-commerce sites. We illustrate this in Figure 17-7.

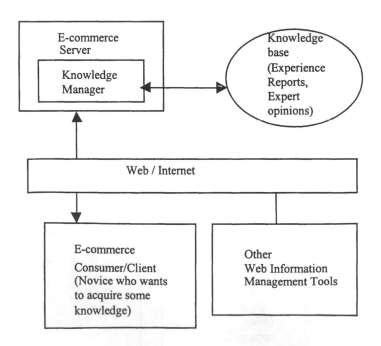

Figure 17-7. Knowledge Management for E-commerce

17.2.12 Web Decision Support

We explained decision support technologies for the web in Chapter 14. With e-commerce one needs effective tools to make decisions on which customers to target, whether to carry out business with a customer and advice on conducting business with other organizations. Since decision support is closely related to data mining, we address this in Section 17.3.

17.2.13 Web Agents

Agents were described in Chapter 14. Agents include retrieval agents, filtering agents and mobile agents. Security for agents as well as ensuring that agents do not corrupt the hosts is critical. Agents play a key role in e-commerce as they may act as brokers or mediators to conduct e-commerce transactions. This is illustrated in Figure 17-8.

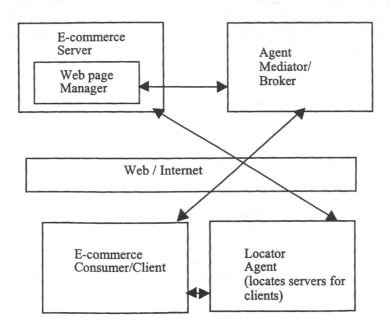

Figure 17-8. Web Agents

17.2.14 Web Interoperability

We discussed interoperability issues in Chapter 8. To conduct successful e-commerce, information has to be integrated from multiple databases. Multimedia databases have to be mined. Different technologies have to interoperate with each other. Therefore, interoperability is critical for e-commerce. This includes not just data interoperability but also systems interoperability. OMG has formed a special interest group for e-commerce and this group is examining various services that have to be provided by ORBs for e-commerce. These services include services for mediators and brokers as well as extensions for IDL. This group is also working closely with OMG's other groups such as security and real-time to ensure that timely and secure e-commerce services are provided. Figure 17-9 illustrates OMG's services.

17.2.15 Web Servers, Clients and Browsers

Almost everything we have discussed so far relies on web client and server technology. One needs browsers to scan through the large quantities of information as well as to issue requests to e-commerce sites. Browsers typically execute in the client environment. Web servers are the backbone of e-commerce sites. Search engines will connect the e-commerce users to the e-commerce sites. That is, they will locate the various servers for the clients. We have discussed web client-server technology throughout this book and therefore will not elaborate on them any further.

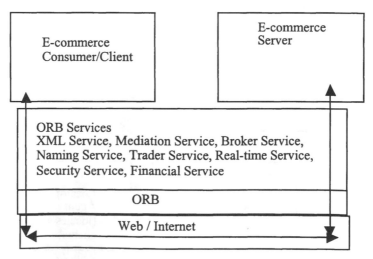

Figure 17-9. Web Interoperability

17.2.16. Other Technologies

We have essentially covered most of the key information management technologies for e-commerce. Other technologies include push/pull models, personal digital assistants, networking, telecommunications and middleware technologies. Some of them were addressed in

Chapter16. Some will be discussed in the remaining chapters as well as in the appendices.

There are also some other technologies that we have not addressed in this book. These include modeling and simulation and benchmarking. Modeling and simulation has shown to be important for various information management activities. The idea is to build simulation models and see how the system would work before actually building the systems. This is illustrated in Figure 17-10. Benchmarks have been developed for various systems such as databases and transaction processing systems. The use of these technologies for e-commerce is being examined. There is still a lot of work to be done on performance for e-commerce. Since the main focus of this book is information management, we have not discussed all relevant technologies for e-commerce. As e-commerce matures, the application of various technologies will be clearer.

Note that essentially almost everything we have learnt in computer science over the past four decades or so has applications in e-commerce. Without the development of these technologies e-commerce would not be possible.

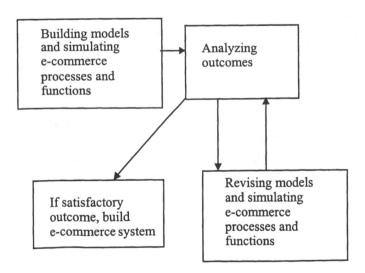

Figure 17-10. Modeling and Simulation for E-commerce

17.3 WEB MINING AND E-COMMERCE

The previous section described how various information technologies support e-commerce. This section gives data mining applications some more consideration. Web mining is about mining the data on the web to make it more manageable for the user by making associations and patterns or it is about mining the usage patterns to help not only the users (i.e., consumers) to carry out e-commerce but also to support the e-commerce sites, the brokers, and the merchants.

First let us reconsider the information provided in Chapter 9. Corporations want to have the competitive edge and are exploring numerous ways to market effectively. Major corporations including retail stores have e-commerce sites and customers can now order products from books to clothing to toys through these sites. A goal for the e-commerce sites is to provide customized marketing. For example, user group A may prefer literature novels whereas user group B may prefer mystery novels. Therefore, new literature novels have to be marketed to group A and new mystery novels have to be marketed to group B. An e-commerce site knows about these preferences by conducting data mining. The usage patterns have to be mined. In addition, the company may mine various public and private databases to get additional information about these users. This is why we included the data miner as part of the functional modules for an e-commerce site. An alternative is to embed the web-mining tool into the agent for the e-commerce site. This agent can be called the e-commerce server agent.

Web mining also helps the consumer by giving information about the various e-commerce sites, what are the best buys and also how consumers could bargain with the seller. Therefore, web miners are also part of the agents for the consumer. So, one could envisage a scenario where web mining tools are embedded into consumer agents and e-commerce agents. They could also be directly embedded into the consumers and e-commerce servers. Web mining could also be part of the brokers and mediators who do not act on behalf of anyone but carry out the functions of an honest broker. Note that we have differentiated between mediators and brokers as brokers are responsible for the brokering between consumers and e-commerce servers or between businesses in the case of business-to-business e-commerce. Mediators mediate between the two parties to resolve heterogeneity and other differences that have to be resolved before any brokering can be done.

Let us examine some specific web mining outcomes that will help e-commerce. With web mining one could form clusters of consumers. That is, members of group A are likely to buy toys (as they have children less than ten years old) and members of group B are likely to buy cosmetics (as they are teenaged girls). Another outcome is an association of the form if one sister prefers a certain brand of clothing then other sisters would also prefer the same brand. On the consumer side, data mining would provide the following type of information: check out company X's web site before purchasing the product from company Y.

As we mentioned in Chapter 9, not only can data mining help e-commerce sites as discussed in the previous paragraph, data mining can also help the users to find information on the web. Let us repeat what we mentioned in Chapter 9. One e-commerce site manager mentioned to us that the major problem he has is users finding his e-commerce site. He has advertised in various magazines, but those who don't have access to the magazines find it difficult to locate his site. One solution here is to have a third party agent making the connection between the site and the user.

There are many such agents on the web who make the connections between the buyer and the seller. For example if I want to buy real estate, I contact the agent. The agent associates me with the potential seller or even a real estate agent. Another solution would be to make the search engines more intelligent. Data mining could also help here. The data miner could take the requirements of the user and try and match the requirements to what is being offered by the e-commerce sites and connect the user to the right site. Work is beginning in this area and we still have a long way to go. We gave an illustration of data mining helping search engines in Figure 9-9. There are two approaches; one is to integrate the data miner with the search engine so that you get an intelligent search engine and this would be tight integration. The other approach is to have a data miner tool on the web that interacts with multiple search engines so that we get a loose integration between the search engine and the data miner. We illustrate a complete view of data mining for e-commerce in Figure 17-11. This figure illustrates both helping the server to carry out targeted marketing as well a helping the client to locate the server.

Another area of data mining that will be important to e-commerce is collaborative data mining. With e-business, corporations are going to work together to carry out business operations. Even within a corporation, different divisions may have to work together. We discussed the various distributed architectures and illustrated them in Chapter 16. The various e-commerce distributed databases have to be mined to extract information. There are two approaches here. One is to mine the individual data sources and then to put the pieces together to form the big picture as shown in Figure 17-12. The other is to carry out distributed data mining as shown in Figure 17-13. Some of the aspects of distributed data mining were discussed in [THUR98a]. Excellent research on this topic is being carried out by Guo et al. at Imperial College in London (see for example [GUO00]).

Closely related to data mining is decision support. As mentioned in Chapter 14 as well as earlier in this chapter, decision support tools have to be integrated with the e-commerce tools so that effective decisions can be made. Figure 17-14 illustrates e-commerce and decision support. One could also integrate the decision support tools with the data miners.

As discussed in Chapter 9, when more developments are made on data mining and the web, we can expect better tools to emerge on web mining both to mine the data on the web and to mine the usage patterns. We can expect to hear a lot about web mining in coming years.

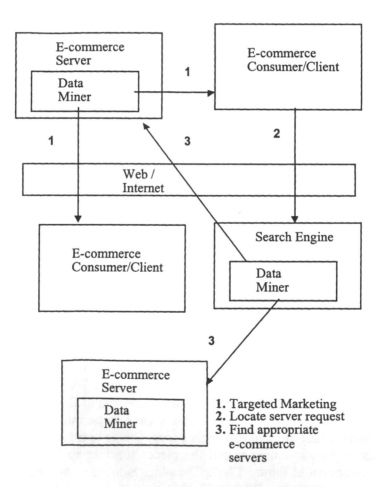

Figure 17-11. Data Mining and E-commerce

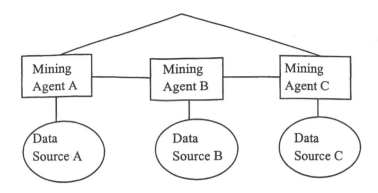

Figure 17-12. Collaborative Data Mining – Approach I

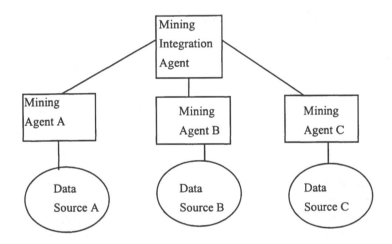

Figure 17-13. Collaborative Data Mining – Approach II

17.4 BUILDING AN E-COMMERCE ORGANIZATION

Now that we have given an introduction to e-commerce and dis-
cused the impact of information management technologies, let us see
how to go about setting up an e-commerce organization. Note that the
ideas presented here are those of the author and do not reflect any
official policies on setting up an e-commerce organization. Furthermore,
to get a complete picture one needs business specialists. Therefore, the
information given here is purely a technologist's point of view Nevertheless, the reader might find some of this information useful. However,
we urge the reader to consult a business specialist before embarking on

setting up an e-commerce organization. The information presented here
is merely suggestions.

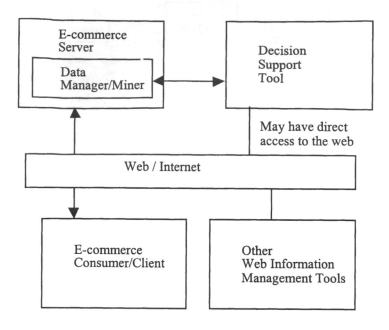

Figure 17-14. Decision Support and E-commerce

There are two aspects here. One is to build an e-commerce organization from scratch and the other is to migrate an existing organization
to an e-commerce-based organization. With the latter, we hear often
about companies spinning off subsidiaries to carry out e-commerce for
the corporation. That is, there is the corporation carrying out business as
usual and the spin-off is supposed to build the e-commence organization
for the corporation. In some ways spinning off an e-commerce organization may be like building an e-commerce organization from scratch.
Below we give our opinions on who the players may be and what
technologies and expertise may be needed for building an e-commerce
organization.

We have stressed in this book that to build an e-commerce organization you need the business specialists and the technologists. The
question is do you separate them into different groups and let them
communicate with each other as needed? On the one hand this may be
good, as it is hard for people with different skills to communicate.
However, we feel that to build an effective e-commerce organization we
need business specialists to be integrated with the technologists.

Figure 17-15 illustrates one approach to organizing the corporation to be effective as an e-commerce organization. You have the usual executives such as the CEO (chief executive officer), COO (chief operating officer), CFO (chief financial officer), CTO (chief technology officer) and CIO (chief information officer). In addition we have introduced a CKO (chief knowledge officer) who will be responsible for knowledge management, CWO (chief web officer) responsible for the corporate web technologies and CBO (chief business officer) who will be responsible for the e-business strategies for the company.

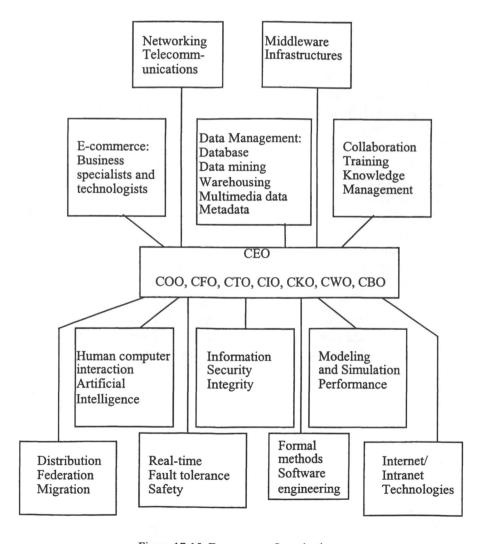

Figure 17-15. E-commerce Organization

There is the question as to whether we need all these officers or whether we can combine the responsibilities. For example, should the CIO have the role of CWO?

Then we have grouped the technical organizations in terms of technologies that we have discussed. A vice president, director, or a team leader, depending on the size of the corporation, could head each group. The e-commerce strategists and technologies are responsible for strategizing as well as investigating technologies. They have to communicate with each of the technology area directors. We have the following areas: data management, mining, and multimedia; collaboration, training and knowledge management; human computer interaction and artificial intelligence; infrastructure and middleware; networking and telecommunications; modeling, simulation and performance; information security and integrity; real-time processing, fault tolerance and safety; formal methods and software engineering; Internet and intranet technologies; and distribution, federations, and migration. The functions of each of these groups are fairly clear from the descriptions of the technologies in the previous chapters. For example, the Internet/Intranet group will ensure that the corporate information infrastructure policies are enforced. These could be timecard reporting on the Intranet, project management on the Intranet as well as carrying out internal business process functions such as logistics, sales, and purchasing on the Intranet. Some of these functions will be clearer when we address business processing and enterprise information management in Appendix C.[36] It is stated in [KRAS00] that learning from experiences and failures with ERP (Enterprise Resource Panning) will ensure e-business success.

Note that this book has addressed most of the technologies except formal methods and software engineering aspects. There has been much debate about the need for formal methods in software. We feel that it is always useful to have even a small group working in this area and examining issues like composability of systems and security and safety aspects. The software engineering team members may still be responsible for developing good software to carry out e-commerce. We have also mentioned that various aspects of middleware such as ORBs, transaction monitors, and message-oriented middleware may have to be integrated to provide a comprehensive capability for enterprise data management and application integration.

---

[36] Products such as SAP-AG's SAP provide complete support for enterprise business process management and enterprise resource planning. We discuss this in Appendix C as we believe that this will be one of the fastest growing areas for e-business for an organization. For a discussion of SAP we refer to [CURR98].

Once the players are set, then it is critical that the different groups communicate with each other. That is, to build an effective e-commerce organization, the different groups have to collaborate with each other. Another point to note is that it is not easy to put together an excellent group of business specialists and technologists because the demand for the professionals is so high that recruiting them will be hard. Since timely actions are critical for success, a suggestion is to start a program with what you have and slowly build the organization. Having the wrong talent could, however, be dangerous. This is where the upper management has to ensure that the right staff is recruited for the job. Even if one does not have all the staff, one also should think about contracting the work out.

17.5 SUMMARY

This chapter has examined the various web data and information management technologies discussed in Part II and described how they could be applied for e-commerce. These technologies include data management, collaboration, multimedia, training, and knowledge management. Finally we paid some special consideration for web mining in e-commerce. With the number of consumers and e-commerce sites growing almost exponentially in recent years and with revenues in e-commerce in billions of dollars at present, and expected to grow by at least twenty percent each year over the next few years at least, we need data mining tools to make the tasks of the consumers and e-commerce site managers as well as merchants easier. As web information management tools improve, we can expect significant progress to be made in e-commerce.

Now that we have described what e-commerce is all about, how information technologies could be applied for e-commerce, and how one can build an e-commerce organization with the technologies, we are now in a position to address two key information technologies for e-commerce and they are security and transactions. These topics will be addressed in Chapters 18 and 19, respectively.

CHAPTER 18

E-COMMERCE SECURITY

18.1 OVERVIEW

This chapter introduces one of the most important aspects of e-commerce and that is security. Since a major part or almost all of e-commerce security has to deal with web security, in this chapter we use the term e-commerce security and web security interchangeably. Some argue that web security encompasses e-commerce security as the web has to be secure to carry out secure e-commerce transactions.

We have found two sources of references to be excellent for e-commerce security. One is the book by Ghosh [GHOS98] where detailed discussions of the various threats and solutions to e-commerce security are given. Essentially the view that is taken here is the following: e-commerce security is web security The second reference we recommend is the tutorial notes on Java for E-commerce and E-commerce Security by Learning Tree International [LEAR99]. The latter reference gives a practical guide to implementing e-commerce security.

In Chapter 6 we provided an overview of data and information security. The issues and solutions discussed in that chapter apply for e-commerce also. That is, access to data has to be controlled and data integrity has to be maintained. In addition, there are numerous other security problems for e-commerce. This chapter will focus on these problems and discuss various solutions being proposed. The problems include access control violations, integrity violations, denial of service and infrastructure attacks, sabotage, and fraud on the Internet. The solutions combine the solutions proposed for operating system security, database security, network security, middleware security, and application security.

Note that in Chapters 16 and 17 we briefly discussed security issues and solutions. For example, we discussed trust issues in chapter 16 and also provided an overview of topics such as Java Wallet. Chapter 17 addressed security as part of our discussion on the application of information management technologies for e-commerce. In this chapter we elaborate on the discussions given previously.

The organization of this chapter is as follows. An overview of the various security problems will be given in Section 18.2. Solutions are discussed in Section 18.3. Essentially we state that we need end-to-end security. That is, the clients, the servers and the infrastructures have to be secure. Since network security is key to e-commerce security, and encryption and cryptography are essential for network security, we provide an overview of cryptography and digital signatures in Section 18.4. We have stressed over and over again the importance of Java for e-commerce. If e-commerce applications are to be programmed in Java, then Java security is critical. We discuss some aspects in Section 18.5. The chapter is summarized in Section 18.6.

18.2 SECURITY PROBLEMS FOR THE WEB

As mentioned in Section 18.1, there are numerous security threats that can occur due to the web. We discuss some of the web security threats in this section. These security threats are illustrated in Figure 18-1.

Access Control Violations: The traditional access control violations could be extended to the web. Users may access unauthorized data across the web. Note that with the web there is so much of data all over the place that controlling access to this data will be quite a challenge.

Integrity Violations: Data on the web may be subject to unauthorized modifications. This makes it easier to corrupt the data. Also, data could originate from anywhere and the producers of the data may not be trustworthy. Incorrect data could cause serious damages such as incorrect bank accounts, which could result in incorrect transactions.

Sabotage: We hear of hackers breaking into systems and posting inappropriate messages. For example, it is reported in [GHOS98] about the sabotage of various government web pages. One only needs to corrupt one server, client or network for the problem to cascade to several machines.

Fraud: With so much of business and commerce being carried out on the web without proper controls, Internet fraud could cause businesses to lose millions of dollars. Intruders could obtain the identity of legitimate users and through masquerading may empty the bank accounts.

Privacy: We have been stressing privacy throughout this book. With the web one can obtain all kinds of information collected about individuals. Also, data mining tools facilitate the compromise of privacy.

Denial of Service and Infrastructure Attacks: We hear about infrastructures being brought down by hackers. Infrastructures could be the telecommunication system, power system, and the heating system. These systems are being controlled by computers and often through the Internet. Such attacks would cause denial of service.

Other Threats: These include violations to confidentiality, authenticity, and nonrepudiation. Confidentiality violations enable intruders to listen in on the message. Authentication violations include using passwords without permissions, and nonrepudiation violations enable someone from denying that he sent the message.

The above are some of the threats. All of these threats collectively have come to be known as **cyberwar** or **cyberterrorism.** Essentially cyberwar is about corrupting the web and all of its components so that the enemy or adversary's system collapses. There is currently a lot of money being invested by the various government agencies in the US and Western Europe to conduct research on protecting the web and preventing cyberwars and cyberterrorism.

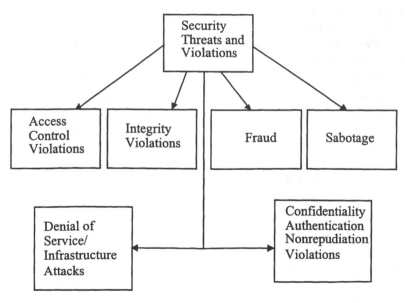

Figure 18-1. Security Threats/Violations

The web threats discussed here occur because of insecure clients, servers and networks. To have complete security, one needs end-to-end security; that means secure clients, secure servers, secure operating systems, secure databases, secure middleware and secure networks. There is a lot of emphasis these days on developing security solutions for clients, servers, databases, middleware, operating systems and networks. Programming languages such as Java and systems such as Microsoft's ActiveX are being made secure. Sophisticated encryption mechanisms are being developed for network security. We discuss some of the specifics in Sections 18.4 and 18.5. Overall approaches to security will be discussed in Section 18.3.

18.3 SECURITY SOLUTIONS FOR THE WEB

Figure 18-2 illustrates the various components that have to be made secure to get a secure web. We need end-to-end security and therefore the components include secure clients, secure servers, secure databases, secure operating systems, secure infrastructures, secure networks, secure transactions and secure protocols. One needs good encryption mechanisms to ensue that the sender and receiver communicate securely. Ultimately whether it be exchanging messages or carrying out transactions, the communication between sender and receiver or the buyer and the seller has to be secure. We discuss encryption in more detail in Section 18.4. Secure client solutions include securing the browser, securing the Java virtual machine, securing Java applets, and incorporating various security features into languages such as Java. Note that Java is not the only component that has to be secure. Microsoft has come up with a collection of products including ActiveX and these products have to be secure also. Securing the protocols includes secure HTTP, and the secure socket layer. Securing the web server means the server has to be installed securely as well as it has to be ensured that the server cannot be attacked. Various mechanisms that have been used to secure operating systems and databases may be applied here. Notable among them are access control lists which specify which users have access to which web pages and data. The web servers may be connected to databases at the backend and these databases have to be secure. Finally various encryption algorithms are being implemented for the networks, and groups such as OMG are envisaging security for middleware such as ORBs. Figure 18-3 illustrates various security solutions.

One of the challenges faced by the web managers is implementing security policies. One may have policies for clients, servers, networks, middleware, and databases. The question is how do you integrate these policies? That is how do you make these policies work together? Who is responsible for implementing these policies? Is there a global administrator or are there several administrators that have to work together?

Security policy integration is an area that is being examined by researchers.

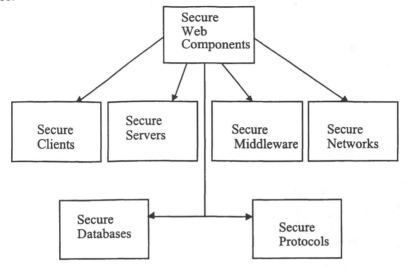

Figure 18-2. Secure Components

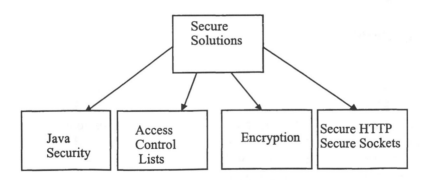

Figure 18-3. Security Solutions

Finally, one of the emerging technologies for ensuring that an organization's assets are protected is firewalls. Various organizations now have web infrastructures for internal and external use. To access the external infrastructure one has to go through the firewall. These firewalls examine the information that come into and out of an organization. This way, the internal assets are protected and inappropriate information may be prevented from coming into an organization. We can expect sophisticated firewalls to be developed in the future. The concept of a firewall is illustrated in Figure 18-4.

This section has briefly examined the various security solutions for the web. The next two sections will elaborate on two areas that are part of the security solutions. These are cryptography and Java security. Note that each of the solutions discussed here could be elaborated further. But a detailed discussion of security is beyond the scope of this book. For a discussion we refer to [GHOS98].

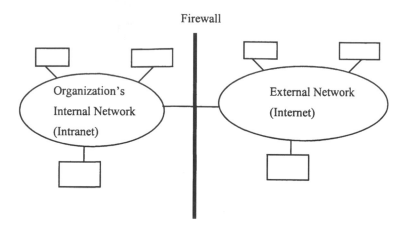

Figure 18-4. Firewalls

18.4 CRYPTOGRAPHY

Numerous texts and articles have been published on cryptography (see for example [DENN82]). Various tutorials have also been published [LEAR99]. In addition, annual cryptology conferences also take place. Yet cryptography is one of the areas that needs continuous research as the codes are being broken with powerful machines and sophisticated techniques. There are also many discussions on export/import controls on encryption techniques. This section will briefly provide an overview of some of the technical details of cryptography relevant to the web and therefore to e-commerce.

The main issue with cryptology is ensuring that a message is sent properly. That is, the receiver gets the message the way it was intended for him to receive. This means that the message should not be intercepted or modified. The issue can be extended to transactions on the web also. That is, transactions have to be carried out in the way they were intended to. Scientists have been working on cryptography for many decades. We hear about codes being broken during World War II. The study of code breaking has come to be known as cryptanalysis. In cryptography, essentially the sender of the message encrypts the message with a key. For example he could use the letter B for A, C for B, - - - - - A for Z. If the receiver knows the key, then he can decode this message. So a message with the word COMPUTER would be DPNQVUFS. Now this code is so simple and will be easy to break. The challenge in cryptography is to find a code that is difficult to break. Number theorists have been conducting extensive research in this area.

Essentially in cryptography encryption is used by the sender to transform what is called a plaintext message into ciphertext. Decryption is used by the receiver to obtain the plaintext from the ciphertext received. This is illustrated in Figure 18-5. Two types of cryptography are gaining prominence; one is public key cryptography where there are two keys involved for the sender and the receiver. One is the public key and is visible to everyone and the other is the private key. The sender encrypts the message with the recipient's public key. Only the recipient can decode this message with his private key. This method is illustrated in Figure 18-6. The second method is private key cryptography. Here both users have a private key. There is also a key distribution center involved. This center generates a session key when the sender and receiver want to communicate. This key is sent to both users in an encrypted form using the respective private keys. The sender uses his private key to decrypt the session key. The session key is used to encrypt the message. The receiver can decrypt the session key with his private key and then use this decrypted session key to decrypt the message. Private key cryptography is illustrated in Figure 18-7.

In the above paragraphs we have discussed just cryptography. The question is, how can we ensure that an intruder does not modify the message and that the desirable security properties such as confidentiality, integrity, authentication, and nonrepudiation are maintained? The answer is in message digest and digital signatures. Using hash functions on a message, a message digest is created. If good hash functions are used, each message will have a unique message digest. Therefore, even a small modification to the message will result in a completely different message digest. This way integrity is maintained. Message digests together with cryptographic receipts which are digitally signed ensure that the receiver knows the identity of the sender. That is, the sender may encrypt the message digests with the encryption techniques described in the previous paragraphs. In some techniques, the recipient may need the public key of the sender to decrypt the message. The recipient may obtain this key with what is called a certificate authority. The certificate authority should be a trusted entity and must make sure that the recipient can legitimately get the public key of the sender. Therefore, additional measures are taken by the certificate authority to make sure that this is the case. A complete security example with message digests, certificate authorities and digital signatures is given in [GHOS98] and [LEAR99]. Some of the essential points are illustrated in Figure 18-8.

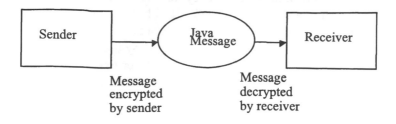

Figure 18-5. Encryption and Decryption

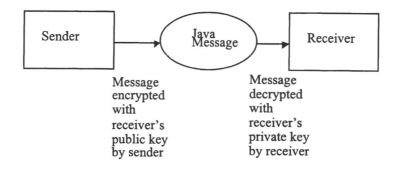

Figure 18-6. Public Key Cryptography

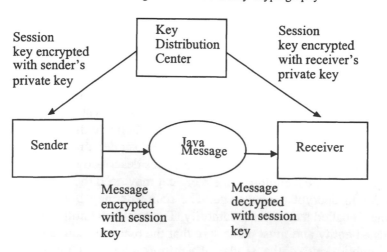

Figure 18-7. Private Key Cryptography

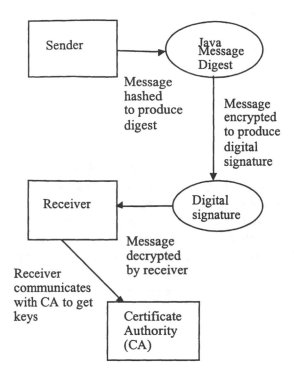

Figure 18-8. Message Digests and Digital Signatures

18.5 A NOTE ON JAVA SECURITY

Without a discussion of the details of the Java language it is difficult to do justice to all the useful security features of the Java language. Since this book is not about Java, we are not going to give the details. We only provide a high level overview of Java security features without discussing the actual constructs. For a detailed discussion we refer to [LEAR99] and [GHOS98].

First of all Java was developed with security in mind at the onset. Usually the trend is to develop a system and then look into security. However, since Java has essentially become the language for the Internet, it would have been nearly impossible to use it had security not been considered right from the beginning.

Java specifies constructs for many of the security features we discussed in the previous section. For example there are general classes for providing the security framework. There are interfaces to encryption algorithms. There are classes for managing certificates as well as access control lists. The interesting point in implementing the security features as classes is that one can separate implementation from the specification.

Later on, one could delete one implementation and replace it by another. Also, one could add more specifications and encryption algorithms. Essentially Java security is provided through the security API (application programming interface). This API has different parts for implementing various encryption algorithms.

While Java has security features, note that Java programs themselves have to be secure. This is another aspect of Java security. For example, Java applets may be downloaded from different machines and they could have embedded Trojan horses. If these programs are executing in the client's machine it could corrupt the client's machine. Therefore, the Java code has to be trusted. Furthermore, in many cases the Java applets have to execute in what is called a sandbox so that they cannot corrupt the local resources. There is a lot of work being reported on applying formal methods to ensure that the Java code is secure (see for example [OOPS98]). Figure 18-9 illustrates both aspects of Java security. This is a topic that will be active for the next several years.

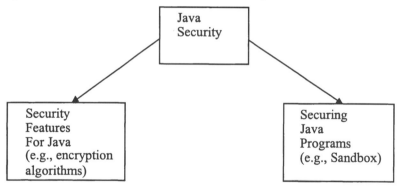

Figure 18-9. Two Aspects of Java Security

18.6 SUMMARY

This chapter has provided a brief overview of security threats and solutions for the web. We started with a discussion of the various threats including violations of integrity, confidentiality, access control, as well as threats such as sabotage and infrastructure attacks. Then we provided a general overview of the solutions. One needs end-to-end security and this means secure clients, servers, and networks. Then we discussed some specific solutions such as secure protocols and firewalls. Then we elaborated on two aspects and these were cryptography and Java security.

Security solutions for the web are in their infancy. We feel that it is only after the advent of the web, and essentially e-commerce, that organizations are very particular about security. Now that the new millennium is upon us and the scare about the Y2K is over, there are speculations that a lot of funding will be available to investigate solutions for the web and e-commerce security. This will come from both the government and the private sectors. We are in the beginning of perhaps one of the most exciting eras for information security in general and web security in particular.

Recently we have read about an emerging new area called quantum information processing that attempts to integrate principles of physics with computer science to develop novel cryptographic algorithms (see for example [IEEE00]). Furthermore biologists are working with computer scientists to use results from immunology to develop solutions for computer viruses. We feel that physicists, computer scientists, biologists and many others have to work together to develop effective solutions for the web and e-commerce security.

CHAPTER 19

E-COMMERCE TRANSACTIONS

19.1 OVERVIEW

The basic unit of an e-commerce function is a data transaction. Essentially any activity on the Internet such as purchasing a car, transferring funds, and negotiating a deal is carried out as a transaction. That is, banking and trading on the Internet will be implemented as a collection of transactions. Each data transaction could contain many tasks. For example, in a banking transaction, the tasks include logging into the system, checking the amount in account A, checking the amount in account B, and transferring X dollars from account A to account B. In the case of trading, the buyer logs into the e-commerce site, chooses the product, clicks on the product, gives his credit card number and then gets a receipt. Both these data transactions are illustrated in Figure 19-1 and 19-2. Note that part of the figure in 19-2 also appeared in Chapter 16 when we introduced the process of e-commerce.

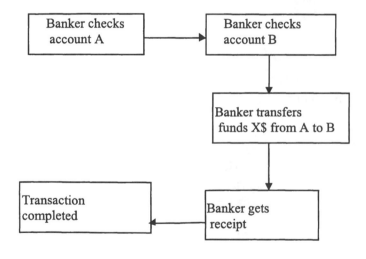

Figure 19-1. Banking on the Internet

In Chapter 2 we discussed a basic transaction. Transactions were revisited in Chapter 8. Database transactions are transactions that execute on databases. Database transactions often have to satisfy various properties such as the ACID properties discussed in Chapter 2. There are atomicity, consistency, isolation and durability. Concurrency control and recovery are two major concerns of database transactions. Database transactions may be built on top of the data transaction service on the web. That is, if the data managed by the web servers are stored in databases, then the data transactions essentially become database transactions.

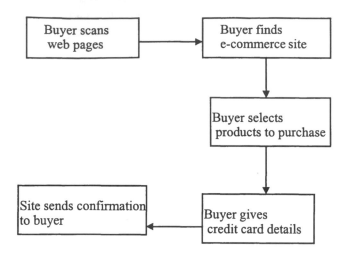

Figure 19-2. Trading on the Internet

The major focus of this chapter is data transactions. We discuss various types of data transactions and some approaches to handling them. Then we provide a note on database transactions. In particular, Section 19.2 describes data transactions while Section 19.3 addresses database transactions. The chapter is summarized in Section 19.4. Our discussion of data transactions is rather brief. A detailed discussion can be found in the book by [GHOS98].

19.2 DATA TRANSACTIONS

This section examines various aspects of data transactions. Two popular transaction payments systems are the Stored Account Payment and the Stored Valued Payment Systems. The Stored Account Payment Systems is about credit and debit card transactions as well as electronic payment systems. For example, systems where buyers give their credit cards are stored account payment systems. In the same way electronic payment systems use the user's bank account to transfer funds to purchase an item.

The stored value payment system is modeled after hard cash payment systems just as if we go to a shop and pay by cash. The essential point here is that there are user bearer certificates. These certificates represent cash and the user pays through certificates (essentially cash) for the goods. We illustrate both types of systems in Figure 19-3.

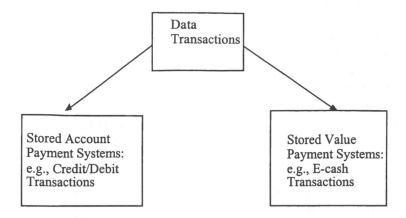

Figure 19-3. Payment Systems

The stored account payment systems essentially transfer funds between accounts through the Internet. For example, electronic banking has been around for a long time. What is new here is that this transaction is being carried out over the Internet instead of telephone lines only. This type of system is less difficult to trace if there are any problems. Therefore, adversaries can use the lack of tracing capability to carry out illegal activities. For example, if an adversary can get hold of a credit card number then he can use this card to purchase goods.

With the stored value payment system, the goal is to replace hard cash with e-cash. No approval from the bank is necessary as a user gives cash to get tokens or certificates. That is, the user purchases these certificates. We hear that this method of transaction on the web will be popular. However, there are still security risks as there is no controlling authority such as a bank to watch over the transaction. Therefore, researchers are examining the use of brokers and agents with this stored value payment system.

As stated in [GOSH98], various types of stored account payment systems and stored value payment systems are emerging in the form of products. These include systems such as *First Virtual, CyberCash,* and *Secure Electronic Transaction* for stored account payment systems and *E-cash, Cybercoin* and *Smartcard* for stored value payment systems.

Since we are hearing a lot abut e-cash, let us look at some of the details. As discussed by [GOS98], Electronic Cash (or e-cash) is stored in a hardware token. The token may be loaded with money such as digital cash from the bank. Buyer can make payments to seller's token (offline). Buyer can pay to seller's bank (online). Both cases agree upon protocols. There are security problems if traceability is difficult. Both parties may use some sort of cryptographic key mechanism discussed in Chapter 18 to improve security.

Before we end this section on data transactions, we describe a protocol stack for data transactions. This stack is illustrated in Figure 19-4. At the bottom layer is the TCP/IP protocol for transmission and the Internet. Then we have the socket protocol for socket communication. Then we have the HTTP protocol for the web. Finally we have the payment protocols. [37]

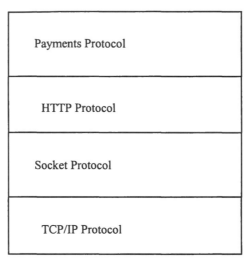

Figure 19-4. Protocols for transactions

19.3 DATABASE TRANSACTIONS

As stated in Chapter 8, transaction management is essential for many applications. There may be new kinds of transactions on the Internet. For example, various items may be sold through the Internet. In this case, the item should not be locked immediately when a potential buyer makes a bid. It has to be left open until several bids are received and the item is sold. That is, special transaction models are needed. Appropriate concurrency control and recovery techniques have to be developed for the transaction models.

Next let us examine web transactions. These transactions may be built on top of the data transactions. Protocols for the database transac-

---

[37] For more details we refer to [GHOS98]).

tions are illustrated in Figure 19-5. For example, database transaction protocols may be built on top of the payment protocols. This subject is still in the research stages. Consider the case where multiple users attempt to update a seller's e-cash token at the same time. This may cause consistency problems. We need some form of concurrency control mechanism. Recovery procedures are needed to handle failed transactions. Enforcing access control rules in transactions processing is also a challenge. That is, the transactions have to operate securely. Essentially in building database transactions, the challenges include concurrency control and recovery mechanisms suitable for the web.

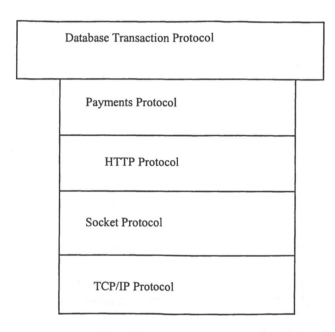

Figure 19-5. Protocols for Database Transactions

Finally let us examine some of the current technologies for e-commerce transactions. One can expect e-commerce transactions to be implemented as business objects based on an extension to the three-tier architecture illustrated in Figure 19-6 where there are four tiers. Clients are connected to TMs and Database servers via e-commerce business objects.

Note that agent technology also may play a role. That is, agents may carry out e-commerce transactions. Both stored account and stored value payment systems may apply here. Agents communicate with each other according to well-defined protocols. The directions for

e-commerce transactions include enhancing the data transactions we
have discussed, investigating the relationship between data and database
transactions, examining the use of technologies such as ORBs and TMs,
and finally integrating security into transaction processing. We also
need many of these transactions to execute in real-time. That is, these
transactions have to meet timing constraints. Consider a transaction that
has to purchase stocks for an investor so that the investor can make
maximum gains. Such a transaction must operate within a certain time
or the investor could lose a lot of money. We can expect to see much
development in this area in the future (see [THUR99b]).

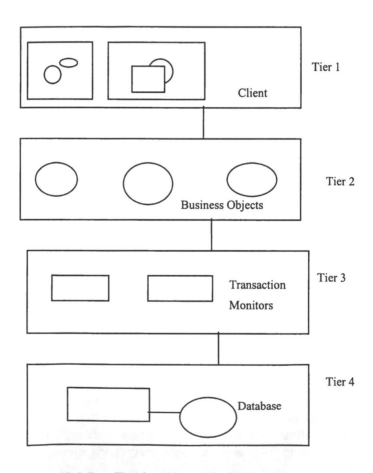

Figure 19-6. Four-Tiered Architecture for Database Transactions

19.4 SUMMARY

Finally we come to the end of this chapter on e-commerce transactions and therefore the end of our chapters on e-commerce. First we provided an overview of data transactions. Both stored account payment systems and stored value payment systems were discussed. We also gave examples of these systems. The next step was to discuss database transactions. We showed how database transactions may be built on top of data transactions. We need to integrate the technologies of Chapter 17 and security mechanisms of Chapter 18 to provide sophisticated and secure data transactions for e-commerce. We have made great strides, but there is still a lot to be done.

The future of e-commerce transactions will be to provide secure and reliable transactions. These transactions have to be timely also. For example, when you want to purchase stocks they have to be done in real-time else you could lose millions of dollars. Therefore, integrating security, real-time and fault tolerance mechanisms into transaction processing will be a challenge.

Conclusion to Part III

This brings us to the end of Part III that was all about e-commerce. Chapter 16 provided an introduction to e-business and e-commerce. In particular, process, models, functions, and architectures were described. Chapter 17 examined each web information management technology and showed how it could help e-commerce. E-commerce security, which is essentially web security, was discussed in Chapter 18. Finally, e-commerce transactions was the subject of Chapter 19.

As we have stressed in this book, technology is only one aspect of e-commerce. We need excellent business practices for e-commerce to succeed. This means that business specialists have to work with technologies. We also expect web information management to merge with e-commerce technologies to provide solutions for essentially e-business. As we have stated, e-business encompasses e-commerce and web information management.

One of the current trends is to integrate the e-commerce processes into enterprise resources planning tools. Some of the issues involved will be discussed in Appendix C. Chapter 20 will provide future directions for web information management as well as e-commerce.

CHAPTER 20

SUMMARY AND DIRECTIONS

20.1 ABOUT THIS CHAPTER

This chapter brings us to closure on this book *Web Data Management and Electronic Commerce*. We have discussed various supporting technologies for web data management, described the concepts and techniques for web data management, and provided an overview of some of the trends in electronic commerce. As stated throughout this book, web data management is an integration of multiple technologies, and has applications in e-commerce. This chapter summarizes the contents of this book and then provides an overview of the challenges and directions in web data management and in e-commerce. We also give the reader some suggestions on where to go from here.

The organization of this chapter is as follows. In Section 20.2 we summarize the contents of this book. Note that each of the Chapters 2 through 19 gave a summary at the end of the chapter. Essentially we have collected these summaries and put them together to form an overall summary of this book. Then in Section 20.3 we discuss the challenges and directions for web data management. In Section 20.4 we discuss the challenges and directions for e-commerce. Essentially, we consider the trends discussed in this book, and for each of the topics addressed, we have discussed future work in the area. One could argue that the directions are also part of the challenges. In addressing the directions, one needs to address the challenges also. Finally, in Section 20.5 we give suggestions to the reader as to where to go from here. Some of the key points in this book are reiterated, and then we encourage the reader to take the steps to make web data management and e-commerce a success.

20.2 SUMMARY OF THIS BOOK

Figure 20-1 duplicates Figure 1-7 to recap what we have described throughout this book. Chapter 1 provided an introduction to web data management and e-commerce. We first provided an introduction to web data management. We discussed data, information and knowledge. Then we provided a brief introduction to the web. Supporting technologies for web data management were described next. These included database systems, data mining, and interoperability, object management, and information security. Then we focused on data management related

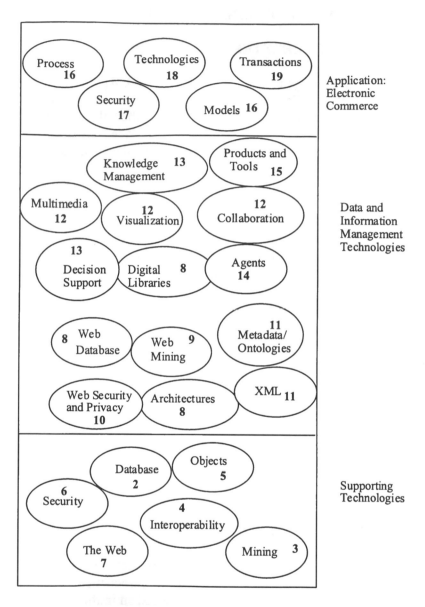

Figure 20-1. Topics Addressed in this Book

technologies for the web. In particular, web database management, web mining, security and privacy issues, metadata and ontologies, and emerging standards were discussed. The next topic was about emerging information technologies for the web which included knowledge management, distributed agents, multimedia and collaboration. Finally we discussed a key application area and that is electronic commerce.

Next we illustrated a framework for web data management and e-commerce and showed how we address the components of this framework in this book. The framework is a three-layer framework. Each layer was described in a part of this book. Part I, which describes the supporting technologies layer, consists of Chapters 2 through 7. Part II, which describes the web data and information management technologies layer, consists of Chapters 8 through 15, and Part III, which describes the trends in e-commerce, consists of Chapters 16 through 19. In the remainder of this section we summarize each of Chapters 2 through 19.

Chapter 2 has discussed various aspects of database systems and provided a lot of background information to understand the other chapters in this book. We began with a discussion of various data models. We chose relational and entity-relationship models as they are more relevant to what we have addressed in this book. Then we provided an overview of various types of architectures for database systems. These include functional and schema architectures. Note that we have focused on centralized systems. Next we discussed database design aspects and database administration issues. This chapter also provided an overview of the various functions of database systems. These include query processing, transaction management, storage management, metadata management, security, integrity, and fault tolerance. Finally we discussed briefly the impact of the web on database management.

Chapter 3 has provided an introduction to data mining. We first discussed various technologies for data mining, and then we provided an overview of the concepts in data mining. These concepts include the outcomes of mining, the techniques employed, and the approaches used. The directions and trends, such as mining heterogeneous data sources, mining multimedia data, mining web data, metadata aspects, and privacy issues, were addressed next. Finally, we provided an overview of data warehousing and its relationship to data mining as well as the impact of data mining on the web.

Chapter 4 has addressed various multi-database issues. We started with a discussion of distributed databases and then addressed heterogeneity. Federated database management was the next topic. This was followed by a discussion of client-server-based interoperability. Finally we addressed legacy database issues as well as discussed some other types of middleware. For each type of multi-database system we described the impact of the web. As stated in this chapter as well as in the previous chapters, the numerous databases on the web have to be integrated and eventually mined to get useful information.

Object technology plays a major role with database integration. The various types of object technologies were the subject of Chapter 5. Essentially this chapter has summarized some of the important object technology developments that have taken place over the past three decades. We started with object models, the very essence of object technology. Then we discussed the evolution of OOPLs. This was followed by a discussion of various types of object database systems. Object-oriented design and analysis was given some consideration. Next we provided an overview of distributed object management. Finally the emerging area of frameworks and components was discussed. The impact of this technology on the web is tremendous.

Chapter 6 has provided a brief overview of the developments in secure systems. We first discussed basic concepts in access control as well as in discretionary and mandatory policies. Then, we provided an overview of secure systems. In particular secure operating systems, secure databases, secure networks, and secure distributed systems were discussed. Next we provided some details on secure databases. Finally we discussed some research trends and the impact of the web.

While Chapters 2 through 6 discussed supporting technologies, Chapter 7 provided an overview of the web itself. We started with a discussion of the evolution of the web and then discussed the importance of Java technology for the web. This was followed by a discussion of hypermedia technologies for the web. Next we provided an overview of the World Wide Web Consortium and then discussed the notion of Corporate Information Infrastructures. With this we ended Part I of this book.

We started Part II with Chapter 8. This chapter provided a broad overview of the developments and challenges on web database management. We first gave an introduction to accessing databases on the web and then gave an overview of JDBC. We also described an example application and that is a digital library. Next we discussed data modeling for web databases. This was followed by a discussion of the functions. Finally we described architectural aspects. Several issues were addressed including architectures for database access, three-tier computing, interoperability, migration, client-server paradigm, push/pull computing and the federated model.

Chapter 9 has discussed the emerging topic of web data mining. First we provided some of the challenges in mining Internet databases which include building warehouses as well as mining multimedia databases. Then we discussed how mining could facilitate the user in browsing the web. Finally we discussed major applications in electronic commerce.

Chapter 10 was devoted to the important area of security and privacy related to the web as well as privacy issues for data mining. First, we gave an overview of the inference problem and then discussed approaches to handle this problem that result from mining. Warehousing and inference issues were also discussed. Then we provided an overview of the privacy issues. Finally we discussed some general security measures for the web.

Chapter 11 was devoted to a discussion of web metadata management and mining. We first provided an overview of the various types of metadata, and then discussed metadata management on the web. Since mining metadata is critical for web data management as one can extract, say, usage patterns by mining metadata, we then discussed metadata mining. Metadata is the central component to many kinds of information systems such as decision support systems, database systems, and machine learning systems. We ended this chapter with a discussion of XML and ontologies.

In Chapter 12, we have described numerous technologies for web data management. First we provided a fairly detailed discussion of collaboration and multimedia. With respect to collaboration we gave examples, discussed the data management needs, focused on a specific type of collaborative application and that is workflow and then described the impact of the web on collaboration. Our discussion on multimedia focused on multimedia data management. It included a discussion of architectures, data models and functions were discussed. Then we paid some attention to multimedia data mining, as this will be an important function for the web. Finally we discussed the impact of the web and described the need for multimedia on the web for applications such as entertainment and training. Then we provided an overview of a number of technologies for the web. We started with a discussion of computer-based training and distance learning. Next we discussed real-time processing and high performance computing. Visualization on the web was the next subject. We discussed issues on integrating visualization tools with databases and data mining systems to better understand the results. Next we focused on Quality of Service. Finally we discussed various other technologies such as knowledge management, decision support and agents and these last three topics were elaborated in Chapters 13 and 14.

Chapter 13 has described two key technologies for the web. They are knowledge management and decision support. We explained what these terms were, the various developments and described the impact of the web. Chapter 14 has provided a brief overview of agents and discussed how they operate on the web. We first defined an agent and then discussed various types of agents and their functions. Agent architecture and communication aspects were described next. Finally we provided an overview of mobile agents and ended with a discussion of information dissemination. Chapter 15 provided an overview of the various tools for information management on the web. We discussed various types of information management technologies, and from each type selected a tool to describe the essential concepts. This ended Part II of this book.

We started Part III with Chapter 16. This chapter has given a broad overview of e-commerce. We started with a discussion of the e-commerce process, which was followed, by a discussion of the differences between e-business and e-commerce. Then we described models, architectures and functions for e-commerce. We also discussed the application of Java as well as telecommunications for e-commerce. Finally we provided an overview of some of the legal and ethical considerations for e-commerce.

Chapter 17 has examined the various web data and information management technologies discussed in Part II and described they could be applied for e-commerce. These technologies include data management, collaboration, multimedia, training, and knowledge management. Finally we paid some special consideration for web mining in e-commerce.

Chapter 18 has provided a brief overview of security threats and solutions for the web. We started with a discussion of the various threats including violations of integrity, confidentiality, access control, as well as threats such as sabotage and infrastructure attacks. Then we provided a general overview of the solutions. One needs end-to-end security and this means secure clients, servers, and networks. Then we discussed some specific solutions such as secure protocols and firewalls. Then we elaborated on two aspects and these were cryptography and Java security.

In Chapter 19, we provided an overview of data transactions. Both stored account payment systems and stored value payment systems were discussed. We also gave examples of these systems. The next step was to discuss database transactions. We showed how database transactions may be built on data transactions. With this we ended Part III of this book.

20.3 CHALLENGES AND DIRECTIONS IN WEB DATA MANAGEMENT

This section examines each chapter in Part II and discusses future directions. In the area of web database management one of the major challenges is scalability. That is, how do you efficiently access large quantities of data on the web? Other challenges include enhancing the traditional database technologies for the web such as query strategies, transaction management, indexing, security and integrity. We need novel architectures for the web. OMG's ORB-based infrastructures are just one aspect. Component-based plug and play technologies as well as integration of ORB-based middleware with, say, Transaction Monitors as well as Message Oriented Middleware may be the direction.

In the area of web mining there are two aspects. First, how do you mine all the data out there and extract useful information and the other is mining to help e-business. We need better mining tools to work with the web. Mining for the e-business will be one of the major directions in information technology. Security and privacy aspects for web mining will also be given some consideration in the future.

XML and Ontologies will continue to explode. Numerous extensions to XML have been proposed and while there will be some type of XML-like language, we could expect to see a radical change when various extensions are combined. The support for complex data structures in XML will be important.[38] In addition to XML and Ontologies, various other aspects of metadata management will be given prominence. The definition metadata will continue to evolve.

Other directions in web data management include better tools for knowledge management, collaboration, decision support and training. Currently these terms are rather vague. We can expect to see standard definitions emerge. Tools for enterprise data management and enterprise application integration will emerge. Finally support for organizations to share and collaborate with each other as well as form partnerships will be critical.

Figure 20-2 illustrates some of the directions for web data/information management. In addition to all of the above areas, we believe that it is time to focus on the foundational aspects. Is there some sort of theory upon which web based systems can be built? For example, XML has origins in areas like the lambda calculus and theoreticians are continuing to pursue in this direction. Query processing and transaction management is built on various theories in general. Do these theories apply for the web also? We need extensive research in this area.

---

[38]   I thank Rich Byrnes for pointing out the need for object representation capability for XML.

20.4 CHALLENGES AND DIRECTIONS FOR E-COMMERCE

Each of the web data management technologies discussed in this book and their future developments will have a significant impact on e-commerce. More and more organizations will be involved in e-commerce. Some other organizations will become involved in e-business. We can expect clearer definitions for e-commerce and e-business to emerge.

To provide better support for e-commerce we need developments in web database management, web mining, knowledge management, collaboration, metadata management, multimedia information management and many of the other technologies discussed in this book. Some of the directions for the technologies were discussed in Section 20.3.

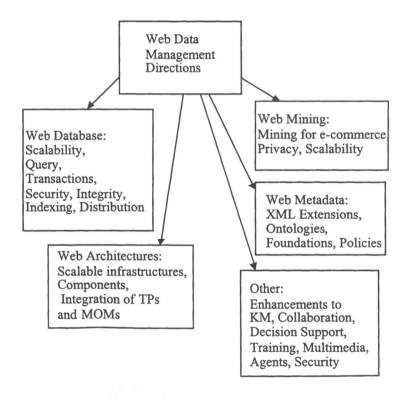

Figure 20-2. Web Data Management Directions

We addressed two aspects of e-commerce. One is e-commerce security and the other is e-commerce transaction. Now that we have entered the new millennium and much of our fear of the Year 2000 problem is over, we can expect to see many developments in e-commerce security. Various research programs are being established in the US and in Western Europe. We need more than information technology. Physicists, biologists, mathematicians and computer scientists will have to work together to produce security solutions for the web.

E-commerce transactions will continue to evolve. In addition to technological advances we also need organizational advances. E-commerce is a new way of doing business. Therefore, many of the business schools do not yet address e-commerce. We can expect to see major programs mainly in business schools combined with information technology to teach e-commerce. Policies and procedures for credit card transactions have to be established. Then these procedures have to be implemented.

Figure 20-3 illustrates directions for e-commerce. Essentially e-commerce and web data management will merge into e-business and this is illustrated in Figure 20-4.

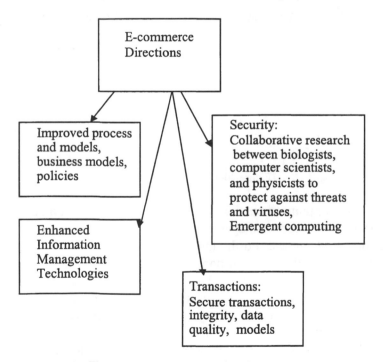

Figure 20-3. E-commerce Directions

20.5 WHERE DO WE GO FROM HERE?

We have provided a broad overview of web data management and e-commerce and discussed technologies, techniques, tools and trends. We have also given many references should the reader need in-depth coverage of a particular topic. However, all the reading is not going to give the reader a better appreciation for what web data management is all about. It is certainly useful to have a good knowledge in web data management and be able to speak intelligently about it. However, if you want to know what technique works, what are the limitations of an algorithm, or how you want to conduct e-commerce, then you need hands-on experience with the tools. As in the case of many technologies, web data management gets better with practice; we urge the reader to work with practical applications in using the web data management tools as well as, if possible, with developing the tools.

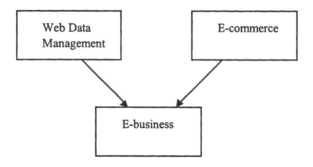

Figure 20-4. Evolution of E-business

Another point to note is that when you want to start an e-commerce project, you need management buy-in. This means financial and personnel resources. Furthermore, you need to decide whether to contract the work or have it done in-house. If you are using a commercial tool, then you need to have frequent communication with the developer. In other words, the customer, the e-commerce tool/solutions developer, and those who carry out e-commerce have to work very closely together, or else the project may be a failure.

This book has also given some brief information about web data management tools. As we have stressed, we have selected these products only because of our familiarity with them. We are not endorsing any of the products. Furthermore, due to the rapid developments in the field, the information about these products may soon be outdated.

Therefore, we urge the reader to take advantage of the various commercial and research material available on these products.

We believe that there are exciting opportunities in e-commerce with the emergence of new web data management technologies. Furthermore, technology integration, such as integration of data management, data mining, objects, and security, is making a lot of progress. As the user gets flooded with more and more data and information, the need to analyze this information, give only the information the user needs, and extract previously unknown information to help the user in the decision making process will become urgent. Also, various laws and policies will be clearer with e-commerce, and corporations as well as consumers will soon become familiar with the process of e-commerce. We can also expect universities to offer special courses and specialization certificates on e-commerce. We feel that the opportunities and challenges in web data management, in general, and e-commerce, in particular, will be endless. Let us stress the key points illustrated in Figure 20-5.

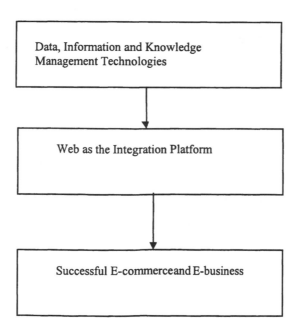

Figure 20-5. The Future

- The web will be the integration platform for all types of data, information and knowledge management technologies.

- The various data, information and knowledge management technologies have to work with the web. This will include database access through the web and collaboration on the web.
- We need infrastructures for the web to support the various data, information and knowledge management technologies.
- E-commerce and e-business will thrive only if we establish the web as the integration platform successfully.
- We need research and development programs to enable the web to be the integration platform. This means that whenever we conduct research on data, information and knowledge management technologies, we cannot ignore the web.

References

REFERENCES

[ACM90] Special Issue on Heterogeneous Database Systems, ACM Computing Surveys, September 1990.

[ACM91a] Special Issue on Next Generation Database Systems, Communications of the ACM, October 1991.

[ACM91b] Special Issue on Computer Supported Cooperative Work, Communications of the ACM, December 1991.

[ACM94] Proceedings of the ACM Multimedia Database System Workshop, October 1994.

[ACM95] Special Issue on Digital Libraries, Communications of the ACM, May 1995.

[ACM96a] Special Issue on Data Mining, Communications of the ACM, November 1996.

[ACM96b] Special Issue on Electronic Commerce, Communications of the ACM, June 1996.

[ACM97] Special Issue on Components and Frameworks, Communications of the ACM, October 1997.

[ACM99] Communications of the ACM, May 1999.

[ADRI96] Adriaans, P. and Zantinge, D., "Data Mining," Addison-Wesley, MA, 1996.

[AFCE97] Proceedings of the First Federal Data Mining Symposium, Washington D.C., December 1997.

[AFSB83] Air Force Summer Study Board Report on Multilevel Secure Database Systems, Department of Defense Document, 1983.

[AGRA93] Agrawal, A. et al., "Database Mining a Performance Perspective," IEEE Transactions on Knowledge and Data Engineering, Vol. 5, December 1993.

[AIPA95] Proceedings of the Symposium on Advanced Information Processing and Analysis, Tysons Corner, March 1995.

[AIPA96] Proceedings of the Symposium on Advanced Information Processing and Analysis, Tysons Corner, March 1996.

[ALON96] Alonso, G. et al., "Exotica/FDMC: A Workflow Management System for Mobile and Disconnected Clients," Distributed and Parallel Databases Journal, 1996.

[BANE87] Banerjee, J. et al., "A Data Model for Object-Oriented Applications," ACM Transactions on Office Information Systems, Vol. 5, 1987.

[BEA] http://www.beasys.com/products/weblogic/.

[BELL75] Bell, D. and L. LaPadula, "Secure Computer Systems: Unified Exposition and Multics Interpretation," Technical Report No: ESD-TR-75-306, Hanscom Air Force Base, Bedford, MA, 1975.

[BELL92] Bell, D. and Grimson, J., "Distributed Database Systems," Addison-Wesley, MA, 1992.

[BENS95] Bensley, E. et al., "Evolvable Systems Initiative for Real-time Command and Control Systems," Proceedings of the 1st IEEE Complex Systems Conference, Orlando, FL, November 1995.

[BENY90] Benyon, D., "Information and Data Modeling," Blackwell Scientific Publications, Oxford, UK, 1990.

[BERN87] Bernstein, P. et al., "Concurrency Control and Recovery in Database Systems," Addison-Wesley, MA, 1987.

[BERR97] Berry, M. and Linoff, G., "Data Mining Techniques for Marketing, Sales, and Customer Support," John Wiley, NY, 1997.

[BERT97] Bertino, E. and S. Jajodia, "Secure Concurrency Control," IEEE Transactions on Knowledge and Data Engineering, 1997.

[BROD95] Brodie M. and Stonebraker, M., "Migrating Legacy Databases," Morgan Kaufmann, CA, 1995.

[BUSI] Business Week, Asian Edition, December 1999.

[CATT91] Cattel, R., Object Data Management Systems, Addison-Wesley, MA, 1991.

[CERI84] Ceri, S. and Pelagatti, G., "Distributed Databases, Principles and Systems," McGraw-Hill, NY, 1984.

[CHEN76] Chen, P., "The Entity Relationship Model - Toward a Unified View of Data," ACM Transactions on Database Systems, Vol. 1, 1976.

[CHES94] Cheswick, W. and S. Bellovin, "Firewalls and Internet Security: Repelling the Wily Hacker," Addison-Wesley, MA, 1994

[CHOR94] Chorafas, D., "Intelligent Multimedia Databases," Prentice-Hall, NJ, 1994.

[CLIF96] Clifton, C., "Text Mining," Private Communication, Bedford, MA, January 1996.

[CLIF97] Clifton, C., "Privacy Issues for Data Mining," Private Communication, Bedford, MA, April 1998.

[CLIF98] Clifton, C., "Image Mining," Private Communication, Bedford, MA, July 1998.

[CLIF99a] Clifton C., "Data Mining and Security," Proceedings of the IFIP Conference on Database Security, Seattle, July 1999.

[CLIF99b] Clifton, C., "Data Mining for Intrusion Detection," IFIP 1999 Database Security Conference Panel, July 1999.

[CODD70] Codd, E. F., "A Relational Model of Data for Large Shared Data Banks," Communications of the ACM, Vol. 13, 1970.

[COOL98] Cooley, R., "Taxonomy for Web Mining," Private Communication, Bedford, MA, August 1998.

[CORR99] Corradi, A., R. Montanari and C. Stefanelli, "Security Issues in Mobile Agent Technology," Proceedings of IEEE FTDCS, Cape Town, December 1999.

[CURR98] Curran, T., G. Keller and A. Ladd, "SAP R/3 Business Blueprint," Prentice-Hall, 1998

[DATE90] Date, C. J., "An Introduction to Database Management Systems," Addison-Wesley, MA, 1990 (6th edition published in 1995 by Addison-Wesley).

[DAVE97] Davenport, T., "Working Knowledge: How Organizations Manage What They Know," Harvard Business School Press, 1997.

[DE98] Proceedings of the 1998 Data Engineering Conference, Orlando, FL, February 1998.

[DECI] Decision Support Journal, Elsevier/North Holland Publications.

[DENN] Denning, D., "Cryptography and Data Security," Addison-Wesley, 1982.

[DEUT99] Deutch, A. et al., "XML-QL: A Query Language for XML," http://w3c1.inria.fr/TR/1998/NOTE-xml-ql-19980819/.

[DIGI95] Proceedings of the Advances in Digital Libraries Conference, McLean, VA, May 1995 (Ed: N. Adam et al.).

[DIPI99] DiPippo, L., E. Hodys and B. Thuraisingham, "Towards a Real-time Agent Architecture: A White Paper," Proceedings of IEEE WORDS, Monterey, CA, 1999.

[DMH94] Data Management Handbook, Auerbach Publications, NY, 1994 (Ed: B. von Halle and D. Kull).

[DMH95] Data Management Handbook Supplement, Auerbach Publications, NY, 1995 (Ed: B. von Halle and D. Kull).

[DMH96] Data Management Handbook Supplement, Auerbach Publications, NY, 1996 (Ed: B. Thuraisingham).

[DMH98] Data Management Handbook Supplement, Auerbach Publications, NY, 1998 (Ed: B. Thuraisingham).

[DOD94] Proceedings of the DoD Database Colloquium, San Diego, CA, August 1994.

[DOD95] Proceedings of the DoD Database Colloquium, San Diego, CA, August 1995.

[ELMA85] Elmasri, R. et al., "The Category Concept: An Extension to the Entity Relationship Model," Data and Knowledge Engineering Journal, Vol. 1, 1985.

[FAYY96] Fayyad, U. et al. "Advances in Knowledge Discovery and Data Mining," MIT Press, MA, 1996.

[FELD95] Feldman, R. and Dagan, I., "Knowledge Discovery in Textual Databases (KDT)," Proceedings of the 1995 Knowledge Discovery in Databases Conference, Montreal, Canada, August 1995.

[FERA00] Ferarri, E. and B. Thuraisinham, "Database Security: Survey," To appear in Book on Advanced Databases by Artech House, 2000.

[FINI94] Finin, T., R. Fritzon, D. McKay and R. McEntire, "KQML as an Agent Communication Language," Proceedings of CIKM, 1994.

[FING00] Fingar, P., H. Kumar and T. Sharma, "Enterprise E-Commerce," Meghan Kiffer Press, 2000.

[FIPA98] FIPA 98 Specification, http://www.fipa.org/spec/fipa98.html.

[FIRE] Building Internet Firewalls Tutorial (author: B. Chapman) http://www.greatcircle.com/tutorials/bif.html

[FOWL97] Fowler, M. et al., "UML Distilled: Applying the Standard Object Modeling Language," Addison-Wesley, MA, 1997.

[FROS86] Frost, R., "On Knowledge Base Management Systems," Collins Publishers, U.K., 1986.

[GHOS98] Ghosh, A., "E-commerce Security, Weak Links and Strong Defenses," John Wiley, NY, 1998.

[GRAH99] Graham, J. and K. Decker, "Towards a Distributed Environment Centered Agent Framework," Proceedings of the International Workshop on Agent Theories, Languages, and Architectures," Orlando, July 1999.

[GRIN95] Grinstein, G. and Thuraisingham, B., "Data Mining and Visualization: A Position Paper," Proceedings of the Workshop on Databases in Visualization, Atlanta, GA, October 1995.

[GRUP98] Grupe, F. and Owrang, M., "Database Mining Tools", in the Handbook of Data Management Supplement, Auerbach Publications, NY, 1998 (Ed: B.Thuraisingham).

[GUO] Guo, Y., "Kensington Data Mining," http://ruby.doc.ic.ac.uk.

[HARV96] Harvard Business School Articles on Knowledge Management, Harvard University, 1996.

[HINK88] Hinke, T., "Inference and Aggregation Detection in Database Management Systems," Proceedings of the 1988 Conference on Security and Privacy, Oakland, CA, April 1988.

[IBM] IBM Zurich Research Laboratory, Private Communication, November 1999.

[ICTA97] Panel on Web Mining, International Conference on Tools for Artificial Intelligence, Newport Beach, CA, November 1997.

[IEEE89] "Parallel Architectures for Databases," IEEE Tutorial, 1989 (Ed: A. Hurson et al.).

[IEEE83] Special Issue in Computer Security, IEEE Computer, July 1983.

[IEEE91] Special Issue in Multidatabase Systems, IEEE Computer, December 1991.

[IEEE98] IEEE Data Engineering Bulletin, June 1998.

[IEEE99] Special Issue in Collaborative Computing, IEEE Computer, September 1993.

[IEEE00] Special Issue in Technologies for the Millennium, IEEE Computer, January 2000.

[IFIP] Proceedings of the IFIP Conference Series in Database Security, North Holland.

[IFIP97] Proceedings of the IFIP 1997 Conference Series in Database Security, North Holland (Panel on Data Warehousing and Data Mining Security).

[IFIP98] Proceedings of the IFIP 1998 Conference Series in Database Security, North Holland (Panel on Data Mining and Web Security).

[ILP97] Summer School on Inductive Logic Programming, Prague, Czech Republic, September 1998.

[INFO1] Information Week, November 1999.

[INFO2] Information World, December 1999.

[INMO93] Inmon, W., "Building the Data Warehouse," John Wiley and Sons, NY, 1993.

[JAVA] Java Programming Language, http://www.javasoft.com/.

[JDBC] Java Database Connectivity, http://java.sun.com/products/jdbc/index.html.

[JENS00] Jensen, D., Real-time Java, Proceedings of ISORC Symposium, New Port Beach, CA, March 2000.

[JONE99] Jones, S., "Collaborative Computing Workspace," Linux Journal, 1999.

[JUNG98] Junglee Corporation, "Virtual Database Technology, XML, and the Evolution of the Web," IEEE Data Engineering Bulletin, June 1998 (authors: Prasad and Rajaraman).

[KDD95] Proceedings of the First Knowledge Discovery in Databases Conference, Montreal, Canada, August 1995.

[KDD96] Proceedings of the Second Knowledge Discovery in Databases Conference, Portland, OR, August 1996.

[KDD97] Proceedings of the Third Knowledge Discovery in Databases Conference, Newport Beach, CA, August 1997.

[KDD98] Proceedings of the Fourth Knowledge Discovery in Databases Conference, New York, NY, August 1998.

[KDDN] http://www.kdnuggets.com/.

[KIM85] Kim, W. et al., "Query Processing in Database Systems," Springer-Verlag, NY, 1985.

[KORT86] Korth, H. and A. Silberschatz, "Database System Concepts," McGraw-Hill, NY, 1986.

[KRAS00] Krasner, H., "Ensuring E-business Success by Learning from ERP Failures," IEEE ITPro, February 2000.

[LEAR99] Java for E-commerce Security, Learning Tree International, Course Notes, July 1999.

[LLOY87] Lloyd, J., "Logic Programming," Springer-Verlag, Heidelberg, 1987.

[LOOM93] Loomis, M., "Object Databases," Addison-Wesley, MA, 1993.

[MAIE83] Maier, D., "Theory of Relational Databases," Computer Science Press, MD, 1983.

[MARS92] Marshak, R., "Workflow Computing," Patricia Seybold's Office Computing, 1992.

[MART99] Martin, D., A. Cheyer and D. Moran, "The Open Agent Architecture: Framework for Building Software System," Applied Artificial Intelligence, Vol. 13, 1999.

[MDDS94] Proceedings of the Massive Digital Data Systems Initiative Workshop, CMS Report, 1994.

[MERL97] Merlino, A. et al., "Broadcast News Navigation using Story Segments," Proceedings of the 1997 ACM Multimedia Conference, Seattle, WA, November 1998.

[META96] Proceedings of the 1st IEEE Metadata Conference, Silver Spring, MD, April 1996 (Originally published on the web, Editor: R. Musick, Lawrence Livermore National Laboratory).

[MICR] http://www.microsoft.com/COMMERCE/km/.

[MIT] Technical Reports on Data Quality, Sloan School, Massachusetts Institute of Technology, Cambridge, MA.

[MOBI97] Proceedings of the Workshop on Mobile Agents, Berlin, Germany, 1997.

[MORE98a] Morey, D., "Web Mining," Private Communication, Bedford, MA, June 1998.

[MORE98b] Morey, D., "Knowledge Management Architecture," Handbook of Data Management, Auerbach Publications, NY, 1998 (Ed: B. Thuraisingham).

[MORE00] Morey, D., M. Maybury and B. Thuraisingham (Editors) "Knowledge Management," MIT Press, 2000 (to appear).

[MORG87] Morgenstern, M., "Security and Inference in Multilevel Database and Knowledge Base Systems," Proceedings of the 1987 ACM SIGMOD Conference, San Francisco, CA, June 1987.

[NETG] http://www.netgen.com/.

[NSF95] Proceedings of the Database Systems Workshop, Report published by the National Science Foundation, 1995 (also in ACM SIGMOD Record, March 1996).

[NWOS96] Nwosu, K. et al. (Editors) "Multimedia Database Systems, Design and Implementation Strategies," Kluwer Publications, MA, 1996.

[ODI] http://www.odi.com/excelon/main.htm.

[ODBC] Open Database Connectivity, http://www.microsoft.com/data/odbc/default.htm.

[ODMG93] "Object Database Standard: ODMB 93," Object Database Management Group, Morgan Kaufmann, CA, 1993.

[OMG95] "Common Object Request Broker Architecture and Specification," OMG Publications, John Wiley, NY, 1995.

[ONTO] http://www-db.stanford.edu/LIC/HPKBtalk/sld002.htm.

[OOPS98] OOPSLA 98 Workshop on Formal Methods for Java, Van Couver, BC, 1998.

[ORAC1] http://www.oracle.com/database/oracle8i/.

[ORAC2] http://www.oracle.com/tools/webdb/.

[ORFA94] Orfali, R. et al., "Essential, Client Server Survival Guide," John Wiley, NY, 1994.

[ORFA96] Orfali, R. et al., "The Essential, Distributed Objects Survival Guide," John Wiley, NY, 1994.

[PAKD97] Proceedings of the Knowledge Discovery in Databases Conference, Singapore, February 1997.

[PAKD98] Proceedings of the Second Knowledge Discovery in Databases Conference, Melbourne, Australia, April 1998.

[PRAB97] Prabhakaran, B., "Multimedia Database Systems," Kluwer Publications, MA, 1997.

[ROSE99] Rosenthal, A., XML Presentation, 1999.

[SHET90] Sheth A. and J. Larson, "Federated Database Systems," ACM Computing Surveys, September 1990.

[SHET93] Sheth, A. and M. Rusinkiewicz, "On Transactional Workflows," IEEE Data Engineering Bulletin, Vol. 16, 1993.

[SIGM96] Proceedings of the ACM SIGMOD Workshop on Data Mining, Montreal, Canada, May 1996.

[SIGM98] Proceedings of the 1998 ACM SIGMOD Conference, Seattle, WA, June 1998.

[SIMO95] Simoudis, E. et al., "Recon Data Mining System," Technical Report, Lockheed Martin Corporation, 1995.

[SQL3] "SQL3," American National Standards Institute, Draft, 1992 (a version also presented by J. Melton at the Department of Navy's DISWG NGCR meeting, Salt Lake City, UT, November 1994).

[THUR87] Thuraisingham, B., "Security Checking in Relational Database Systems Augmented by an Inference Engine," Computers and Security, Vol. 6, 1987.

[THUR89] Thuraisingham, B., "Security for Object-Oriented Database Systems," Proceedings of the ACM OOPSLA Conference, 1989.

[THUR90a] Thuraisingham, B., "Recursion Theoretic Properties of the Inference Problem," MITRE Report, June 1990 (also presented at the 1990 Computer Security Foundations Workshop, Franconia, NH, June 1990).

[THUR90b] Thuraisingham, B., "Nonmonotonic Typed Multilevel Logic for Multilevel Secure Database Systems," MITRE Report, June 1990 (also published in the Proceedings of the1992 Computer Security Foundations Workshop, Franconia, NH, June 1991).

[THUR90c] Thuraisingham, B., "Novel Approaches to Handle the Inference Problem," Proceedings of the 1990 RADC Workshop in Database Security, Castile, NY, June 1990.

[THUR91a] Thuraisingham, B., Security for Distributed Database Systems, Computers and Security, 1991.

[THUR91b] Thuraisingham, B., "On the Use of Conceptual Structures to Handle the Inference Problem," Proceedings of the 1991 IFIP Database Security Conference, Shepherdstown, WV, November 1991.

[THUR93] Thuraisingham, B. et al., "Design and Implementation of a Database Inference Controller," Data and Knowledge Engineering Journal, North Holland, Vol. 8, December 1993.

[THUR94] Thuraisingham, B., "Security for Federated Database Systems, Computers and Security," 1994.

[THUR95] Thuraisingham, B. and Ford, W., "Security Constraint Processing in a Multilevel Secure Distributed Database Management System," IEEE Transactions on Knowledge and Data Engineering, Vol. 7, 1995.

[THUR96a] Thuraisingham, B., "Internet Database Management," Database Management, Auerbach Publications, NY, 1996.

[THUR96b] Thuraisingham, B., "Data Warehousing, Data Mining, and Security," Proceedings of the 10th IFIP Database Security Conference, Como, Italy, 1996 (Version I).

[THUR96c] Thuraisingham, B., "Interactive Data Mining and the World Wide Web," Proceedings of Compugraphics Conference, Paris, France, December 1996.

[THUR97] Thuraisingham, B., " Data Management Systems Evolution and Interoperation," CRC Press, FL, May 1997.

[THUR98a] Thuraisingham, B., "Data Mining: Technologies, Techniques, Tools and Trends," CRC Press, FL, December 1998

[THUR98b] Thuraisingham, B., "Data Warehousing, Data Mining, and Security," Keynote address at PAKDD, Melbourne, Australia, 1998.

[THUR99a] Thuraisingham, B., "Web Information Management and Electronic Commerce," AI Tools Journal, July 1999.

[THUR99b] Thuraisingham, B. and J. Maurer, "Information Survivability for Real-time Command and Control Systems," IEEE Transactions on Knowledge and Data Engineering, January 1999.

[THUR00] Thuraisingham, B., "A Primer for Understanding and Applying, Data Mining," IEEE ITPro, February 2000.

[TKDE93] Special Issue on Data Mining, IEEE Transactions on Knowledge and Data Engineering, December 1993.

[TKDE96] Special Issue on Data Mining, IEEE Transactions on Knowledge and Data Engineering, December 1996.

[TSIC82] Tsichritzis, D. and Lochovsky, F., "Data Models," Prentice-Hall, NJ, 1982.

[TSUR98] Tsur, D. et al., "Query Flocks: A Generalization of Association Rule Mining," Proceedings of the 1998 ACM SIGMOD Conference, Seattle, WA, June 1998.

[TURB97] Turban, E. and J. Aronson, "Decision Support Systems and Intelligent Systems," Prentice-Hall, NJ, 1997.

[ULLM88] Ullman, J. D., "Principles of Database and Knowledge Base Management Systems," Volumes I and II, Computer Science Press, MD, 1988.

[VIS95] Proceedings of the 1995 Workshop on Visualization and Databases, Atlanta, GA, October 1997 (Ed: G. Grinstein).

[VLDB98] Proceedings of the Very Large Database Conference, New York City, NY, August 1998.

[WDM99] Web Data Mining Workshop at KDD99, San Diego, 1999.

[WIDO98] Widom, J., "Lore DBMS," Stanford Database Workshop, 1998.

[WIED92] Wiederhold, G., "Mediators in the Architecture of Future Information Systems," IEEE Computer, March 1992.

[WOEL86] Woelk, D. et al., "An Object-Oriented Approach to Multimedia Databases," Proceedings of the ACM SIGMOD Conference, Washington, DC, June 1986.

[WOLF00] Wolfe, W., R. Johnston and B. Thuraisingham, "Real-time CORBA," To appear in IEEE Transactions on Parallel and Distributed Systems, 2000.

[XML1] http://www.W3c.org.

[XML2] http://www.xml.org/.

[YANG88] Yang, D. and T. Torey, "A Practical Approach to Transforming ER Diagrams into the Relational Model," Information Sciences, Vol. 42, 1988.

Appendices

APPENDIX A

DATA MANAGEMENT SYSTEMS:
DEVELOPMENTS AND TRENDS

A.1 OVERVIEW

In this appendix we provide an overview of the developments and trends in data management as discussed in our previous book *Data Management Systems Evolution and Interoperation* [THUR97]. Since data play a major role in web data management, a good understanding of data management is essential for web data management.

Recent developments in information systems technologies have resulted in computerizing many applications in various business areas. Data have become a critical resource in many organizations and therefore efficient access to data, sharing the data, extracting information from the data, and making use of the information have become urgent needs. As a result, there have been several efforts on integrating the various data sources scattered across several sites. These data sources may be databases managed by database management systems or they could simply be files. To provide the interoperability between the multiple data sources and systems, various tools are being developed. These tools enable users of one system to access other systems in an efficient and transparent manner.

We define data management systems to be systems that manage the data, extract meaningful information from the data, and make use of the information extracted. Therefore, data management systems include database systems, data warehouses, and data mining systems. Data could be structured data such as that found in relational databases or it could be unstructured such as text, voice, imagery, and video. There have been numerous discussions in the past to distinguish between data, information, and knowledge.[39] We do not attempt to clarify these terms. For our purposes, data could be just bits and bytes or it could convey some meaningful information to the user. We will, however, distinguish between database systems and database management systems. A database management system is that component which manages the database containing persistent data. A database system consists of both the database and the database management system.

A key component to the evolution and interoperation of data management systems is the interoperability of heterogeneous database

---

[39] More recently the area of knowledge management is receiving a lot of attention. We addressed knowledge management in Chapter 13. More details are given in [MORE98].

systems. Efforts on the interoperability between database systems were reported since the late 1970s. However, it is only recently that we are seeing commercial developments in heterogeneous database systems. Major database system vendors are now providing interoperability between their products and other systems. Furthermore, many of the database system vendors are migrating towards an architecture called the client-server architecture which facilitates distributed data management capabilities. In addition to efforts on the interoperability between different database systems and client-server environments, work is also directed towards handling autonomous and federated environments.

The organization of this appendix is as follows. Since database systems are a key component of data management systems, we first provide an overview of the developments in database systems. These developments are discussed in Section A.2. Then we provide a vision for data management systems in Section A.3. Our framework for data management systems is discussed in Section A.4. Note that data mining, warehousing as well as web data management are components of this framework. Building information systems from our framework with special instantiations is discussed in Section A.5. The relationship between the various texts that we have written (or are writing) for CRC Press is discussed in Section A.6. This appendix is summarized in Section A.7. References are given in Section A.8.

A.2 DEVELOPMENTS IN DATABASE SYSTEMS

Figure A-1 provides an overview of the developments in database systems technology. While the early work in the 1960s focused on developing products based on the network and hierarchical data models, much of the developments in database systems took place after the seminal paper by Codd describing the relational model [CODD70]. Research and development work on relational database systems was carried out during the early 1970s and several prototypes were developed throughout the 1970s. Notable efforts include IBM's (International Business Machine Corporation's) System R and University of California at Berkeley's Ingres. During the 1980s, many relational database system products were being marketed (notable among these products are those of Oracle Corporation, Sybase Inc., Informix Corporation, Ingres Corporation, IBM, Digital Equipment Corporation, and Hewlett Packard Company). During the 1990s, products from other vendors have emerged (e.g., Microsoft Corporation). In fact, to date numerous relational database system products have been marketed. However, Codd has stated that many of the systems that are being marketed as relational systems are not really relational (see, for example, the discussion in [DATE90]). He then discussed various criteria that a system must satisfy to be qualified as a relational database system. While the early work focused on issues such as data model, normalization theory, query processing and optimization strategies, query languages, and access strategies and indexes, later the focus shifted toward supporting a multi-user environment. In particular, concurrency control and recovery techniques were developed. Support for transaction processing was also provided.

Research on relational database systems as well as on transaction management was followed by research on distributed database systems around the mid-1970s. Several distributed database system prototype development efforts also began around the late 1970s. Notable among these efforts include IBM's System R*, DDTS (Distributed Database Testbed System) by Honeywell Inc., SDD-I and Multibase by CCA (Computer Corporation of America), and Mermaid by SDC (System Development Corporation). Furthermore, many of these systems (e.g., DDTS, Multibase, Mermaid) function in a heterogeneous environment. During the early 1990s several database system vendors (such as Oracle Corporation, Sybase Inc., Informix Corporation) provided data distribution capabilities for their systems. Most of the distributed relational database system products are based on client-server architectures. The idea is to have the client of vendor A communicate with the server database system of vendor B. In other words, the client-server computing paradigm facilitates a heterogeneous computing environment. Interoperability between relational and non-relational commercial database systems is also possible. The database systems community is also involved in standardization efforts. Notable among the standardization efforts are the ANSI/SPARC 3-level schema architecture,[40] the IRDS (Information Resource Dictionary System) standard for Data Dictionary Systems, the relational query language SQL (Structured Query Language), and the RDA (Remote Database Access) protocol for remote database access.

Another significant development in database technology is the advent of object-oriented database management systems. Active work on developing such systems began in the mid-1980s and they are now commercially available (notable among them include the products of Object Design Inc., Ontos Inc., Gemstone Systems Inc., Versant Object Technology). It was felt that new generation applications such as

---

[40] ANSI stands for American National Standards Institute. SPARC stands for Systems Planning and Requirements Committee.

multimedia, office information systems, CAD/CAM,[41] process control, and software engineering have different requirements. Such applications utilize complex data structures. Tighter integration between the programming language and the data model is also desired. Object-oriented database systems satisfy most of the requirements of these new generation applications [CATT91].

According to the Lagunita report published as a result of a National Science Foundation (NSF) workshop in 1990 [NSF90], relational database systems, transaction processing, and distributed (relational) database systems are stated as mature technologies. Furthermore, vendors are marketing object-oriented database systems and demonstrating the interoperability between different database systems. The report goes on to state that as applications are getting increasingly complex, more sophisticated database systems are needed. Furthermore, since many organizations now use database systems, in many cases of different types, the database systems need to be integrated. Although work has begun to address these issues and commercial products are available, several issues still need to be resolved. Therefore, challenges faced by the database systems researchers in the early 1990s were in two areas. One was next generation database systems and the other was heterogeneous database systems.

Next generation database systems include object-oriented database systems, functional database systems, special parallel architectures to enhance the performance of database system functions, high performance database systems, real-time database systems, scientific database systems, temporal database systems, database systems that handle incomplete and uncertain information, and intelligent database systems (also sometimes called logic or deductive database systems).[42] Ideally, a database system should provide the support for high performance transaction processing, model complex applications, represent new kinds of data, and make intelligent deductions. While significant progress has been made during the late 1980s and early 1990s, there is much to be done before such a database system can be developed.

41　CAD/CAM stands for Computer Aided Design/Computer Aided Manufacturing.

42　For a discussion of the next generation database systems, we refer to [SIGM90].

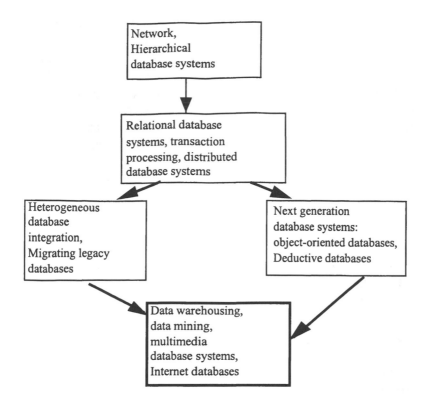

Figure A-1. Developments in Database Systems Technology

Heterogeneous database systems have been receiving considerable attention during the past decade [ACM90]. The major issues include handling different data models, different query processing strategies, different transaction processing algorithms, and different query languages. Should a uniform view be provided to the entire system or should the users of the individual systems maintain their own views of the entire system? These are questions that have yet to be answered satisfactorily. It is also envisaged that a complete solution to heterogeneous database management systems is a generation away. While research should be directed towards finding such a solution, work should also be carried out to handle limited forms of heterogeneity to satisfy the customer needs. Another type of database system that has received some attention lately is a federated database system. Note that some have used the terms heterogeneous database system and federated database system interchangeably. While heterogeneous database systems can be part of a federation, a federation can also include homogeneous database systems.

The explosion of users on the Internet and the web as well as developments in interface technologies has resulted in even more challenges for data management researchers. A second workshop was sponsored by NSF in 1995, and several emerging technologies have been identified to be important as we go into the twenty-first century [NSF95]. These include digital libraries, managing very large databases, data administration issues, multimedia databases, data warehousing, data mining, data management for collaborative computing environments, and security and privacy. Another significant development in the 1990s is the development of object-relational systems. Such systems combine the advantages of both object-oriented database systems and relational database systems. Also, many corporations are now focusing on integrating their data management products with Internet technologies. Finally, for many organizations there is an increasing need to migrate some of the legacy databases and applications to newer architectures and systems such as client-server architectures and relational database systems. We believe there is no end to data management systems. As new technologies are developed, there are new opportunities for data management research and development.

A comprehensive view of all data management technologies is illustrated in Figure A-2. As shown, traditional technologies include database design, transaction processing, and benchmarking. Then there are database systems based on data models such as relational and object-oriented. Database systems may depend on features they provide such as security and real-time. These database systems may be relational or object-oriented. There are also database systems based on multiple sites or processors such as distributed and heterogeneous database systems, parallel systems, and systems being migrated. Finally, there are the emerging technologies such as data warehousing and mining, collaboration, and the Internet. Any comprehensive text on data management systems should address all of these technologies. We have selected some of the relevant technologies and put them in a framework. This framework is described in Section A.5.[43]

---

[43] In our previous book *Data Management Systems Evolution and Interoperation* we selected certain topics in data management and explained the various concepts.

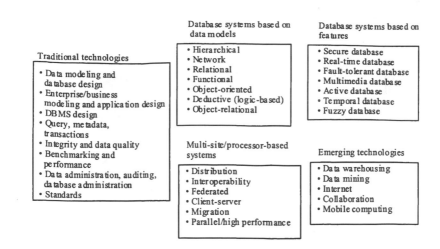

Figure A-2. Comprehensive View of Data Management Systems

A.3 STATUS, VISION AND ISSUES

Significant progress has been made on data management systems. However, many of the technologies are still stand-alone technologies as illustrated in Figure A-3. For example, multimedia systems are yet to be successfully integrated with warehousing and mining technologies. The ultimate goal is to integrate multiple technologies so that accurate data, as well as information, are produced at the right time and distributed to the user in a timely manner. Our vision for data and information management is illustrated in Figure A-4.

The work discussed in [THUR97] addressed many of the challenges necessary to accomplish this vision. In particular, integration of heterogeneous databases, as well as the use of distributed object technology for interoperability, was discussed. While much progress has been made on the system aspects of interoperability, semantic issues still remain a challenge. Different databases have different representations. Furthermore, the same data entity may be interpreted differently at different sites. Addressing these semantic differences and extracting useful information from the heterogeneous and possibly multimedia data sources are major challenges. This book has attempted to address some of the challenges through the use of data mining.

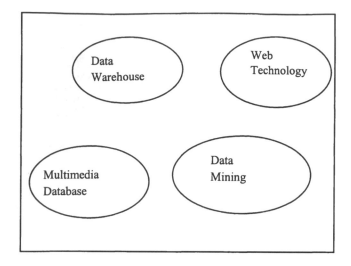

Figure A-3. Stand-alone Systems

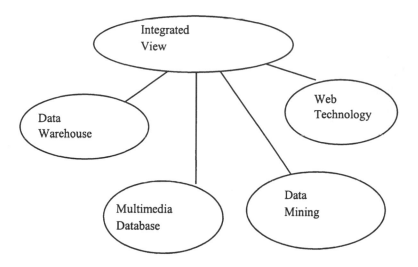

Figure A-4. Vision

A.4 DATA MANAGEMENT SYSTEMS FRAMEWORK

For the successful development of evolvable interoperable data management systems, heterogeneous database systems integration is a major component. However, there are other technologies that have to be successfully integrated with each other to develop techniques for efficient access and sharing of data as well as for the extraction of information from the data. To facilitate the development of data management systems to meet the requirements of various applications in fields such as medical, financial, manufacturing, and military, we have proposed a framework, which can be regarded as a reference model, for data management systems. Various components from this framework have to be integrated to develop data management systems to support the various applications.

Figure A-5 illustrates our framework, which can be regarded as a model, for data management systems.[44] This framework consists of three layers. One can think of the component technologies, which we will also refer to as components, belonging to a particular layer to be more or less built upon the technologies provided by the lower layer. Layer I is the Database Technology and Distribution Layer. This layer consists of database systems and distributed database systems technologies. Layer II is the Interoperability and Migration Layer. This layer consists of technologies such as heterogeneous database integration, client-server databases, and multimedia database systems to handle heterogeneous data types, and migrating legacy databases.[45] Layer III is the Information Extraction and Sharing Layer. This layer essentially consists of technologies for some of the newer services supported by data management systems. These include data warehousing, data mining [THUR98], Internet databases, and database support for collaborative applications.[46,47] Data management systems may utilize lower level technologies such as networking, distributed processing, and mass storage. We have grouped these technologies into a layer called the

---

[44] Note that this three-layer model is subjective and is not a standard model. This model has helped us in organizing our views on data management.

[45] We have placed multimedia database systems in Layer II, as we consider it to be a special type of a heterogeneous database system. A multimedia database system handles heterogeneous data types such as text, audio, and video.

[46] Note that one could also argue whether database support for collaborative applications should be discussed here. This is because collaborative computing is not part of the data management framework. However, such applications do need database support, and our focus has been on this support.

[47] Although Internet database management is an integration of various technologies, we have placed it in Layer III because it still deals with information extraction. *This is really the subject of this present book.* Note that the data management framework consists of technologies for managing data as well as for extracting information from the data. However, what one does with the information, such as collaborative computing, sophisticated human computer interaction, natural language processing, and knowledge-based processing, does not belong to this framework. They belong to the Application Technologies Layer.

Supporting Technologies Layer. This supporting layer does not belong to the data management systems framework. This supporting layer also consists of some higher-level technologies such as distributed object management and agents.[48] Also, shown in Figure A-5 is the Application Technologies Layer. Systems such as collaborative computing systems and knowledge-based systems which belong to the Application Technologies Layer may utilize data management systems. Note that the Application Technologies Layer is also outside of the data management systems framework.

The technologies that constitute the data management systems framework can be regarded to be some of the core technologies in data management. However, features like security, integrity, real-time processing, fault tolerance, and high performance computing are needed for many applications utilizing data management technologies. Applications utilizing data management technologies may be medical, financial, or military, among others. We illustrate this in Figure A-6, where a three-dimensional view relating data management technologies with features and applications is given. For example, one could develop a secure distributed database management system for medical applications or a fault tolerant multimedia database management system for financial applications. [49]

Integrating the components belonging to the various layers is important to developing efficient data management systems. In addition, data management technologies have to be integrated with the application technologies to develop successful information systems. However, at present, there is limited integration between these various components. Our previous book *Data Management Systems Evolution and Interoperation* focused mainly on the concepts, developments, and trends belonging to each of the components shown in the framework. Furthermore, our current book on web data management, which we also refer to as Internet data management, focuses on the Internet database component of Layer 3 of the framework of Figure A-5.

---

[48] Note that technologies such as distributed object management enable interoperation and migration.

[49] In some cases one could also consider multimedia data processing and reengineering which is an essential part of system migration to be at the same level as features like security and integrity. One could also regard them to be emerging technologies.

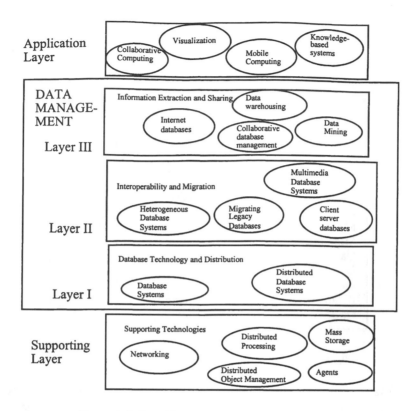

Figure A-5. Data Management Systems Framework

A.5 BUILDING INFORMATION SYSTEMS FROM THE FRAMEWORK

Figure A-5 illustrates a framework for data management systems. As shown in that figure, the technologies for data management include database systems, distributed database systems, heterogeneous database systems, migrating legacy databases, multimedia database systems, data warehousing, data mining, Internet databases, and database support for collaboration. Furthermore, data management systems take advantage of supporting technologies such as distributed processing and agents. Similarly, application technologies such as collaborative computing, visualization, expert systems, and mobile computing take advantage of data management systems.[50]

---

[50] Note that databases could also support expert systems as in the case of collaborative applications.

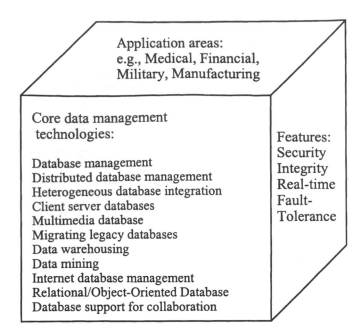

Figure A-6. A Three-dimensional View of Data Management

Many of us have heard of the term information systems on numerous occasions. These systems have sometimes been used interchangeably with data management systems. In our terminology, information systems are much broader than data management systems, but they do include data management systems. In fact, a framework for information systems will include not only the data management system layers, but also the supporting technologies layer as well as the application technologies layer. That is, information systems encompass all kinds of computing systems. It can be regarded as the finished product that can be used for various applications. That is, while hardware is at the lowest end of the spectrum, applications are at the highest end.

We can combine the technologies of Figure A-5 to put together information systems. For example, at the application technology level, one may need collaboration and visualization technologies so that analysts can collaboratively carry out some tasks. At the data management level, one may need both multimedia and distributed database technologies. At the supporting level, one may need mass storage as well as some distributed processing capability. This special framework is illustrated in Figure A-7. Another example is a special framework for interoperability. One may need some visualization technology to display the integrated information from the heterogeneous databases. At the data management level, we have heterogeneous database systems technology. At the supporting technology level, one may use distributed object management technology to encapsulate the heterogeneous databases. This special framework is illustrated in Figure A-8.

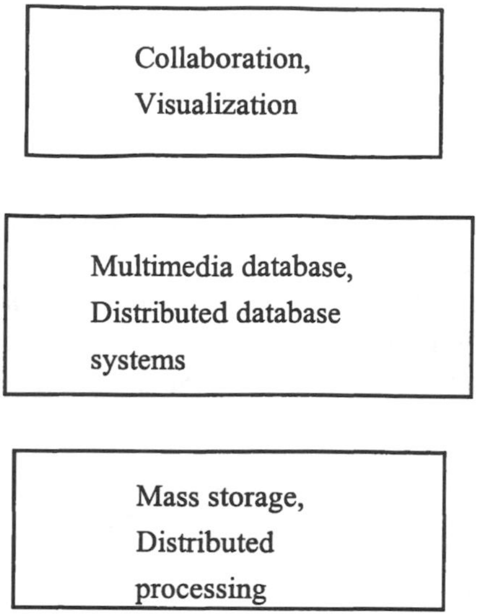

```
┌──────────────────────────────────────┐
│                                      │
│           Collaboration,             │
│           Visualization              │
│                                      │
└──────────────────────────────────────┘

    ┌──────────────────────────────────────┐
    │                                      │
    │      Multimedia database,            │
    │      Distributed database            │
    │      systems                         │
    └──────────────────────────────────────┘

    ┌──────────────────────────────────────┐
    │           Mass storage,              │
    │           Distributed                │
    │           processing                 │
    └──────────────────────────────────────┘
```

Figure A-7. Framework for Multimedia Data Management for Collaboration

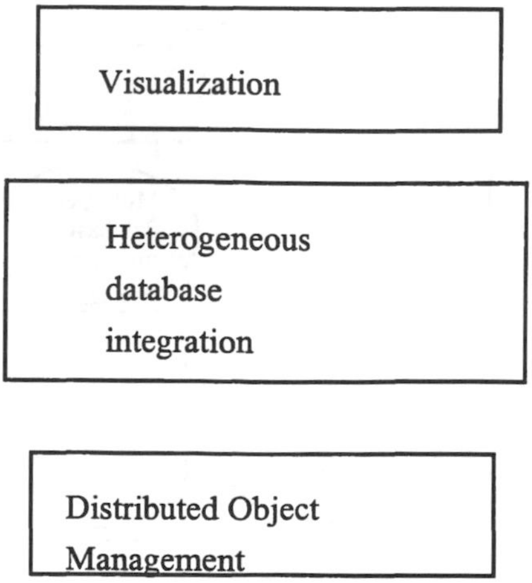

```
    ┌──────────────────────────────────────┐
    │                                      │
    │        Visualization                 │
    │                                      │
    └──────────────────────────────────────┘

    ┌──────────────────────────────────────┐
    │        Heterogeneous                 │
    │        database                      │
    │        integration                   │
    └──────────────────────────────────────┘

    ┌──────────────────────────────────────┐
    │     Distributed Object               │
    │     Management                       │
    └──────────────────────────────────────┘
```

Figure A-8. Framework for Heterogeneous Database Interoperability

Finally, let us illustrate the concepts that we have described above by using a specific example. Suppose a group of physicians/surgeons want a system where they can collaborate and make decisions about various patients. This could be a medical video teleconferencing application. That is, at the highest level, the application is a medical application and, more specifically, a medical video teleconferencing application. At the application technology level, one needs a variety of technologies including collaboration and teleconferencing. These application technologies will make use of data management technologies such as distributed database systems and multimedia database systems. That is, one may need to support multimedia data such as audio and video. The data management technologies in turn draw upon lower level technologies such as distributed processing and networking. We illustrate this in Figure A-9.

In summary, information systems include data management systems as well as application-layer systems such as collaborative computing systems and supporting-layer systems such as distributed object management systems.

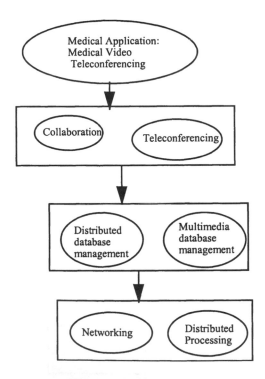

Figure A-9. Specific Example

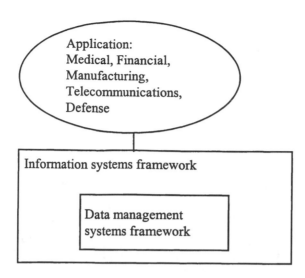

Figure A-10. Application-Framework Relationship

While application technologies make use of data management technologies and data management technologies make use of supporting technologies, the ultimate user of the information system is the application itself. Today numerous applications make use of information systems. These applications are from multiple domains such as medical, financial, manufacturing, telecommunications, and defense. Specific applications include signal processing, electronic commerce, patient monitoring, and situation assessment. Figure A-10 illustrates the relationship between the application and the information system.

A.6 RELATIONSHIP BETWEEN THE TEXTS

We have published three books on data management and mining and currently are writing one more. These books are *Data Management Systems Evolution and Interoperation* [THUR97], *Data Mining Technologies, Techniques, Tools and Trends* [THUR98], *Web Data Management and Electronic Commerce* [THUR00a] (which is this book) and *Managing and Mining Multimedia Databases* [THUR00b] (expected to be published later in the year 2000). All of these books have evolved from the framework that we illustrated in this appendix and address different parts of the framework. The connection between these texts is illustrated in Figure A-11.

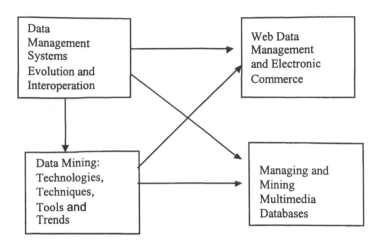

Figure A-11. Relationship between Texts

A.7 SUMMARY

In this appendix we have provided an overview of data management. We first discussed the developments in data management and then provided a vision for data management. Then we illustrated a framework for data management. This framework consists of three layers: database systems layer, interoperability layer, and information extraction layer. Web data management belongs to Layer 3. Finally, we showed how information systems could be built from the technologies of the framework.

Let us repeat what we mentioned in Chapter 1 now that we have described the data management framework we introduced in [THUR97]. The chapters in this book not only discussed web data management concepts, they also showed how web data management could be applied to the various applications such as electronic commerce. We also showed how the other technologies support web data management. For example, Chapter 8 described relationships between the web and databases. Chapter 10 described relationships between mining and the web. That is, many of the technologies discussed in the framework of Figure A-5 have been useful in the discussion of web data management. These include database systems, distributed database systems, interoperability of heterogeneous database systems, migrating legacy databases, multimedia database systems, data warehousing, and data mining. In addition, some other features for data management such as metadata and security also play a role in various chapters of this book. For example, metadata and onotologies for the web were the subject of Chapter 11. Security and privacy issues were discussed both with respect to the web as well as with respect to electronic commerce. Therefore, much of the discussions in this book have a strong orientation toward data and data management.

While data is the main concern for us, we have not ignored some of the other essential technologies and features of web data management. For example, Chapter 5 discussed other web technologies such as objects. Chapters 4 and 8 discussed architectures, and Chapter 13 described various knowledge management concepts and techniques. Chapter 15 provided an overview of various web data management tools. Therefore, we have tried to give a fairly balanced view of what is out there in web data management. Since networking has also contributed much to the web, we address this in Appendix B.

A.8 REFERENCES

[ACM90] Special Issue on Heterogeneous Database Systems, ACM Computing Surveys, September 1990.

[CATT91] Cattell, R., "Object Data Management Systems," Addison-Wesley, MA, 1991.

[CODD70] Codd, E. F., "A Relational Model of Data for Large Shared Data Banks," Communications of the ACM, Vol. 13, #6, June 1970.

[DATE90] Date, C. J., "An Introduction to Database Management Systems," Addison-Wesley, MA, 1990 (6th edition published in 1995 by Addison-Wesley).

[MORE98] Morey, D., "Knowledge Management Architecture," Handbook of Data Management, Auerbach Publications, New York, 1998 (Ed: B. Thuraisingham).

[NSF90] Proceedings of the Database Systems Workshop, Report published by the National Science Foundation, 1990 (also in ACM SIGMOD Record, December 1990).

[NSF95] Proceedings of the Database Systems Workshop, Report published by the National Science Foundation, 1995 (also in ACM SIGMOD Record, March 1996).

[SIGM90] "Next Generation Database Systems," ACM SIGMOD Record," December 1990.

[THUR97] Thuraisingham, B., "Data Management Systems Evolution and Interoperation," CRC Press, FL, 1997.

[THUR98] Thuraisingham, B., "Data Mining: Technologies, Techniques, Tools and Trends," CRC Press, FL, 1998.

[THUR00a] Thuraisingham, B., "Web Data Management and Electronic Commerce," CRC Press, FL, 2000.

[THUR00b] Thuraisingham, B., "Managing and Mining Multimedia Databases" CRC Press, FL (to be published).

APPENDIX B

CONCEPTS IN NETWORKING

B.1 OVERVIEW

In this appendix we provide an overview of the developments and trends in computer networks. Networking technologies have evolved since the 1960s. The Department of Defense funded much of the early work. Then in the 1970s we began to see commercial products emerge. Many standards organizations were also formed to address networking at all levels. Networking and information management technologies essentially resulted in the Internet and the web as we see it today.

We provide a brief overview of networking in this appendix. In Section B.2, we start with the discussion of networks for distributed databases since one of the major topics of this book is data management for the web. A quick overview of the developments of networking starting from ARPANET to active networks as well as networks for multimedia is provided in Section B.3. For completeness we duplicate some of the information in Chapter 7 (about the evolution of the web) in section B.4. The appendix is summarized in Section B.5. References are given in Section B.6.

B.2 NETWORKS FOR DATA MANAGEMENT

As stated earlier, networks play a major role in data management and especially in distributed database management systems (DDBMS). This is because a network connects the different nodes in a distributed environment. Distributed database systems may utilize long haul networks or local area networks. The bandwidth of the network will impact the design of the architecture of the distributed database system. Furthermore, many of the algorithms, such as the commit protocols, depend on the reliability of the network.

It appears that distributed database systems research has proceeded more or less independently of the networking issues. There are some papers that have been published on the impact of network protocols, network topology, and the design of networks on distributed databases (see, for example, [LARS84]). Various performance studies have also been conducted. For example, replicating relations in a distributed database as well as computing costs of various query optimization strategies have some dependency on the network topology (see for example [CERI84] and [OSZU91]). As distributed and heterogeneous database systems become common practice, integration with network-ing technology will play a major role.

Figure B-1 illustrates three types of networks that are intercon-nected to form some sort of super network. Each circle is a node and could host a DBMS. These various DBMSs may be interconnected to form a DDBMS. In network A, the nodes are connected through a single node. It can be regarded as a star network. In network B, all the nodes are connected to one another. The DDBMS based on our choice architecture is assumed to be hosted on such a network. In network C, some of the nodes are connected to one another.

Some applications that require distributed database support may also have special requirements for the network. For example, in the case of mobile applications discussed in our previous book *Data Manage-ment Systems Evolution and Interoperation*, it is important that the network be secure and reliable. Details of networking support for distributed database systems are beyond the scope of this book.

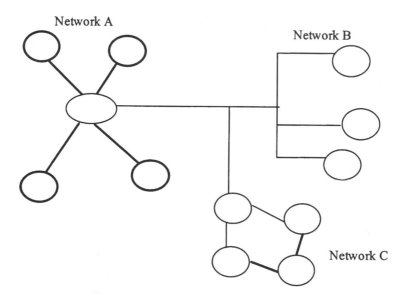

Figure B-1. Networks for Distributed Databases

B.3 EVOLUTION OF NETWORKS

Network technology has evolved a great deal over the last two dec-ades. Some of the early network systems included the U.S. Department of Defense's (DoD) ARPANET, IBM's SNA and Digital Equipment Corporation's DECNET. Various types of networks such as X.25 were also emerging in the 1970s. Xerox PARC conducted extensive research on Ethernet and various transport protocols. BBN Corporation developed networking documents for the government in the 1970s and 1980s. At that time the International Standards Organization (ISO) began an effort to define standards for networking. ISO's effort has come to be known as the seven layer protocol stack and is described in detail in [TANN91]. We illustrate this protocol stack in Figure B-2. Early developments in networking also include the token ring and the token bus networks.

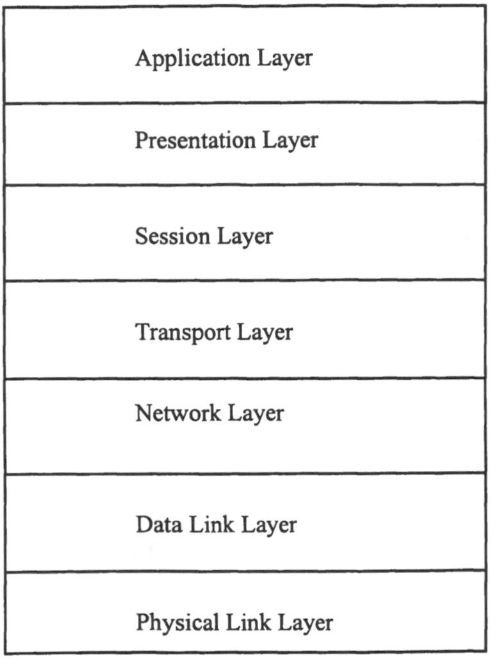

| Application Layer |
| Presentation Layer |
| Session Layer |
| Transport Layer |
| Network Layer |
| Data Link Layer |
| Physical Link Layer |

Figure B-2. ISO Seven Layer Protocol Stack

The US DoD funded research on TCP/IP (Transmission Control Protocol / Internet Protocol) which began in the 1960s and really took off in the 1980s and beyond with the development of what is now called the Internet. We often interchange the terms Internet and the Web, but Internet is actually the network while the web includes not only the network, but also the servers and everything that is connected to the Internet.

More recent developments in networking technology include FDDI (Fiber Optics Networks), Frame relays, and ATM (Asynchronous Transfer Mode). Considerable advances have also been made on packet switches, bridges, and routers. More recently there are research efforts by DARPA on active networks [IEEE99]. Other developments with networking include telecommunications technologies. Telephones, one of the basics of telecommunications, have played a major role for networking, the web and now e-commerce. Currently much of the e-commerce is being carried out in text format. There is a lot of push to move toward voice portals for e-commerce. In Part III of this book we provided an overview of how telecommunications technology has helped the web and e-commerce. One of the current challenges is to transmit multimedia data such as live audio and video on the Internet in a seamless fashion. There are also developments in specialized packet switches, bridges and routers for the Internet [INFO99].

This section has provided only the basics on the evolution of networks. For more details we refer the reader to books such as [TANN91] and [MAGE96].

B.4 EVOLUTION OF THE WEB

We duplicate some of the information we presented in Chapter 7 for completeness of this appendix. The inception of the web took place at CERN in Switzerland. Although different people have been credited to be father of the web, one of the early conceivers of the web was Timothy Bernes-Lee who was at CERN at that time. He now heads the World Wide Web consortium (W3C). The consortium specifies standards for the web including data models, query languages, and security.

As soon as the WWW emerged in the early 1990s, a group of graduate students at the University of Illinois developed a browser, which was called MOSAIC. This was around 1993-4. A Company called Netscape Communications then marketed MOSAIC and since then various browsers as well as search engines have emerged. These search engines, the browsers, and the servers all now constitute the WWW. Internet became the transport medium for communication.

Various protocols for communication such as HTTP (Hypertext Transfer Protocol) and languages for creating web pages such as HTML (Hypertext markup language) also emerged. Perhaps one of the significant developments is the Java programming language by Sun Microsystems. The work is now being continued by Javasoft, a subsidiary of Sun. Java is a language that is very much like C++ but avoids all the disadvantages of C++ like pointers. It was developed as a programming language to be run platform independent. It was soon found that this was an ideal language for the web. So now there are various Java applications as well as what is known as Java applets. Applets are Java programs residing in a machine and can be called by a web page running on a separate machine. Therefore applets can be embedded into web pages to perform all kinds of features. Of course there are additional security restrictions as applets could come from untrusted machines. Another concept is a servlet. Servlets run on web servers and perform specific functions such as delivering web pages for a user request.

Middleware for the web is continuing to evolve. If the entire environment is Java, that is connecting Java clients to Java servers, then one could use RMI (Remote Method Invocation) by Javasoft. If the platform consists of heterogeneous clients and servers then one could use Object Management Group's CORBA (Common Object Request Broker Architecture) for interoperability. Some argue whether client-server technology will be dead because of the web. That is, one may need different computing paradigms such as the federated computing model for the web.

Another development for the web is components and frameworks. Component technology such as Enterprise Java Beans (EJB) is becoming very popular for componentizing various web applications. These applications are managed by what is now known as application servers. These application servers (such as BEA's Web Logic) communicate with database management systems through data servers (these data servers may be developed by the Database vendors such as Object Design Inc.). Finally one of the latest technologies for integrating various applications and systems, possibly heterogeneous, through the web is JINI. It essentially encompasses Java and RMI as its basic elements.

The web is continuing to expand and explode. Now there is so much data, information, and knowledge on the web that managing all this is becoming critical. Web information management is all about developing technologies for managing this information. One particular type of information system is a database system. One of the major problems with the Internet is information overload. Because humans can now access large amounts of information very rapidly, they can quickly become overloaded with information and in some cases the information may not be useful to them. Furthermore, in certain other cases, the information may even be harmful to the humans. The current search engines, although improving steadily, still give the users too much information. When a user types in an index word, a lot of irrelevant web pages are also retrieved. What we need is intelligent search engines. The technologies that we have discussed in this book, if implemented successfully, would prevent this information overload problem. For example, agents may filter out information so those users get only the relevant information. Data mining technology could extract meaningful information from the data sources. Security technology could prevent users from getting information that they are not authorized to know. In addition to computer scientists, researchers in psychology, sociology, and other disciplines are also involved in examining various aspects of Internet database management. We need people in multiple disciplines to collaboratively work together to make the Internet a useful tool to human beings. One of the emerging goals of web technology is to provide appropriate support for data dissemination. This deals with getting the right data/information at the right time to the analyst/user (directly to the desktop if possible) to assist in carrying out various functions.

B.5 SUMMARY

In this appendix we have provided a brief overview of networks. We started with a discussion of networks for distributed databases since the main topic addressed in this book is data management on the web. Then we discussed some of the developments on networks. Finally we duplicated the overview of the web that we provided in Chapter 7 for completion.

Networks will continue to play a major role in computing. It is really the heart of computer communications. We have seen significant improvements in networking and telecommunications technologies. With the continued research efforts in networking and distributed processing, this is an area that will continue to see significant developments for the next several years.

B.6 REFERENCES

[CERI84] Ceri, S. and Pelagatti, G., "Distributed Databases, Principles and Systems," McGraw-Hill, NY, 1984.

[IEEE99] IEEE Computer, Special Issue on Active Networks, March 1999.

[INFO99] Information World, December 1999.

[LARS84] Larson, J. and S. Rahimi, "Distributed Databases," IEEE Tutorial, 1984.

[MAGE96] Magedanz, T. and R. Popescu-Zeletin, "Intelligent Networks," Coriolis Group, 1996.

[OSZU91] Oszu, T. and P. Valduriez, "Principles of Distributed Database Systems," Prentice-Hall, NY, 1991.

[TANN91] Tannenbaum, A., "Computer Networks", Prentice-Hall, 1991.

APPENDIX C

ENTERPRISE BUSINESS PROCESS MANAGEMENT

C.1 OVERVIEW

For organizations to conduct effective e-commerce, they have to first ensure that their internal business processes are run properly. Internal business processing may include time card reporting, purchasing, project management, inventory management, sales order processing, general ledger and other similar processes.

Numerous commercial products such as those by Oracle, Peoplesoft, Baan, J. D. Edwards, and SAP-AG have emerged to provide a comprehensive set capabilities to manage an organization's business processes (see for example [KRAS00]). With the advent of corporate information infrastructures, many organizations are now managing their business processes on the web. The three-tier architecture for the web is being developed for managing the business processes. Since enterprise business process management and enterprise resource planning are key aspects of e-business, and many organizations are now formulating their strategies for e-business, we provide a brief discussion of enterprise business process management in this appendix. Many of the organizations are focusing on developing e-business capabilities so that they can succeed in the e-commerce marketplace.

The organization of this appendix is as follows. The evolution of enterprise business processing is given in Section C.2. An example of an enterprise business process product is given in Section C.3. The role of the web in enterprise business process management is discussed in Section C.4. The appendix is summarized in Section C.5. References are given in Section C.6.

C.2 EVOLUTION OF BUSINESS PROCESS MANAGEMENT

Business process management has existed from the time organizations were set up. In the early years all of these processings were carried out manually. Organizations would have numerous clerks manipulating numbers and carrying out the business functions supervised by accountants, administration and other management personnel.

As early as the 1960s organizations started to automate their business processes. Early automation systems were simply computer programs that replaced the manual processing. In the 1970s with the advent of database technology and modeling tools, significant advances were made for business processing. Corporations such as SAP-AG were founded precisely for this purpose. Even corporations such as Oracle have now ventured into developing software for business processing.

Numerous developments for business processing were made in the 1980s. Various data as well as process modeling tools were being developed. Organizations could use these tools for supply chain management, sales order processing, purchasing and other administrative functions. BPR (business process reengineering) became a well-known term and tools were developed to help organizations to reengineer the legacy business processes. These tools were integrated with databases so that data from heterogeneous sources could be accessed for BPR.

The trends in the 1980s continued throughout the early 1990s with tools such as SAP/R3 emerging. Such tools were based on so-called client-server computing. One of the significant developments in the 1990s was knowledge management. Some call knowledge management to be an enhanced version of BPR. Nevertheless with the advent of the web, organizations are attempting to automate their business processes through corporate Intranets. Products like SAP are being enhanced to carry out BPR on the web. The functions include tracking the sales, purchasing, time card reporting and project management all carried out through the corporate information infrastructures. Three-tier client-server computing for the web is becoming popular. We duplicate Figure 8-15 in Figure C-1 to recap three-tier client-server computing.

C.3 AN EXAMPLE OF A BUSINESS PROCESS MANAGEMENT TOOL

Several products are now on the market for business process management. One of the products that we are familiar with is SAP/R3. SAP/R3 is the product of SAP-AG in Waldorf, Germany. SAP-AG first marketed a product called SAP/R2 for mainframe systems. Then around 1992 they migrated toward three-tier client-server computing and developed SAP/R3. Several books have been published on SAP/R3 including the one by [CURR98].

Essentially SAP/R3 is based on a business blueprint. The blueprint has compiled a collection of best practices through several years of experiences. These best practices could be purchasing a car, selling a product, managing a project, and other organizational activities. As customers gain more experiences with SAP and report these experiences, some of them will go into the blueprint.

SAP/R3 comes with a suite of tools to implement the blueprint. These tools help to model the business processes, reengineer the processes as well as give the corporation an edge to compete in the marketplace. It is essentially a complete solution for enterprise business management.

After an organization purchases SAP/R3, it uses the modeling tool to model the business processes that are already available from SAP. In cases where the capability is not provided for a particular process, such as, say, marketing on the web, then the organization has to develop the models for the corresponding process and make enhancements to SAP/R3.

Once the business processes are modeled, the next step is to implement the processes. SAP/R3 also provides tools to automate the business processes in the middle tier. Back-end is the database tier and could interface to many commercial database systems. Front tier is the client-tier that includes the presentation logic. Several industries are using SAP/R3 for their business process reengineering activities. For a detailed discussion we refer to [CURR98].

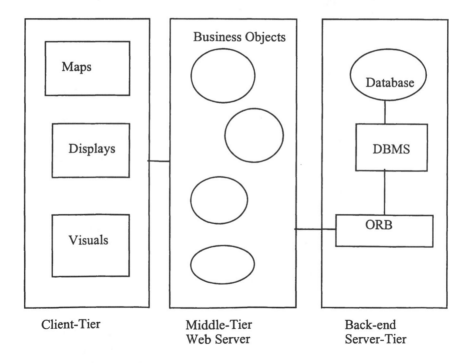

Figure C-1. Three-Tier Computing for the Web

C.4 IMPACT OF THE WEB

The web has impacted business process management in two ways. One is that organizations are not only automating their business processes, but many organizational activities such as time card reporting, sales order processing, and product management are carried out on the web. This means products such as SAP/R3 should have the capability to be integrated with the organization's information infrastructure. Another more important aspect of the impact of the web is for the business process management products to provide support for e-commerce. In Part III we listed a variety of functions for e-commerce. These include advertising, mining to obtain intelligence about the customer, developing cool web pages to attract customers, and many other activities that are specific to e-commerce. Therefore, a blueprint of products such as SAP/R3 has to be enhanced to provide support for e-commerce business processing.

One of the challenges today is to identify the e-commerce business processes. These processes may vary depending on whether the activity is business-to-business or business-to-consumer. We also need to develop standards for e-commerce business processes. Once the processes are identified then products have to be enhanced to support these business processes. Finally the e-commerce business processes have to be implemented possibly using the three-tier client-server architecture. Figure C-2 modifies Figure 16-11 for three tier computing for e-commerce. The business processes include e-commerce marketing, web mining, and other related activities to support e-commerce.

C.5 SUMMARY

In this appendix we have described business process reengineering and showed how the web impacts it. We first gave a brief overview of the evolution of enterprise business process management and then discussed a commercial product. Finally we described how e-commerce business processes need to be integrated with the business processing capability of the product.

One of the fastest growing areas in e-business is supply chain management and business process reengineering. In addition to all the traditional business processes, e-commerce has introduced several other processes. Since the area is still in its infancy, a lot of work has to be done to identify the business processes. Once they are identified then they have to be integrated into the business process tools of the organization. As developments are made in e-commerce and web information

management, we can expect various tools to be developed for managing
the business processes for e-commerce.

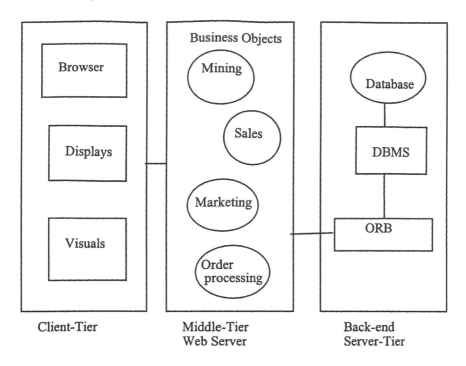

Figure C-2. Business Processing for E-commerce

C.6 REFERENCES

[BENY90] Benyon, D., "Information and Data Modeling," Blackwell
Scientific Publications, Oxford, UK, 1990.

[CURR98] Ceri, S. and Pelagatti, G., "Distributed Databases, Principles and Systems," McGraw-Hill, NY, 1984.

[KRAS00] Krasner, H., "Ensuring E-business Success by Learning
from ERP Failures," IEEE ITPro, February 2000.

Index

Index